IT Virtualization Best Practices

IT Virtualization Best Practices

A Lean, Green Virtualized Data Center Approach

Mickey Iqbal
Mithkal Smadi
Chris Molloy
Jim Rymarczyk

MC Press Online, LLC
Ketchum, ID 83340

IT Virtualization Best Practices
Mickey Iqbal, Mithkal Smadi, Chris Molloy, and Jim Rymarczyk

First Edition
First Printing—November 2010

MC Press Online, LLC
  Corporate Offices
  P.O. Box 4886
  Ketchum, ID 83340-4886 USA
For information regarding sales and/or customer service, please contact:
  MC Press
  P.O. Box 4300
  Big Sandy, TX 75755-4300 USA
  Toll Free: 1-877-226-5394
For information regarding permissions or special orders, please contact:
  mcbooks@mcpressonline.com

ISBN: 978-158347-354-2

To my mother, Parveen.
— *Mickey Iqbal*

To my mother, Amneh, for her guidance and sharp vision.
— *Mithkal Smadi*

To my wife, Jenny, for her years of love, support,
and friendship.
— *Chris Molloy*

To my mother, Edna; my wife, Barbara; my daughters,
Beth and Sharon; and my granddaughter, Paige.
— *Jim Rymarczyk*

Acknowledgments

The authors would like to acknowledge the following people for their contributions:

- Richard Baum, IBM Fellow Emeritus, who collaborated during the 2002–2005 timeframe on the virtualization concepts explained in Chapter 1
- The following IBM team members, whose research work and contributions led to the content development related to Chapter 4's pattern specification: Thomas Jobson, Jr., Gang Chen, Kyle Brown, Alexandre Polozoff, Bobby Woolf, Paul Verschueren, Pieter Lindeque, and Peter Bahrs
- IBM Senior Technical Staff Member Praduemn Goyal, Ph.D., whose research work and contributions led to the content development for Chapter 5
- IBM Senior Technical Staff Member Brian Snitzer, whose research work and contributions led to the content development for Chapter 6
- IBM Senior Technical Staff Member Rajeev Puri, whose research work and contributions led to the content development for Chapter 9
- Soumen Chowdhury of VMware, for his contributions to the development of the content for Chapter 10
- IBM Enterprise Architect Thirumal Nellutla, for research contributions to Chapter 11
- Stephen Ward, Ph.D., of IBM Austria, whose research work and contributions led to the content development for Chapter 13
- The authors and reviewers of *IT Optimization and Virtualization Management*, an IBM technical paper: Donna N. Dillenberger, Alex Donatelli, Brad Brech, Chris Finden-Browne, Mark Ernest, Dave Lindquist, and Pratik Gupta

- Robert G. Simko, President of International Technology Group, Los Altos, California, and his extended team's contribution to the white paper *Aligning Platform and Service Management with IBM Systems Director and Tivoli Solutions* (January 2009), which we have leveraged in the development of content for Chapter 8 and Appendix A

We would also like to thank Marianne Krcma and Andy Oram for their help with editing this book.

About the Authors

Mickey Iqbal is an IBM Distinguished Engineer responsible for leading architecture and technology deployment strategy for IBM's Strategic Outsourcing (SO) business. As a technology leader and an executive at IBM, he leads the global programs for hardware and software infrastructure resource optimization and for technology deployment in IBM's global data centers, which span more than 8 million square feet of raised floor space. Mickey has led several large transformation projects for some of IBM's largest clients and is globally sought by clients for consultation in the areas of IT strategy, IT transformations, virtualization, cloud computing, green data centers, IT architecture, and operations management. Mickey developed the strategy and architecture for IBM SO's global operating systems provisioning and for IBM's electronic software distribution services, which are deployed worldwide in support of IBM's clients. Mickey has filed 12 patents on behalf of IBM and is the co-author of two IBM Redbooks. He championed and led the development of software technology that resulted in two IBM commercial software products. Mickey holds an MBA and a Master of Science in Management Information Systems from the University of Illinois at Chicago, as well as a Bachelor of Science in Mechanical Engineering from UET, Lahore. He is a member of the IBM Academy of Technology, which focuses on the technical underpinnings of IBM's future.

Dr. Mithkal Smadi is an IBM Distinguished Engineer in Integrated Service Delivery. Recently, he played a leading role in the early development and deployment of IBM lean transformation methodology across Integrated Technology Delivery (ITD) and Integrated Managed Business Process Delivery (IMBPD). Mithkal is a recognized technical leader in quality control, design, qualification, and manufacturing across IBM products and services. Mithkal joined IBM in 1987 and has held a variety of technical and management positions in technology, product development, supply chain engineering, and IT services. Mithkal has led many quality improvement projects in logic commodities, OEM products, and now in IBM Services, resulting in substantial savings and improvements to IBM product competitiveness. He leads the Global Defect Prevention Process development and deployment.

Chris Molloy is an IBM Distinguished Engineer, responsible for optimizing the 8 million square feet of data center space used around the world to support IBM's outsourcing customers. Chris drives the worldwide strategy for these data centers, leveraging the patented process he put in place for distributed capacity planning now being used for over 100,000 servers. With an MBA from Duke University to complement his computer science degree from the University of Florida, Chris blends his understanding and use of the technology with the economic business value benefit needed by today's corporations to mitigate the growth of IT demand with the IT budget. Chris is also a member of IBM's Academy of Technology.

Jim Rymarczyk, an IBM Fellow, is the Chief Virtualization Technologist for IBM's Systems and Technology Group. He leads the corresponding development community and co-leads the architecture board for IBM's New Enterprise Data Center products. He also conducts frequent customer briefings on the expanding role virtualization will play in reducing IT complexity and cost. Since joining IBM in 1968, Jim has played a key role in numerous IBM technologies, including serving as a principal designer of the S/390 PR/SM Logical Partitioning facility, leading the design of a precursor to the RS/6000 SP, and serving as a principal architect of the S/390 Parallel Sysplex. He also led the highly successful effort to bring mainframe virtualization technologies to IBM's Power Systems™ family of servers. Jim researches a broad range of future server technologies and designs, predicts IT technology trends and disruptions, leads product competitiveness studies, and drives changes to the system-level design of future IBM servers. He received a BSEE from the Massachusetts Institute of Technology and has served as Adjunct Professor of Computer Science with Union College. He is a member of the IEEE, the ACM, and the IBM Academy of Technology.

Contents

Introduction

As the energy and climate crises loom throughout the globe, we are also witnessing an explosive growth in the demand for energy-hungry IT computing infrastructure resources. Most of the global IT data centers that host the IT infrastructure are at the brink of capacity for both energy and floor space.

Building new data centers is an extremely expensive proposition, with costs running anywhere from tens of millions to upwards of a hundred million dollars in capital and operational expenses. Meanwhile, industry analysts estimate that several billion dollars worth of investment in existing server hardware in global data centers is not properly utilized. These under-utilized resources are still consuming expensive energy and floor space in data centers, without doing much value-added work.

The need for more computing power and the inability of organizations to tap into existing, under-utilized hardware resources is driving the demand for more hardware, energy, and floor space. This trend is leading to the building of more energy-hungry data centers. This paradigm, if left unchecked, will no doubt lead to additional unused infrastructure resources, which negatively affect an organization's economic bottom line, stifle its ability to invest in its core business, and contribute to a significant increase in the carbon footprint that is a growing peril for our planet.

Virtualization for a Smarter Planet

Through smarter use of IT resources, an organization can become more instrumented, interconnected, and intelligent. To address the challenges described above, organizations across the world have already started to leverage smarter technologies, such as *virtualization.* This technology allows us to "slice" a single piece of physical hardware (a server and storage) and the associated physical network resources into pools of many virtual resources. This allows a single physical resource to act as and host many virtual resources, with the promise of reducing IT infrastructure complexity and costs.

Virtualization reduces the energy and floor space footprint required to host the otherwise many physical hardware resources. Mature technologies from several vendors exist in the marketplace today, allowing IT organizations to adopt virtualization and to exploit several infrastructure-related benefits. However, virtualization technologies alone, without the benefit of a smartly engineered transformation effort, have fallen short of providing their promised benefits. These technologies, alone, do not provide the return on investment that resonates with an organization's lines of business (LOBs). For LOBs, data centers are one of the several enablers of their mission to improve margins, slice down operational costs, reduce their carbon footprint, and attain business efficiencies to fuel their business growth.

Organizations that have adopted virtualization technology have, in general, seen a reduction in their energy, hardware, and floor space spending. However, the successful extraction of overall business value and benefits from virtualization technology has been extremely challenging to realize for the LOB stakeholders. Research and industry experience have revealed that these challenges arise due to an organization's inability to properly plan, engineer, and manage the transformation effort. These challenges are exacerbated by the complexity inherent in transforming legacy IT infrastructure, applications, business processes, management systems, and the organizational structure, which are all affected by a virtualization transformation. Often, the net results are significant delays in virtualization project schedules, a substantial increase in operations costs to transform the IT infrastructure to a virtualized state, and a higher-than-expected cost to manage them, going forward. The unwanted increase in transformation and ongoing operations costs lead to the erosion of net benefits and cost savings, which would otherwise be compelling business drivers for all key stakeholders of a virtualization transformation.

This book provides an approach based on service patterns to transform IT infrastructures to a virtualized state. It also discusses how to manage IT infrastructures, while optimizing both technical and organizational resources to derive compelling business value for the organization. Our service patterns are derived from our globally acknowledged technical and thought leadership in several areas, including the following:

- Leadership, insights, and experiences from successfully executing virtualization projects and from virtualizing thousands of infrastructure resources (servers, storage, and network) for global organizations across all industry sectors
- Global experience and leadership in applying organizational theory, business process reengineering, and lean methodologies to optimize the organizational constructs and labor models required to support very complex organizational transitions and business environments
- Leadership in the development and management of hardware, software, and systems management technologies for virtualization
- Global leadership in developing and applying "green" technologies for managing global data centers built over several millions of square feet of raised floor space

This book provides an end-to-end approach for virtualization transformations, leading to efficient and cost-optimized virtualized infrastructures and data centers. Our goal is to ensure that virtualized data centers are transformed to provide business value, which transcends the traditional infrastructure cost-optimization business proposition for a CIO.

For organizations embracing virtualization technologies to address the energy and infrastructure resource challenges of the data center, our approach enables their several lines of business to do the following:

- Become more productive in managing their overall costs
- Be agile in provisioning new business services and improving time to market
- Be proactive in catering to rapidly changing business models and client demands
- Become more "charged" as an engine for fueling business growth, with innovation in technology and business process change
- Produce direct value to their clients by optimizing their value chain
- Become more successful at improving their shareholders' equity

Without the benefit of leveraging an approach such as our service-patterns methodology for virtualization transformations, most organizations will continue to stumble as they navigate their way through. They will continue to face extreme challenges in realizing the business value from developing and managing virtualized infrastructures.

The Organization of this Book

This book is organized as follows:

- Chapter 1 describes various types of virtualization technologies. It also describes how emerging technologies, such as cloud computing, will leverage virtualization and the Web, to play a valuable role in the implementation of IT infrastructures of the future.
- Chapter 2 addresses why virtualization is important for green data centers, which are a critical component of our strategy for building a smarter planet and for reducing the carbon footprint generated by IT resources globally.
- Chapter 3 introduces the concept of a lean transformation. It discusses the eight commonly known types of waste and describes the seven lean levers that are the building blocks of our patterns for virtualization.
- Chapter 4 describes a template for patterns, which we use to document and illustrate our service patterns for virtualization.
- Chapters 5 through 11 present the seven patterns for virtualization in terms of the seven lean levers, namely: Segmenting Complexity, Redistributing Activities, Pooling Resources, Flexible Resource Balancing, Reducing Incoming Hardware Infrastructure and Work, Reducing Non-Value-Added Work, and Standard Operations.
- Chapter 12 describes the essential components of a lean implementation.
- Chapter 13 provides guidance toward building a virtualization business case to demonstrate the financial return that your virtualization project can bring to your organizational stakeholders.

1

How Virtualization Will Save IT

O ver the past dozen years, IT organizations have been fighting a losing battle against server sprawl—the essentially irresistible proliferation of commodity servers that are cheap and easy to deploy, but complex and costly to manage in substantial numbers. The cost of managing these distributed servers has grown from a small fraction of the IT budget to the dominant IT cost component, far exceeding the cost of the servers themselves! This growing cost, coupled with tightened IT budgets because of the recent worldwide financial downturn, increases the urgency to find an alternative methodology for IT resource management.

While facing these problems of growing resource management costs and shrinking budgets, IT groups are being asked to do more than ever before. New pressures have come from four major directions:

- *Exploding volumes of data, information, and new applications*. Digital data, both raw and processed, is being generated at a dramatically increasing rate. As our world becomes highly instrumented and interconnected, data is also coming from a growing number of distributed sources (including such diverse sources as supermarket checkout stations, Web-click tracking software, and highway traffic sensors). By the end of 2011, one estimate indicates that the worldwide amount of digital data will be doubling every 11 hours! Accompanying this sea of new data, highly valuable new applications continue to emerge, many of which were previously impractical. In a growing number of situations, the new applications are being used to control complex distributed systems, evolving our world toward the promise of a smarter planet. This broad expansion in the role of IT is driving a huge increase in the need for storage, network, and computing resources—all of which add to the IT resource management challenge.

- *Growing requirements for business resilience and security.* As IT has become a critical underpinning of most businesses and government agencies, even partial IT outages can have traumatic consequences. While this dependence on IT continues to increase, contemporary IT infrastructures are fraught with critical vulnerabilities. The threats to IT are grave and increasing. Some threats come from within the IT organization itself, whereas new threats arise from distant groups, including terrorists and agents of political cyberwar. The magnitude of this problem is reflected in the landslide of security and business resilience regulations that must be followed.

- *New mandates to reduce energy consumption.* Until recently, energy efficiency was a low priority on most IT requirements lists (generally a third-tier requirement). Now, it has risen to the top. In part, this is due to rises in both energy cost and energy demand. In some situations, the energy required for additional IT resources is simply unavailable from existing energy suppliers. Power and thermal issues have also begun to inhibit IT operations—the addition and configuration of hardware resources is no longer just a matter of fitting into the available space. It must also take into account complex power and cooling constraints. Additionally, IT providers face environmental compliance and governance requirements, including the growing societal pressure to be "green."

- *The accelerating pace of technological innovations.* Technological innovations are occurring at an increasing rate, and many of these innovations have compelling IT value. Examples include the rapidly improving virtualization technologies, converged networks, solid-state storage, IT appliances, storage de-duplication, the increasing numbers of cores and threads per chip, low-cost high-bandwidth fiber optics, petaflop supercomputers, cloud computing services, real-time data streams, cloud computing architectures, and distributed sensors/actuators (as used in transportation grids, power grids, and other real-time control systems). The best products available at any point will soon become the old, deficient products that lack many valuable functions and features. As a result, most IT infrastructures will consist of a diversity of product types and generations, rather than becoming homogeneous.

This book opens the door to solutions for all these problems. It explains how to plan and implement advances in virtualization technologies and management software to enable a vital breakthrough in IT effectiveness, efficiency, resiliency, and security.

This chapter explains the various types of technologies that fit under the rubric of virtualization, the advances in virtualization that have historically changed IT centers, and emerging technologies that continue to work major transformations in administrators' jobs and resources. You will also learn how emerging forms of cloud computing will leverage virtualization and the Web to play a valuable and expanding role in the implementation of the IT infrastructures of the future.

The Current IT Crisis

The strains in data centers large and small spring from a number of pressures that we'll explore in this section.

IT Infrastructures Have Become Too Labor-Intensive

Figure 1.1 illustrates a key problem faced by most IT providers. At the top of the figure is a depiction of the business processes whose implementation is the main purpose of IT. Unfortunately, the cost of managing the underlying IT resources has grown to the point where it consumes the lion's share of the IT budget, leaving limited funds to spend on business processes and applications.

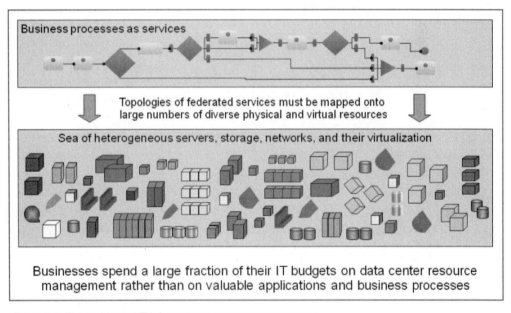

Figure 1.1: The problem of IT infrastructure resource management.

Studies have shown that IT operational overhead has grown to account for 70 percent of the enterprise IT budget, leaving precious few resources for new initiatives. Much of this problem stems from the fact that physical configurations, unless well virtualized, have many hard constraints that are impediments to routine operational tasks such as the deployment of new applications or the adjustment of workload resource levels. The amount of resource provided per server is usually fixed when the server is deployed and rarely matches the actual needs of the assigned workload, which may vary dynamically. Industry-wide studies of Windows® and Linux® systems have indicated that their average server utilization is well below 10 percent, which results in a significant waste of data center hardware, floor space, power, and cooling.

Figure 1.2 depicts the non-virtualized resource configuration for a medium-sized business. This figure illustrates the problems that need to be overcome:

- Rigid configurations
- Fixed resources per server
- Low server utilization
- Wasted energy and floor space
- Hardware changes affecting software assets
- Servers managed individually

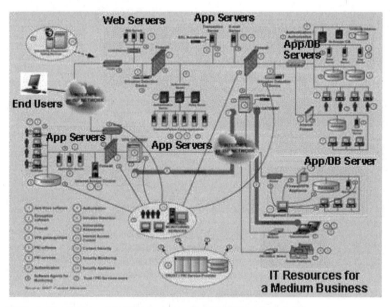

Figure 1.2: Without virtualization, IT infrastructures are inflexible and wasteful.

Non-virtualized IT environments also typically require substantial labor for software maintenance. The ongoing installation of new hardware generations requires corresponding upgrades to operating system software, which has a ripple effect in driving the need to upgrade middleware and to recertify applications prematurely.

Furthermore, without virtualization, the IT staff must deal with each physical server individually. Workloads must be assigned to specific servers, and achieving balanced resource utilization is a difficult and never-ending task. Whenever a given server malfunctions or needs to be taken offline for service, the IT staff must deal with it manually via a complex but temporary redistribution of workloads.

Many IT Infrastructures Violate Engineering Principles

For large enterprises, IT management is especially difficult due to the numbers of applications deployed and the complexity of their ad hoc configuration methods. Figure 1.3 illustrates the application topology at one large enterprise—and this is just one of two pages! Note that the diagram illustrates the application topology level only; it does not even extend to the underlying physical and virtual resources. It is not hard to appreciate the difficulty of managing such a configuration, especially when changes are needed or when problems must be found and fixed. This configuration is not atypical.

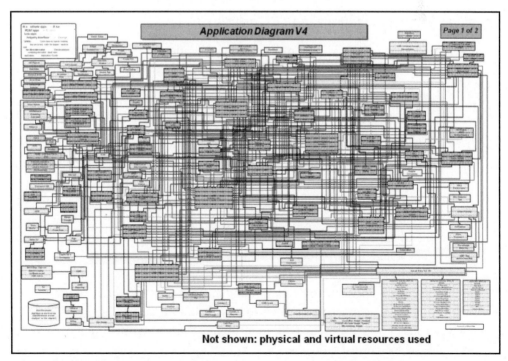

Figure 1.3: Enterprise application complexity.

In fact, the feedback from some IT executives indicates that this diagram understates their complexity problems and is more indicative of their desired IT simplification goal! As one IT executive remarked, "If only my application diagram would fit on two pages!"

Other types of large systems, such as aircraft and automobiles, are arguably even more complex than IT data centers, but such systems are generally much simpler to maintain and use. The historical difficulty with IT data centers is that most are unique, and each typically has an extensive history of piecewise evolution, rather than a "fresh sheet of paper" design that complies with well-established engineering design principles and best practices. Significant IT complexity results from the coupling of numerous independent IT components in ways that are overly rigid and ad hoc.

The coming advances in IT resource virtualization and its management will lead to improved IT architectures that exhibit greater modularity and reduced complexity. Moreover, the transition to these future virtualized IT architectures can be done incrementally, yielding positive returns on investment along the way to a full IT transformation.

Prevailing Trends Will Increase IT Complexity

Looking beyond these existing IT conditions, a consideration of IT trends leads us to believe that the situation will get progressively worse unless actions are taken to transform the approach to IT. In particular, four noteworthy trends will increase IT's complexity and cost:

- The *numbers* of systems deployed will continue to increase, driven largely by new applications (such as Web-based, surveillance, and operational asset management apps) and improving hardware price/performance. In the near term, the worldwide financial downturn and the initial wave of server consolidations have combined to put a temporary halt to the historically increasing numbers of servers deployed. However, all indications are that the deployment of new applications and systems will resume a high rate of growth.
- The *diversity* of IT products will increase as competing suppliers continue to introduce new applications, systems, and management software. Today's innovation soon becomes tomorrow's legacy. It almost goes without saying that the IT products you buy today will, in just a few years, lack important capabilities available on the newest products.

- The *coupling* of IT components is extensive and increasing, driven by application tiering, advances in high-performance standard networks, and so on. A growing range of distributed devices are becoming intelligent and networked.
- While it has compelling benefits, the *virtualization* of resources will affect nearly all existing IT processes and can lead to virtual server sprawl. Introducing virtualization can have significant "hidden costs" and requires considerable skills, planning, and discipline. You will learn later in this book how to alleviate these potential downsides of virtualization.

The Power of Virtualization

The term "virtualization" is widely used in the computer industry and is applied to many different things. Virtual memory, virtual machines, and virtual disks have become common IT technology elements, but in each case the process used and result produced are very different. Just what does it mean to be "virtual," and why is this beneficial?

Conceptually, virtualization is a process of substitution. It takes real resources that have well-defined interfaces and functions and creates substitutes for those resources that have the same interfaces and functions. Figure 1.4 shows the relationship between

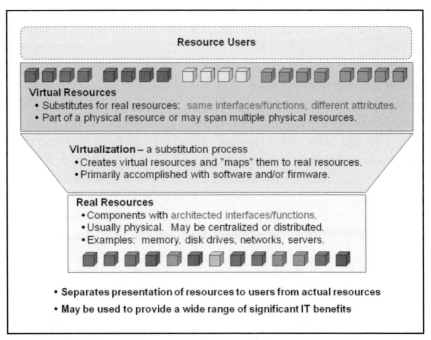

Figure 1.4: The concept of virtualization.

the real resources and the resources presented to the users. To a user, a virtual resource looks and behaves just like its real counterpart. However, a virtual resource can have different attributes—such as size, cost, or adjustability—that make this substitution worthwhile.

Virtualization is often applied to hardware resources, such as servers or storage devices, but any resource with well-defined interfaces and functions can be virtualized. It is increasingly common to find virtualization being applied to software resources, such as operating systems, middleware, and applications.

Virtualization is very powerful, providing four major capabilities that are interrelated and often coexist:

- *Sharing*—Virtualization may be used to create multiple virtual resources from a single real resource. Users of the virtual resources may be unaware of the sharing. In addition to increasing the utilization of real resources, this provides the ability to control and adjust how much of the shared real resource each user consumes. Additional benefits are the ability to create and destroy virtual resources on the fly and to isolate users from one another more securely (although not as well as if each user had his or her own private, real resource). This use of virtualization for resource sharing has become so widespread that it is sometimes considered the only definition of virtualization.
- *Aggregation*—Virtualization also allows us to go in the opposite direction, making multiple real resources look like one resource to users. A classic example of this is a virtual disk. The user sees a single logical disk and doesn't need to worry about the numbers and sizes of the underlying physical disks. This can greatly simplify life for both end users and storage resource managers. Such aggregation also allows a virtual resource to scale well beyond an underlying hardware resource and to survive unplanned and planned hardware outages (e.g., via RAID or clustering techniques).
- *Emulation*—Virtualization may be used to create virtual resources whose interfaces and functions differ from those of the underlying real resources. Major benefits include compatibility with older real resources and the protection of a software investment. Architecture emulators have been widely used since the 1960s; for example, microcode-based emulators enabled IBM® System/360 computers to run the same binary programs that were written for earlier computer generations. Other

examples include iSCSI, which provides a virtual SCSI bus on an IP network; virtual tape built upon disk drives; and the new virtual Fibre Channel networks over Ethernet.

- *Insulation*—Virtualization introduces a layer of abstraction and indirection that decouples virtual resources from the underlying real resources. As a result, virtual resources and their users need not be affected by changes to real resources. This enables administrators to dynamically replace, upgrade, and service the real resources in a manner that is transparent to the virtual resources. More importantly, it can insulate software stacks, which are the most valuable and labor-intensive IT components, from the ongoing stream of hardware changes. A noteworthy special case of insulation is *encapsulation*, in which virtualization is used to insulate the users of a virtual resource from its internals.

Figure 1.5 illustrates each of the four functions of virtualization.

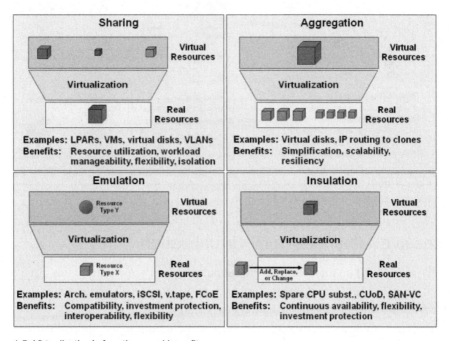

Figure 1.5: Virtualization's functions and benefits.

By decoupling and insulating software assets from their underlying hardware, then, virtualization can overcome many problems. IT administrators benefit because they can deploy and manage applications more dynamically and easily. The IT personnel who manage and maintain the underlying hardware also benefit because hardware resources can be taken off line non-disruptively, making hardware/firmware changes easier and more timely—and avoiding the need to beg IT users for hardware "change windows." Figure 1.6 shows the distinction between common configurations in non-virtualized environments and the improvements possible in a well-planned virtualization project. As the figure illustrates, virtualization technologies and emerging management software will significantly improve the efficiency and effectiveness of IT data centers.

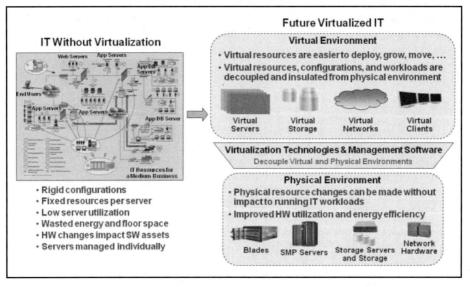

Figure 1.6: The vision of a fully virtualized IT.

Progressive Advances in IT Virtualization

Originally introduced on mainframe computers, virtualization technologies have been employed since the 1960s as a means for sharing resources such as servers and storage. These technologies have evolved over the years, and in the past decade they have proliferated to systems and resources of all types, including high-volume distributed systems. The widespread availability and increasing maturity of these technologies, together with the surge in pressure to cut IT costs, has led to the widespread use of virtualization, especially in server consolidation scenarios.

Historically, the focus of industry efforts has been on technologies that virtualize individual resources. In recent years, the industry has begun to develop new management software that builds upon these virtualization technologies to achieve two key advances in IT functionality:

- *Resource pools* that approximate the manageability of single resources
- *Virtual resource objects* that encapsulate virtual machines, virtual storage resources, and virtual networks as files, which can be stored in libraries, provisioned, versioned, and so on using new management tools

This advanced management software will play a major role in overcoming the escalating IT labor costs that have resulted from "distributed server" sprawl. Although these new capabilities (shown in Figure 1.7) are becoming available and beginning to be used today, they have not yet matured and are not yet widely used.

The following sections describe the foundational technologies used to virtualize individual IT resources, as well as the higher-level software technologies used to implement multi-system resource pools and encapsulated virtual resource objects.

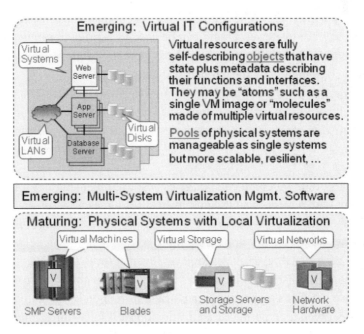

Figure 1.7: The expanding IT role of virtualization.

Virtualization of Individual IT Resources

Because virtualization came to most computer systems long after CPUs were developed, virtualization has always started as a software layer. However, when the importance of virtualization became clear, hardware manufacturers responded by building support into firmware and the chips themselves (such as Intel® Virtualization Technology). The trend toward moving support for virtualization deeper into hardware resources (servers, storage drives, networks, I/O adapters, and so on) is called *self-virtualization*.

Self-virtualization was fully achieved on mainframe computer systems in the late 1980s. In recent times, these virtualization capabilities have proliferated to industry-standard hardware resources.

Server Virtualization

The virtualization of servers began on mainframe computers in the mid-1960s, long before those machines became known as "servers." Two classic techniques have beenused:

- *Hardware partitioning*—The server is subdivided into fractions, each of which functions as a complete server and can be used in parallel to run its own instance of an operating system. This partitioning is generally done at the hardware level through a combination of special hardware and firmware.
- *Hypervisors*—A layer of code (software or firmware) is added to a server to create multiple virtual servers (often called *virtual machines*, but sometimes called *logical partitions*) that dynamically "timeshare" the server hardware resources.

The hardware partitioning method can be the easiest to implement, but it has limitations in the granularity with which it can assign physical resources to hardware partitions. Early implementations were only able to partition a server into two halves. Over time, the granularity has progressively improved to the board level, the processor "core" level, and even to the hardware thread level. However, even at these finer levels of hardware allocation, the hardware partitioning method is limited in its ability to share hardware resources because it assigns a partition to a particular fraction of the hardware. As a result, during any given time period, if a partition doesn't fully utilize the hardware resources that have been assigned to it, those unused resources cannot be used by some other partition.

In contrast, hypervisors can achieve much more effective resource sharing, by assigning physical resources to virtual resources for bursts of time. The shared physical resources need not become idle whenever their current user no longer needs them. Instead, they can be assigned immediately to another user under the control of some user priority mechanism. Furthermore, a hypervisor makes it possible to create arbitrarily large numbers of virtual resources, which can be very valuable for interactive workloads that spend most of their time waiting for the next human command, or that are otherwise I/O bound.

Hypervisors are often classified into *bare-metal hypervisors* and *hosted hypervisors*. Bare-metal hypervisors run directly on the server hardware. Hosted hypervisors run as extensions to, or applications upon, some underlying operating system that runs directly on the server hardware.

With hosted hypervisors, the underlying operating system is, in effect, a huge single point of failure that can easily reach many tens of millions of instructions in size. Due to its size and rich functionality, the operating system below a hosted hypervisor must be serviced often to fix bugs, apply security patches, add new device support, and so on. This makes hosted hypervisors poorly suited for business-critical roles. However, they can be attractive in some situations, such as in single-user client systems, where reboots are common and where it can be simpler to have the hypervisor piggyback on OS services such as device support.

For most server usage scenarios, bare-metal hypervisors are preferable because they can be purpose-built and very lean (e.g., 100K instructions, versus 10M instructions for an operating system), thereby minimizing the probability of failure due to latent bugs or service failures. In general, hypervisor malfunctions will cause all the active virtual machines to crash, so it is very desirable to minimize the cross-section of this inherent single point of failure. For this reason, bare-metal hypervisors are most widely used to run business-critical workloads.

To keep the size and complexity of a bare-metal hypervisor to a minimum, it is common practice to use a set of special virtual machines to implement specific aspects of virtualization, such as I/O device virtualization, as a "service VM" layer above the core hypervisor. If done right, failures in this service VM layer will be contained to a given service VM and will not cause the hypervisor to crash. Additionally, multipathing techniques are sometimes used, so that the loss of a service VM can be transparent to its users. This technique has been used for the IBM POWER® Hypervisor™ and its multiple Virtual I/O Servers since 2004, and it is becoming adopted widely in the industry as a general method for providing functions as extensions to a hypervisor.

Bare-metal hypervisors make it attractive to integrate the hypervisor with the server hardware as firmware. This has been done on the IBM System z® Processor Resource/System Manager (PR/SM) since 1988 and on IBM Power Systems since 2004.

Figure 1.8 illustrates the various architectures for server virtualization. Table 1.1 characterizes the advantages and disadvantages of these three approaches to server hardware virtualization and gives some examples of each approach.

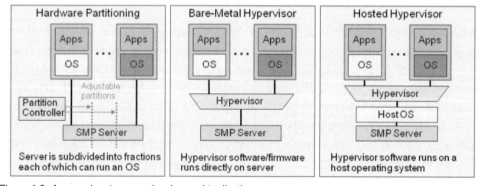

Figure 1.8: Approaches to server hardware virtualization.

The outlook is that bare-metal hypervisors will become the preferred and pervasive approach for servers, and these hypervisors will increasingly become integrated as part of the server firmware. Hosted hypervisors will continue to be used widely, but mainly in client devices such as home PCs, where their ability to piggyback on the host OS is important as a means to device support and where continuous availability is not a critical requirement. Hardware partitioning is expected to die out as an approach, due to its resource-sharing deficiencies, especially where server hardware becomes more integrated onto fewer chips.

Table 1.1: Comparison of Server Hardware Virtualization Approaches			
	Hardware Partitioning	Bare-Metal Hypervisor	Hosted Hypervisor
Pros	Board-level partitioning may provide electrical isolation.	Granularity may be very fine. The sum of virtual resources may far exceed physical resources. There is dynamic timesharing of all physical resources. Virtual machines may have dedicated hardware resources.	Granularity may be very fine. The sum of virtual resources may far exceed physical resources. The hypervisor can exploit OS services and device drivers.
Cons	Granularity is generally coarse, but can be at the hardware thread level. The number of virtual machines is limited, but may be sufficient. Hardware fractions become dedicated to partitions.	The hypervisor is a single point of failure.	The hypervisor is a single point of failure. The host OS is a large single point of failure and overhead factor.
Examples	• 1970s mainframe physical partitioning • POWER4™ LPARs • HP vPars • Sun Logical Domains	• IBM System z PR/SM and z/VM® • IBM PowerVM™ • VMware ESX • Xen Hypervisor • Microsoft® Hyper-V™	• VMware GSX • Microsoft Virtual Server • HP Integrity VM • User Mode Linux

The ubiquitous x86 category of servers (both Intel and AMD) still support virtualization largely through add-on software products, but the expectation is that server virtualization will soon become an integral capability of those platforms, with hypervisors becoming firmware, like the BIOS. VMware introduced this capability for its "ESX i" hypervisor family, which was first delivered on the IBM System x® 3950 M2 servers in 2007. Other hypervisor vendors also have begun to offer integrated versions of their products.

I/O Adapter Virtualization

Industry-standard I/O adapters are also becoming self-virtualizing through the use of architectures such as Single Root I/O Virtualization (SR-IOV), an extension of the PCI

Architecture for PCI-family I/O adapters, and N_Port ID Virtualization (NPIV), an extension of the Fibre Channel SAN Architecture for Fibre Channel storage networks. These architectures allow a single adapter to be shared concurrently by multiple operating systems, each running in its own virtual machine. By means of these architectures, individual I/O adapters are able to host multiple virtual I/O adapters that can be dynamically created, destroyed, reconfigured, and even moved while active from one physical server to another.

Network Virtualization

Virtual networks have long been available within mainframe computers. They are now becoming widely available on servers of all types. Typically, these have been implemented within the physical memory of a given server, as is done with Hypersockets on the IBM System z. Now, using new I/O virtualization capabilities, and corresponding virtualization capabilities that are being provided in network switches, virtual networks will be able to span large pools of servers, entire data centers, and even multiple data centers for some usage scenarios.

Storage Virtualization

Storage is virtualized in multiple ways that will continue to evolve and become more powerful. First, storage virtualization will continue to be provided as a basic function of the storage resources and storage systems (arrays or controllers) themselves. This has become standard practice on most storage products. In fact, one could argue that even the ability to partition a single hard drive is a primitive form of storage virtualization.

Second, storage virtualization will continue to be provided within servers as an efficient local way to rapidly provision shared storage resources. This is a popular way for server administrators to sub-allocate and manage virtual storage resources from a block of assigned physical storage resources, avoiding the need to make frequent discrete requests of the IT storage administrators.

Third, in the many real-world IT environments that have a diversity of server and storage resource types, it can be helpful to provide a storage virtualization function as an intermediary networked function that exists between the various servers and the various storage systems. Efforts to do this by placing the storage virtualization function within the network switch devices have not been successful in the past. In recent years, however, specialized networked appliances such as the IBM SAN Volume Controller have become effective and popular solutions.

OS and Middleware Virtualization

While hypervisors have become the most widely used approach for server virtualization, alternative approaches are also popular and may be preferable in some situations. Overall, these server virtualization approaches may be grouped into categories based on the level of the system stack at which the virtualization is accomplished. Starting at the bottom, the three main categories are as follows:

1. *Hardware virtualization*—The hardware resources (processors, memory, I/O adapters, storage, networks, and so on) are virtualized using hardware partitioning or a hypervisor. Each operating system runs on its own partition or virtual machine.
2. *OS virtualization*—The interfaces and resources of an operating system are virtualized via enhancements and extensions to the OS itself, creating virtual OS instances on which applications and middleware can be run. This is especially useful as a means to greater efficiency when running multiple copies of applications and middleware. It is very valuable for applications and middleware that can have only one instance per OS instance. By reducing the number of real OS instances that must be deployed, this approach can reduce the required amount of hardware resources. Examples include Workload Partitions (WPARs) for AIX® and Containers for Solaris.
3. *Middleware virtualization*—Middleware runtime environments can be highly abstract by their nature. For example, IBM WebSphere® applications run in Java™ Virtual Machines (JVMs) that decouple the applications from any specific real instance of WebSphere and even hide the underlying hardware instruction set architecture.

Virtualization at all three of these levels can provide significant benefits, including the efficient use of hardware resources and rapid application provisioning. However, each layer of virtualization brings its own complexity, and the combination of these layers requires coordinated management. Therefore, these approaches are typically not combined on a given server. Instead, one approach is usually chosen, based on the nature of the workloads that the given server will run.

Hardware virtualization is the most general-purpose approach because it can support the full range of software that can run on the server hardware. As one moves up the stack and virtualizes at a higher level, the virtualization is capable of supporting a narrower range of workloads. On the other hand, virtualizing higher in the stack (closer to the application) can be much more lightweight (not dragging extra copies of OS software per application) and efficient. It can also be more independent of the ever-changing hardware.

Resource Pools

Recently developed forms of management software enable the aggregation of multiple virtualized resources to form an integrated pool that looks, in most respects, like a single resource from a management perspective. Normal day-to-day management operations are performed at the pool level, treating the pool as one large server. Of course, some operations, such as servicing physical hardware, still need to be done at the server level. But these integrated resource pools constitute an important new class of IT building blocks that can play a major role in reducing the complexity and cost of managing distributed systems.

A server resource pool would typically integrate the following components:

- *Multiple server nodes*—These are normal servers packaged as blades, drawers, or towers. To facilitate the manageability of the pool as a single server, the nodes would generally need to be compatible from the viewpoint of the software workloads they run. This can be accomplished by making the nodes homogeneous, but it is desirable to allow the pool to include more than one generation of server nodes, for the purposes of flexibility and growth. Heterogeneity enables IT groups to create pools from existing hardware resources and then expand the pools later to incorporate newer servers.
- *Resource virtualizers*—These may be available for all types of hardware, depending on the type of pool required: hypervisors, self-virtualizing I/O adapters, network virtualizers, and storage virtualizers.
- *Virtual resource mobility*—This enables the non-disruptive movement of active virtual resources between nodes of the pool.
- *Local network*—This might be optimized for particular workload scenarios. Most local networks consist of the Ethernet du jour, but some roles benefit from more specialized networks.

- *System pool manager*—This can provide a single system-management interface, including both GUIs and APIs. The APIs permit scripting and custom automation of tasks.
- *Virtual resource placement optimizer*—This can automate the distribution of virtual resources within the pool.
- *Multi-system services*—These can provide such things as cluster locking, caching, and queuing at the pool level. The System z Parallel Sysplex introduced such "data sharing" cluster capabilities in the early 1990s. The IBM® DB2® pureScale™ offering for IBM Power Systems is a more recent example.
- *Platform-level tools*—These can be used for such tasks as capacity planning, image management, and physical-to-virtual migration (P2V). They can make a huge difference in reducing the amount of manual labor required.

The Benefits of Resource Pools

The benefits of resource pools can be very significant. The most prominent benefit is to relieve the IT organization from doing capacity planning and ongoing management for each individual server in the pool. Instead, integrated pool management software makes the pool look like one large server, both to personnel at a console and to service management software. Provisioning software can target the pool rather than a specific server node in the pool. The pool manager automatically places the new virtual resource within the pool and automatically redistributes the workload within the pool. Similarly, an administrator at a console sees a single dashboard for the pool, as if it were a single, large SMP server.

Additionally, by using pools that are prebuilt by a supplier, IT organizations can reduce the amount of labor spent on component selection, assembly, and testing to create a pool. The resulting pool can also be more standardized, resulting in less diversity, risk, and test/certification cost.

The virtual resource placement-management software that comes integrated with the pool can automate policy-based placement and redistribution of workloads within the pool. This achieves multiple IT objectives that are often in conflict, including the following:

- Optimized utilization of physical resources
- Fulfillment of workload performance requirements
- Maximum energy efficiency

- High resilience (no planned downtime, greater fault tolerance, and so on)
- Enforcement of security isolation requirements

To minimize complexity and required IT staff skills, future management software will build in intelligent behavior patterns that can be selected from menus, rather than exposing lots of knobs that require significant expertise in resource pool optimization.

This aggregation of multiple servers to form one logical server resembles what has happened with SMP servers over the years: as servers grew from uniprocessors to large-scale N-way multiprocessors, the software hid the numbers of processors in a given server, as well as which processor was being used by a given application. Unlike single SMP servers, however, resource pools can scale to many thousands of processors and can readily expand and contract without disrupting workloads or operations.

The Limitations of Resource Pools

Although virtualization-based resource pools promise huge benefits, they address only a fraction of the problems in IT complexity and introduce some new challenges of their own. They facilitate server hardware management, but they do not reduce the number of virtual machines to be managed.

There are practical limitations on how frequently one should move an active virtual machine within the pool, due to performance impacts on the moved VM and its neighbors. Also, automated workload placement and redistribution must observe constraints for security separation, performance co-location, and software licensing. These factors will tend to restrict the adoption of resource pools to particular usage scenarios.

Virtual Resource Objects

Virtual resource objects are the primary means by which virtualization will reduce the labor required to build, maintain, and manage the sprawl of software stack instances. The most common example of a virtual resource object is a single virtual machine "image" that consists of a file containing all the binary code and data needed to boot a virtual machine. The file includes metadata that describes what the virtual machine does, what it requires in terms of underlying resources and connectivity to other resources, and enough about its internal structure to allow the image to be edited. This metadata enables configuration, instantiation, startup, and servicing of the VM.

Today, these objects are simple atoms, such as a single VM image. However, industry standards for object formats (such as OVF) and emerging management software will support combinations of multiple virtual resource objects that are bound together like a molecule. New tools will create these atoms and molecules, store them in libraries, and provision them into virtualized IT environments. (IBM's OS/360 introduced similar functionality for System/360 in the 1960s, in the form of object modules, load modules, and the Linkage Editor—yet another example of how mainframes have led the way forward.)

Virtual resource objects will provide several important benefits:

- They provide a known good state of deployed software, reducing build errors.
- They facilitate provisioning, hibernation, backup, cloning, and versioning.
- They enable distribution of software as ready-to-run virtual appliances.
- Installation can be as simple as a copy operation, but configuration is still needed.

However, with these benefits come some challenges:

- The objects proliferate easily—just copy a file.
- Dormant objects need maintenance, too (e.g., security patches).
- Objects can lock in a good deal of hardware platform affinity. Strong compatibility across hardware generations will become very important.
- The tools, skills, and processes required to manage virtual resource objects are different from those widely used today.

New tools are being developed to manage—that is, to design, build, store, maintain, and deploy—virtual resource objects and to provide image libraries and service catalogs for these objects.

Integration for IT Simplification

Although resource pools and virtual resource objects have compelling benefits, their introduction to an existing IT environment can significantly increase complexity and cost. This can be blamed partly on IT process changes needed to accommodate and then reap the benefits of virtualization, and partly on the need for the IT staff, rather than the IT platform providers, to shoulder the burden of choosing, configuring, testing, and maintaining the virtualization technology and management software.

To simplify the deployment of virtualization and its ongoing costs, the industry has begun to deliver resource pools with virtual resource objects as integrated, standardized products that come preassembled from the factory in racks, or even shipping containers. Many clients will still want to build their own customized configurations or reuse existing IT assets, but the use of these integrated, standardized building blocks is expected to become widespread as a cost-effective approach for building or growing data centers.

Figure 1.9 shows the historical evolution of product offerings in virtualization and the ways they improve utilization.

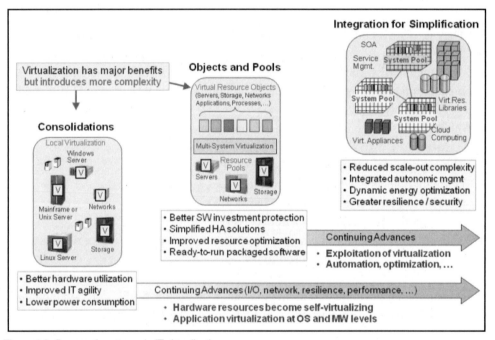

Figure 1.9: Progressive stages in IT virtualization.

New Challenges Introduced by Virtualization

IT administrators must learn new strategies for dealing with security, resilience, and resource sharing as they virtualize their environments. This section covers those concerns.

The IT Security Implications of Virtualization

The growing use of virtualization introduces new security risks and challenges. The sharing of physical resources, by itself, creates new exposures for unauthorized interactions that were not possible when users had their own dedicated resources. In addition, the virtualization technologies themselves may be compromised, especially if they are complex add-on software elements requiring frequent updates.

Despite these challenges, virtualization technologies will come to play a critical role as a foundation for achieving high levels of IT security. To limit their vulnerability, basic virtualization technologies will be provided as integrated and protected hardware features. Higher-level security functions will be provided as virtual appliances that run as service VMs on top of a secure hypervisor, safely isolated from vulnerable operating system VMs. Figure 1.10 shows the security that can be applied at each level of the virtualization stack.

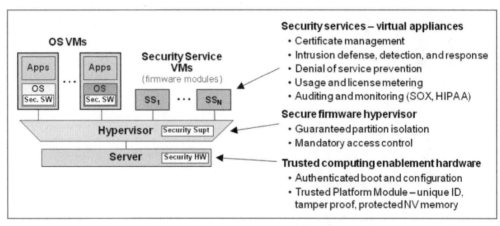

Figure 1.10: The security role of hypervisors.

General-purpose operating systems make weak foundations for secure computing because they are large and complex, with many latent bugs. They are also constantly changing, so security certifications are just pedigrees advertising that a level of security was achieved at a point in time by some version of the operating system's code. In addition, the OS role requires the implementation of a range of complex communication interfaces that make OS environments vulnerable to attack by viruses, worms, and hackers.

In contrast, the role of hypervisors is much more limited. Their primary role is the controlled sharing of hardware resources, so they are well suited to serve as a solid foundation for secure computing. A purpose-built hypervisor can be small enough to be fully inspected and certified. Because of its limited functionality, it may rarely need to be changed, and it can be integrated as firmware (e.g., a BIOS extension) that may not need to be changed for the life of the server.

However, even with the best possible foundation, the security of a system is determined by its weakest link, which may exist at higher levels in the system software stack or in the personnel who use the system. New virtualization-based management software is being developed and deployed to reduce the risk of security exposures and enable security policy enforcement. The term *Trusted Virtual Data Center* (*TVDc*) was introduced by IBM to describe its technology developed to address the security needs for virtualized IT environments. As shown in Figure 1.11, a TVDc consists of two major parts:

- Isolation Management enforces restrictions on administration and resource sharing.
- Integrity Management maintains a resource inventory and acts as an early warning system for anomalies to be detected and reported.

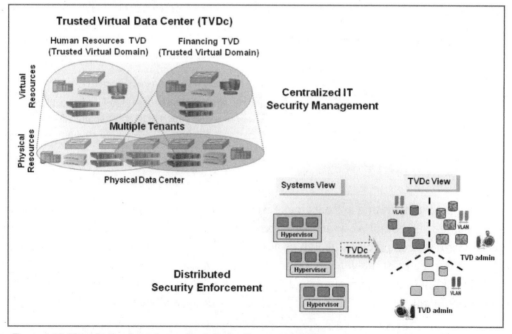

Figure 1.11: Virtualization-based security and security management.

The centralized IT security-management functions include the following:

- Trusted Virtualization Domain support, which is the grouping of virtual server, network, and storage resources that support common objectives (such as customers or workloads)
- Policy-driven, consistent security-configuration management
- Mediating between the views of data center administrators and TVD administrators

The distributed enforcement functions include the following:

- Very strong, coarse-grained security guarantees that cannot be bypassed by VMs
- Data center security-policy implementation across different platforms and hypervisors
- Event containment (for such things as malware and insider attacks)

The Resilience Implications of Virtualization

IT resilience can best be defined as the readiness to take advantage of good changes and to bounce back from bad changes. This includes a wide range of scenarios and solutions, ranging from transparent fault handling within a hardware component to multi-data-center disaster tolerance. Mitigation of planned outages can be as important as fault handling, and automation is often critical.

As with IT security, IT resilience requires the right processes and technologies at multiple levels in the system hierarchy. Again, virtualization introduces some challenges to be overcome (e.g., new single points of failure such as a hypervisor) but provides the means to make significant advances.

For example, consider the problem of keeping an application running, despite both planned and unplanned outages of its underlying server. Upon an outage, you must somehow relocate the application from its current server to a backup server, perhaps via a restart of the application and its underlying system software.

Traditionally, this is accomplished by using add-on high availability (HA) software that must be installed and configured at the OS, middleware, or application level to deal with the outage. The user of the HA software generally must also provide scripts that specify the actions to be taken for each event. This is a powerful approach that can provide rich HA functionality, including tight integration with the application, middleware, or OS. However, this approach can be costly to deploy and manage, as well as brittle. Periodic testing must be done to confirm that the desired HA actions will work as intended and have not been subverted by the effects of some change to the configuration parameters.

New virtualization-based HA software provides advanced capabilities at the VM level, without requiring modifications to the software stacks within the VMs themselves. Instead of writing scripts, the IT staff member selects behaviors from a menu of event-handling options. For example, the user might choose to enable the automatic redistribution of VMs within a resource pool, to deal with the many circumstances under which a server must be taken offline. For failure events, the user might choose to have the affected VMs restarted automatically on other servers in the pool. Virtualization-based mirroring technologies can checkpoint VMs so that they may be resumed with minimal disruption to service or loss of data.

In general, these new HA mechanisms are easier to deploy and manage. They can also work consistently for a wide diversity of software stacks. However, they have less HA functionality than traditional HA approaches (e.g., they can't recover from application failures).

The Importance of System Stack Integration

Ideally, the users of virtualized resources are unaware that the virtualization is happening. In some cases, however, it is desirable for the user to interact with the virtualization mechanisms, in order to optimize performance or to achieve some function that depends upon cooperation between the user and the virtualizer.

Software that has been designed under the assumption that it has exclusive control of the underlying hardware resources may perform poorly when run in a VM. For example, middleware that implements JVMs is typically designed to do "garbage collection" periodically, as a low-priority process that makes use of the wasted processor cycles in a non-virtualized server. Unfortunately, a virtualized server might not leave many spare processor cycles, and the garbage collection process can significantly degrade server throughput. For higher performance, such middleware needs to be "hypervisor aware." It may even communicate with the underlying hypervisor to keep background processes from having an unintended impact on foreground processes.

The implementation of many important system capabilities and attributes depends upon cooperation across multiple layers of the server system stack. Noteworthy examples include the following:

- Spin-lock handling
- Memory keys
- Transparent use of spare hardware
- Dynamic hardware expansion and contraction (CUoD)
- Selective memory mirroring
- Dynamic memory sharing
- Adjustable VM resources (DLPAR)
- Processor folding

Mechanisms such as these are already available on System z and Power Systems and will play an important role in future virtualized IT data centers in general.

Server Virtualization Products

This section is not a buyer's guide, or even an industry survey of virtualization products. Instead, it provides a brief history of server virtualization and then describes noteworthy products that are available today. References are made to these particular products throughout this book. Because product capabilities continue to improve rapidly, you should always consult the latest vendor product specifications when choosing a specific product.

History

Server virtualization originated in the mid-1960s as part of a novel approach to interactive computing. Most computing in those days was done using batch jobs. Although well-suited for running preplanned production workloads, batch jobs were very inefficient for doing work that required lots of interactions between the user and the computer. For example, when doing software development using batch jobs, even trivial programming errors would cause a software compilation job to fail, and the programmer would learn of the error only after a lengthy delay.

To facilitate software development and enable interactive computing in general, many industry projects were undertaken to develop advanced operating systems, called "time-sharing" systems, which would provide multiple users with concurrent interactive access to a shared computer. Notable examples included Project Multics at the Massachusetts Institute of Technology (MIT) and IBM's TSS/360.

One project stood out for its unique approach. Rather than develop a complex time-sharing OS, a project at the IBM Cambridge Scientific Center (in Cambridge, Massachusetts) divided the implementation into two parts:

- A hypervisor, called the Control Program (CP), gave each user a virtual machine and controlled the VMs' sharing of hardware resources.
- A simple OS, called the Cambridge Monitor System (CMS), ran within a VM and supported a single interactive user. CMS did not need to solve the challenging technical problems involved in supporting multiple interactive users and their sharing of computer resources.

CP/CMS was very successful as a time-sharing system. It led to a succession of widely used mainframe products, including VM/370, VM/XA, VM/ESA®, and today's z/VM.

The following are noteworthy milestones in the history of hypervisor development.

- 1966: The CP/CMS research project at IBM Cambridge Scientific Center develops an experimental hypervisor (CP-40) on a modified System/360 Model 40.
- 1968: IBM releases CP-67, the world's first publicly available hypervisor, for use on the System/360 Model 67.
- 1972: IBM introduces VM/370, the successor to CP-67/CMS, commercially available for the full System/370 computer family.
- 1985: Amdahl introduces Multiple Domain Facility (MDF), the first integrated hypervisor, as firmware, supporting up to four OS domains per 580-series computer.
- 1988: IBM delivers PR/SM (LPAR), an integrated firmware derivative of VM/370.
- 2001: IBM iSeries V5R1 introduces the first hypervisor based on PowerPC® hardware.
- 2001: VMware hypervisors (GSX, ESX) use incremental binary translation to run unmodified Windows and Linux in VMs on x86 servers, with good efficiency.
- 2003: The Xen hypervisor uses paravirtualization to run Linux guests at high efficiency, but it cannot run Windows.

- 2004: The IBM POWER Hypervisor is introduced as a standard feature of all POWER5™ servers. It contributes to significant market-share growth for AIX.
- 2005: Intel ships VT-x (Virtualization Technology) in Pentium 4 chips.
- 2005: Hewlett-Packard (HP) delivers the Integrity Virtual Machines (IVM) hypervisor, a hosted hypervisor based on HP-UX, for its Itanium-based server family.
- 2006: Advanced Micro Devices (AMD) ships AMD-V virtualization technology in Athlon 64 chips.
- 2007: Sun Microsystems introduces the Logical Domains feature for its low-end servers, partitioning the server hardware at the hardware thread level.
- 2007: The Kernel-based Virtual Machine (KVM) hypervisor becomes available as part of the Linux kernel, using VT-x/AMD-V (as now does Xen).
- 2008: Microsoft releases Hyper-V with Windows Server 2008, using VT-x/AMD-V.

Mainframe Server Virtualization

The hypervisors provided on mainframes have undergone decades of enhancements and have been required to meet the highest levels of efficiency, resiliency, and security. It comes as no surprise, then, that these hypervisors are generally acknowledged today as being the best.

IBM z/VM

A direct descendent of the original CP-67 hypervisor, z/VM and its underlying System z hardware have pioneered and perfected most of today's server virtualization technologies. z/VM is used in many different roles, but in recent years its most noteworthy use has been in running large numbers of Linux VMs per server with enterprise-grade qualities of service. The efficiency of z/VM, combined with the resiliency, security, and management strengths of the System z platform, have made Linux consolidations on z/VM attractive for many customers in terms of total cost of ownership (TCO).

IBM PR/SM

The Processor Resource/Systems Manager feature was introduced on the IBM System/370 processor family in 1988 and is widely used on System z servers today. It consists of integrated firmware that was derived from the IBM VM/XA hypervisor (a precursor to z/VM in the 1980s). PR/SM integration provides ease of use but also limits the functionality that PR/SM provides. For example, PR/SM is limited to running up to 60 VMs (called LPARs), whereas z/VM is often used to run thousands. z/VM also provides very rich VM software debugging capabilities, whereas PR/SM does not. In many situations, both PR/SM and z/VM are used on the same server.

Unix Server Virtualization

Given the many benefits of virtualization, all of the major Unix® server vendors have begun to provide server hardware virtualization capabilities for their product lines.

IBM PowerVM

The first hypervisor for Unix servers was the POWER Hypervisor, which became available as an integrated feature of all POWER5 servers in 2004 (under the name "Micro-Partitioning"). It was derived from an integrated PowerPC-based hypervisor delivered in 2001 for the IBM iSeries® server family. With the introduction of the IBM POWER6® family in 2008, this integrated hypervisor was rechristened "PowerVM." On POWER6 servers, it provides LPAR mobility—the ability to move a running LPAR from one POWER6 server to another without disrupting its operation.

HP Integrity VM

The HP Integrity VM hypervisor was released in 2005 for HP's Integrity series of servers, which are based on the Itanium architecture. It is a hosted hypervisor that runs on HP-UX. HP has made good headway in reducing the problems with availability and performance normally associated with hosted hypervisors. In 2009, the Online VM Migration capability was added, allowing customers to migrate active guests from one VM host to another without service interruption.

Sun Logical Domains (LDOMs)

In 2007 Sun introduced Logical Domains (LDOMs) as an integrated capability of its T1000/T2000 family of 1-2 socket servers. Unlike other hypervisors, this feature assigns virtual processors to specific hardware threads, allowing multiple LDOMs to share a given core or chip. This novel approach can make efficient use of the hardware threading mechanism. However, it has a noteworthy drawback: if an LDOM doesn't fully use the hardware threads assigned to it, they cannot be used by other LDOMs. Also, at least initially, the hypervisor firmware function needs one or more dedicated hardware cores, which affects the system's net efficiency.

x86 Server Virtualization

Prior to 2005, it was very difficult to virtualize the x86 architecture. One key impediment was the existence of x86 instructions that perform different functions depending on whether they are executed in Ring 0 (the most privileged architecture mode intended for use by an OS kernel) or Ring 3 (the most unprivileged architecture mode for use by application programs). Because of this, it was not possible for an x86-based hypervisor to dispatch a VM in Ring 3 mode and then gain control by a trap/interrupt whenever the VM issued one of these instructions that required special handling. The dual use of opcodes may have resulted from the origins of the x86 architecture on 8-bit microprocessors in the 1970s.

With the introduction of hardware support for virtualization by Intel in 2005 and AMD in 2006, it has become much easier to develop a hypervisor for x86 systems.

VMware

VMware ESX is the most widely used hypervisor today, with about an 86 percent share of the x86 server hypervisor market, according to market analysts such as Gartner. It was the first commercial hypervisor to run unmodified operating systems, including Windows. It accomplished this by using an incremental binary translation technique, in which the VMware hypervisor replaced the nasty "dual role" x86 instructions with explicit trap instructions as VM pages were loaded from storage to the server memory.

This approach continues to enable VMware ESX to work on older hardware that lacks virtualization support. In addition, VMware now exploits the virtualization support offered by newer x86 server hardware.

Through an enhanced management center called vSphere, VMware now leads in a range of valuable IT management capabilities that include, and build upon, the resource pools and virtual resource object functionality described earlier in this chapter.

Xen

Like VMware, the Xen hypervisor was introduced before Intel and AMD began to provide virtualization support in their microprocessor hardware. Unlike VMware, Xen used the paravirtualization approach, in which the OS running in a VM must interact with the hypervisor to accomplish the server virtualization. This precluded the first product release of Xen in 2003 from running Windows, so Xen was limited to running modified Linux systems. Subsequently, with the advent of x86 hardware support for virtualization, Xen became capable of running unmodified operating systems, including Windows. Still, its primary use has been in support of Linux, and it has been adopted and enhanced by both Citrix and Sun.

Microsoft Hyper-V

The Microsoft Hyper-V hypervisor was not introduced until 2008 and lags behind VMware and vSphere today in various respects. However, industry analysts expect it to gain significant market share because it will be included in widely used Windows product offerings.

KVM

The KVM hypervisor is a feature of the Linux kernel that was introduced in 2007. Like Hyper-V, KVM was designed from the outset to use the x86 hardware support for virtualization. Being relatively new, it has very little market share today. Because it is a mainstream component of the Linux kernel, it is popular with the Linux development community, and it is expected to become the predominant hypervisor for Linux. The capabilities of KVM and its accompanying management software have advanced greatly in a short time and will soon meet most IT needs.

IBM WebSphere Cloudburst Appliance

In April 2009, IBM introduced two new products that facilitate the use of IBM WebSphere software in virtualized IT infrastructures and cloud computing environments:

- *IBM WebSphere Cloudburst™* is a hardware appliance that allows customers to virtualize, deploy, and manage SOA in a cloud computing environment, cost-effectively and securely. WebSphere CloudBurst streamlines the process of creating WebSphere application environments and significantly reduces the time to set up, maintain, and tear down environments, while also reducing the potential for errors in the process.

- *IBM WebSphere Application Server Hypervisor Edition* is a version of IBM WebSphere Application Server software optimized to run in virtualized hardware server environments running hypervisors, such as VMware and PowerVM. This product comes preloaded in IBM WebSphere Cloudburst.

Together, these products are an excellent illustration of trends in the use of virtualization and cloud computing. They demonstrate virtualization at the WebSphere J2EE™ level, virtual resource object technologies, pools of servers that are manageable like a single system, and integrated service management functionality, including self-service provisioning and automated optimization.

Storage Virtualization Products

Storage virtualization has been widely available for many years as a software or firmware feature on most servers and storage controllers. Rather than describe the many traditional storage virtualization products available today, this section highlights three products that are representative of a significant shift in the virtualization of IT infrastructures: the IBM SAN Volume Controller (SVC), the VMware Virtual Machine File System (VMFS), and the IBM Scale-out File System (SoFS).

IBM SAN Volume Controller

As IT infrastructures continue to become more highly parallel and employ a growing variety of servers and storage systems, it has become advantageous to move the storage virtualization function into the network, where it is not bound to any particular type of server or storage product. The IBM SAN Volume Controller is a highly successful storage virtualization facility that accomplishes this, attaching to a Storage Area Network (SAN) and acting as an intermediary between the servers and the storage arrays/controllers on that SAN.

At a high level, SVC provides four main functions:

- Aggregation of the capacity from multiple storage arrays, which can be diverse offerings from many vendors, into a single pool of storage from which logical volumes/blocks/LUNs may be allocated

- Management of the storage pool from a central point
- Advanced copy services across the storage pool
- Insulation of host applications from changes to the physical storage resources that could otherwise be disruptive

VMware VMFS

As pools of servers with dynamic virtual resource mobility become widely used, it is no longer adequate for each server to do its own local storage virtualization. Instead, it becomes important to do the storage virtualization at the server pool level, facilitating the aggregation and sharing of virtualized storage resources, and allowing virtual machines to move about within the server pool, without actually moving their virtual storage resources. One way to accomplish this is by using a cluster file system as the shared repository for virtualized storage resources.

Introduced in 2006, the VMware Virtual Machine File System has become widely used as a base mechanism for storage virtualization and an enabler of VMotion, Storage VMotion, and HA/DR functions. More recently, it has been enhanced to use the vStorage APIs as a means of invoking advanced storage functions, such as copy services, that are implemented outboard within storage systems.

IBM SoFS

Most traditional cluster file systems and network file systems are quite limited in scalability. For example, VMware VMFS today allows no more than 32 servers to have access to a given shared virtual disk (virtual LUN). This constraint is typical of most NFS storage servers. Although acceptable in many scenarios, this limitation becomes a major issue as IT virtualization proceeds to extend across entire data centers. As a result, many clients today find themselves struggling to manage their NFS storage server scale-out sprawl. To overcome this issue, support cross-enterprise virtualization, and meet the needs of cloud computing that are described in the next section, a much more scalable virtual resource file system is required.

The IBM Scale-out File System is a highly scalable, efficient, and robust cluster file system that was developed to meet the needs of highly parallel supercomputers made of thousands of servers.

Network Virtualization

As with server virtualization, network virtualization has been emerging in stages, beginning with virtual networks local to a system and progressing to virtual networks that span pools of systems, whole data centers, and even multiple data centers.

Server-local network virtualization is exemplified by the HiperSockets™ technology that has been on IBM mainframes since the 1980s. This technology implements a virtual TCP/IP LAN within the memory of the server, providing in-memory TCP/IP connections for the virtual machines (LPARs) running on that server. The benefits of this are significant and include higher performance communications, lower hardware costs, and avoidance of the need for an external LAN with its physical cabling. As a result, server-local virtual LANs have become widely available throughout the industry as extended functions of hypervisors.

As the scope of IT virtualization expands to the data center level, it becomes necessary to provide end-to-end network virtualization capabilities for entire data center networks. To accomplish this, network hardware vendors have begun to provide major new capabilities in their network switches (e.g., the Cisco Nexus 1000V), including support for the following:

- *Sharing of the distributed physical network by multiple distributed virtual networks.* This requires the ability to create and manage the virtual networks, isolate them from one another, and ensure that each virtual network is provided with its required qualities of service (such as performance and resilience).
- *Binding of virtual network endpoints to virtual server and storage resources.* The virtual machines and virtual storage resources implemented within the many systems in the data center need to be able to bind to endpoints of the virtual networks, not just to physical network endpoints. Also, given that virtual resources will be moveable while active from one physical system to another, the virtual resource mobility-management software and underlying virtualization technologies must interact with the data center network-virtualization software to coordinate and unify the management of server, storage, and network resources, both physical and virtual.
- *Emulation of Fibre Channel networks over Ethernet networks (FCoE).* To reduce the cost and complexity of having a separate SAN physical network, the industry has developed an ANSI-standard architecture for emulating Fibre Channel SANs on Ethernet networks. This network virtualization enables a consolidation of these

networks and is of increasing value as increasing numbers of virtual machines become consolidated per physical server. However, there are performance and quality of service issues with FCoE, which will slow its rate of adoption as an FC SAN replacement.

Cloud Computing: The Next Phase in IT

Like virtualization, cloud computing has many definitions. We define it as an emerging approach to IT, in which applications, information, and resources are provided as services to users over the Web. So, one may ask, what's new about cloud computing? After all, the Web has long been used to deliver software and information. With the introduction of grid computing during the past decade, the Web is already being used to provide controlled sharing of remote physical resources.

Cloud computing is indeed an evolutionary advance and may be viewed as the next phase in the evolution of sharing over the Internet, as depicted in Figure 1.12. However, enabled by the combination of many technology improvements, including various uses of virtualization, cloud computing has begun to cause a sea change in how IT services are delivered to consumers and deployed by providers.

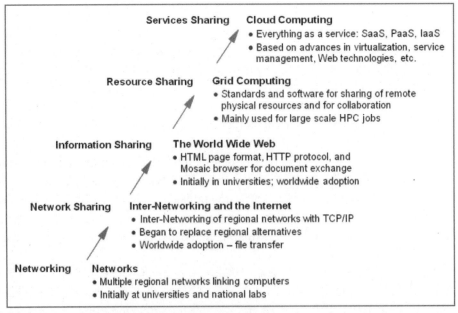

Figure 1.12: The evolution of sharing on the Internet.

Cloud computing enables users to obtain services over the Web from infrastructure providers, instead of having to implement those services on the user's own computer hardware. Examples of popular cloud services today include office productivity suites (a form of software as a service) and virtual disks (a form of virtual hardware resources). The types of services they provide vary widely and are categorized hierarchically as follows:

- *Infrastructure as a Service* (IaaS) is the bottom layer. It consists of virtualized hardware resources, such as VMs, virtual disks, and virtual desktops provided as cloud services.
- *Platform as a Service* (PaaS) is an intermediate level of application runtime environment that may be used as a base for implementing cloud applications. Google App Engine and the new WebSphere and .NET cloud service offerings occupy this tier, as do a range of new middleware platforms developed to support particular cloud applications.
- *Software as a Service* (SaaS) is the top level of the service hierarchy. It includes such things as office productivity suites, collaboration tools, and even business processes as cloud services.

Such cloud services can be very attractive to users, due to the following characteristics:

- *Low cost.* This results in part from the dynamic sharing of pooled cloud resources, together with the vendor's ability to do "thin provisioning" of just enough virtualized cloud resources. In addition, large clouds can achieve major economies of scale in both capital expense and operational expense.
- *Elastic scaling, with a low entry point and massive scaling capabilities.* A cloud service may be as small as an application that gets downloaded to mobile phones or as large as a virtual IT data center used to host high-performance computing workloads. Many cloud services are adjustable in capacity and performance.
- *Flexible pricing.* Cloud service pricing is typically usage-based and progressive. (Users pay more as their usage grows.)
- *Rapid provisioning through browser-based self-service portals.* To obtain a service, users need not install the service software or hardware themselves or request that the service be installed by some intermediary group. Instead, the service can be chosen and configured from a menu, and, thanks in large part to virtualization, the service can become available within minutes.

- *Standardized functions and interfaces.* Cloud services are usually designed to be attractive to a multitude of users, rather than tailored to each user. Also, popular cloud services and their interfaces tend to become de facto standards, by virtue of their familiarity to large numbers of users.
- *High availability.* Cloud services can be as highly available as the Web, but true continuity of service requires special hardware and software infrastructures and thus generally comes at a premium price.
- *Global accessibility.* The ubiquity of the Web enables users to access clouds from almost anywhere, and even while mobile.

From the perspective of IT providers, cloud computing is a valuable but potentially disruptive advance because of the following:

- It can be more efficient than traditional IT implementation methods for a significant and growing subset of IT services.
- It enables a new business model for IT as a dynamic utility, rather than as a dedicated resource. IT providers may choose to buy some adjustable fraction of their infrastructure as cloud services. Conversely, they may sell some of their own infrastructure capacity to others as cloud services.
- It has the potential to expand the IT provider's addressable market to a global scale. This may include the vast range of emerging user devices, such as mobile appliances, as well as the new instrumentation and control devices that are becoming a critical part of what IBM has termed our "Smarter Planet™."

Given all these upsides, one might jump to the conclusion that cloud computing will quickly replace traditional IT implementation methods. The reality is that cloud computing faces huge challenges, most notably these:

- *Achieving security and resiliency.* These attributes are highly dependent on the IT environment of the cloud provider. A string of cloud outages and security breaches have grabbed headlines in recent years. Today's cloud implementations, while acceptable for running some important and growing workloads, generally fall far short of meeting the demanding security and resiliency needs of business-critical workloads.
- *Ensuring scalability and responsiveness.* Latency to remote services and resources is important for many workloads. The proximity of storage to an application's location can be critical for some workloads.

- *Supporting audits and certifications.* Compliance with Sarbanes-Oxley, HIPAA, the Payment Card Industry (PCI) Data Security Standard, and other regulations becomes problematic when parts of a required IT infrastructure are "out there in a cloud someplace."
- *Federating diverse clouds.* There is a growing need to integrate cloud services with one another and with existing enterprise services. The required reference architectures and interoperability standards are progressing but are still in an early stage of development.
- *Application licensing and tracking.* This can be a significant problem for cloud providers, and for some cloud users who desire to move software resources across licensing boundaries. Virtualization-friendly and cloud-friendly software licensing is needed but will take time to evolve and become widespread.
- *Providing technical support across clouds.* It can be extremely difficult to diagnose and resolve problems, even within the confines of a single IT data center. Extending IT infrastructures to include external clouds can make matters worse.
- *The human element. ("Mine!")* Change is especially difficult when it requires someone to relinquish control of something he or she owns.

The industry is developing architectures, standards, and service management software to deal with these and other issues, but it will be many years before all of these challenges are overcome. Even with these difficult issues, however, public clouds from vendors such as Google, Amazon, Yahoo!, Microsoft, and IBM are already handling important workloads such as collaboration, Web serving, high-performance computing, virtual desktops, and development/test environments.

To meet the more stringent needs of business-critical workloads, enterprises have begun to employ private clouds that reside within their own data centers and comply with their IT processes for security, resiliency, change control, auditability, and so on. Cloud providers such as IBM will work with enterprises to create private clouds that meet specific enterprise needs and will also optionally host such clouds, as a trusted enterprise cloud provider.

Over time, both public and private clouds will improve to handle a growing range of workloads. Ultimately, the industry will establish a cloud capability maturity model (CMM) that will serve as the basis for cloud certifications by an ecosystem of licensed auditors.

Summary

IT must undergo a major transformation to overcome the growing management costs of distributed server sprawl and to meet challenging new requirements. Virtualization will play a vital role in this transformation, by facilitating IT infrastructure management and enabling new solutions to the expanding set of IT requirements.

Introducing virtualization where it has not been used before affects nearly every existing IT process, including the processes for capacity planning, software licensing, usage accounting, chargeback, and resource lifecycle management, to name a few. It is therefore important, when planning for IT virtualization, to carefully weigh both the benefits and impacts of virtualization up front and to apply best practices and service patterns such as those described in this book.

Although virtualization provides compelling benefits today, it still has a long way to go to fulfill its ultimate role. Nearly all IT resources will be virtualizable, and many will become self-virtualizing within the next several years, but adoption of these technologies within existing IT environments will progress in stages over many years. Moreover, the management software that controls the use of these virtualization technologies and provides most of the overall benefits is still in an early stage of maturity. It is improving rapidly, but it is many years away from being standardized.

Cloud computing is a major beneficial, but disruptive, approach that will play a huge role in the coming IT transformation. It will employ virtualization to provide a wide range of IT functions (applications, information, and infrastructure) as services over the Web. In so doing, it will finally deliver on the longstanding promise of what has been called "utility computing."

Cloud computing is already gaining widespread use within homes and small businesses. Concerns with cloud security and resiliency today limit its use by enterprises to non-business-critical roles, but these issues will be overcome. For many enterprise workloads today, the economics of private clouds look compelling, and advances in technology will enable a growing range of usage scenarios for both private and public clouds.

CHAPTER 2

Why Virtualization Matters for Green Data Centers

O ver the past decade, we have all witnessed changes to our lives made possible by IT. Cell phones have been upgraded to smart phones, which are now being used for almost everything except making a phone call. Hybrid cars can parallel-park themselves. Personal video recorders allow you to watch days of prerecorded programming at your convenience. New laws require medical information to be kept for the life of the patient. Just imagine how much data will be kept on someone who is born today and lives to be over 100!

Similar new applications have arisen at the corporate level. However, because IT organizations often spend over 70 percent of their budgets just to maintain previously installed applications, less than 30 percent is left for tactical and strategic improvements.

At the same time, customers have become more dependent on these applications, requiring an increase in requirements for business continuity and security. Many people are familiar with the phrase "mission critical," whose origins lie in IT applications sent aboard space missions that were not allowed to fail, such as life support systems. Availability was improved with the addition of redundant systems. Today, every industry has mission-critical applications. From neo-natal monitoring in a hospital, to stock-market trading, to monitoring the energy grid, redundant systems are put in place to prevent failure. This redundant equipment requires data center resources, which drive up the cost of IT support.

The dependence on applications has also driven the need to make them more secure. While IT organizations have voluntarily increased security, regulations have been put in place in several industries to minimize the risks associated with a security breach. In the medical profession, for example, the U.S. Health Insurance Portability and Accountability Act of 1996 (HIPAA) contains provisions for the security and privacy of health data. These additional security requirements, and the resources required to support and audit them, continue to drive up the cost of operational IT support.

The demand for new applications, combined with the need to secure them, has also increased the amount of IT equipment required. Data volumes and network bandwidth are doubling every 18 months. Devices accessing data over the Internet are doubling every 2.5 years. This increase in IT equipment has driven a corresponding increase in data center requirements, as there needs to be a place to put all this new equipment.

This equipment also needs to be powered. Studies have shown that IT equipment used about 180 billion kilowatt-hours of electricity in the United States in 2005, roughly two percent of the energy generated in the country. At current growth rates, IT's power requirements are expected to double by 2012. At ten cents per kilowatt-hour, this equates to $36 billion in IT energy costs. Unfortunately, studies have also shown that the cost of energy has increased by 44 percent from 2004 to 2009, with estimates of annual double-digit growth for the next several years. Meanwhile, most IT organizations have flat or decreasing IT budgets, so this increase in energy costs is often offset by decreases in tactical and strategic improvements to the IT environment.

To summarize, the operational challenges surrounding IT organizations are approaching a breaking point because of these trends:

- Electronic data processing demand is increasing for new applications.
- Electronic data processing demand is increasing due to business-continuity redundancy requirements.
- Electronic data processing demand is increasing due to security requirements.
- IT equipment and electricity use is tied to increased demand, raising data center costs.
- Energy costs are also going up, due to per-unit price increases.
- IT organizations must compensate for these increased costs to stay within flat or declining budgets.

The critical lesson to take from this is that IT must reduce its hardware footprint. IT must learn to make more efficient use of hardware, software, and personnel resources.

Opportunities Abound for the Greening of IT

Fortunately, there are significant opportunities, through virtualization, to address the demand and cost issues in the IT environment. First, let's start by defining green information technology ("green IT"). Green data centers are those that make better use of facilities and information technology integration, resulting in lower energy costs, a reduced carbon footprint, and reduced demands for power, space, and cooling resources. Using this definition, it's clear that green is as much about the economics as it is about the environment.

Opportunities for "going green" exist on both the facilities and IT sides of the data center. Many people were surprised when reports were published indicating that two-thirds of the power that came into a data center never reached a piece of IT equipment. The power that did make it in ended up running servers that used, on average, less than 10 percent of their capacity. In effect, companies were paying for 10 times more than they needed to power equipment and data center resources. There are also power losses associated with the power distribution from the power plant to the data center. Figure 2.1 depicts these inefficiencies. The pie chart on the left shows the ratio between power devoted to computers and power devoted to other elements of the data center. The pie chart on the right shows the ratio of the power used for a server's processor versus other parts of the computer.

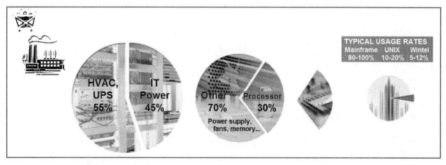

Figure 2.1: Energy loss from the power plant to the processor.

The inefficiencies represented in this figure are actually opportunities for the greening of IT. Let's go over them, from the source of the power to its ultimate use:

1. From the power plant to the data center, there is typically a reduction of 100 units of power down to 33 units of power.
2. From the data center to the IT equipment, there is typically a reduction from 33 units of power down to 15 units. This is because about half of the energy is used for cooling the IT equipment and for additional power distribution within the data center.
3. From the IT equipment to the processor, there is typically a reduction from 15 units down to 4.5 units, because the processor requires only about 30 percent of the energy used by the server.
4. From the overall processor to the amount used by the processor to perform productive work, there is typically a reduction from 4.5 units down to 0.45 units, as processors run at 10 percent utilization.

The combined effect of these inefficiencies is that, for every 100 units of energy produced at a power plant, only half a unit is used for productive processing within a server. Put another way, 99.5 percent of the energy generated for IT use is consumed prior to being productively used by the processor. Consider that in relation to the $36 billion in estimated energy costs for IT in 2012. Clearly, companies that can find ways to become more efficient can apply their savings to keep IT budgets flat or even reduced.

Virtualization focuses on improving the fourth inefficiency, by improving processor utilization. In a simple case, doubling the CPU utilization to 20 percent not only cuts the energy requirements in half at the processor level but has a ripple effect across the entire end-to-end energy use. In other words, doubling the CPU utilization for the same amount of IT load can also halve the amount of server hardware needed and, in turn, the amount of data center resources (power, space, and cooling) needed to house the servers. The savings in hardware and data center costs are actually more significant than the associated energy savings.

So, what do we do with the equipment that is no longer needed because of virtualization? It is estimated that one billion computers will become potential scrap by 2010. Older servers were manufactured with a small portion of hazardous substances that pose a toxic risk if not disposed of properly. About half of the companies in the United States already have eco-friendly disposal plans. This figure is likely to increase as government regulations tighten on the proper disposal of IT equipment.

Many companies are starting to offer IT equipment-recycling programs. IBM is one such company. It receives about 40,000 pieces of IT equipment a week. This equipment is either refurbished to be put out for reuse, disassembled to be used as replacement parts for failed components, or sent to landfills after hazardous materials have been removed. Less than one percent of the material received by IBM in this process goes to landfills, with none of the material toxic. This process is a combination of good economic and environmental practices. Reused servers and parts are resold, and the environment is improved by significantly reducing IT equipment in landfills and properly treating hazardous substances.

IBM Data Center Expertise and "Big Green"

IBM operates hundreds of data centers with over 8 million square feet of data center space on behalf of its customers. Over half of this space is operated by the Information Technology Delivery (ITD) organization, which provides outsourcing services for IBM. ITD's shared data centers span a large range of sizes, from the 300,000-square-foot facility in Boulder, Colorado, to much smaller single-customer data centers. The remaining data center space is operated by IBM's Business Continuity and Recovery Services (BCRS), which provides disaster recovery services, and by its Systems and Technology Group (STG), which provides compute-on-demand services, where customers can lease computing resources on IBM premises. (Cloud computing is not a recent concept for IBM.)

One of the largest accounts that ITD supports is for IBM itself, the IBM Global Account (IGA). Between 1997 and 2007, however, IGA's production workload drastically decreased, as shown in Table 2.1.

Table 2.1: Decrease in IGA Workload		
Metric	**1997**	**2007**
Chief Information Officers	128	1
Traditional Data Centers	155	7
Web Hosting Data Centers	80	5
Networks	31	1
Applications	15,000	4,700

The IGA moved from 235 data centers to a dozen, converging into one network in the process and implementing virtualization techniques for server and storage consolidation. By combining organizations, IGA was also able to converge to fewer applications. The reduction in applications improved labor costs; in the previous distributed environment, for instance, each data center required its own IT organization and Chief Information Officer. It also reduced the amount of data center and IT resources required to support the consolidated organization.

Leveraging what it had learned from IGA and other accounts, IBM announced the Project Big Green initiative in May 2007. The announcement stated that IBM would reallocate $1 billion per year to accelerate green technologies. The investment had two components:

- To develop new hardware, software, and services for green IT
- To invest in our internal data centers to inject these newly developed technologies

Based on its own experiences, IBM would offer a roadmap for clients to address IT energy costs. The initiative also provided for the training of a thousand energy specialists within IBM, to help customers address their energy concerns.

The emphasis on energy conservation was not a new one for IBM. From 1990 to 2005, energy conservation efforts at IBM resulted in a 40 percent reduction in carbon dioxide emissions and more than a billion dollars in energy savings. The Project Big Green initiative specified that $100 million of the $1 billion investment would be spent on infrastructure to support best practices in remanufacturing and recycling.

The ability to grow IT business while saving costs through the injection of new technology was a key value proposition for customers. A 25,000-square-foot data center with an average density of 40 watts of energy per square foot consumes $2.6 million in energy costs annually. The use of the new technologies promoted by IBM cuts the energy use of this data center in half, saving $1.3 million per year. Companies with larger data centers save even more. The economic energy savings are matched by the corresponding environmental savings of a reduced carbon footprint.

New Models for Efficient IT Delivery

With the rapid improvements in IT technology, many IT organizations have established a process for continuous improvement. In fact, the Information Technology Information

Library (ITIL®), the most popular industry guideline for running an IT service, has a whole book devoted to continuous service improvement. The following three models show an evolution of the data center and the vital role that virtualization plays in the continuous improvement paradigm:

- New Enterprise Data Center (NEDC) model
- Dynamic Infrastructure model
- Smarter Planet model

The New Enterprise Data Center Model

In February 2008, IBM launched an updated strategy around the data center that formalized the direction it has taken over the last several years. Based upon previous initiatives, such as Service Oriented Architecture (SOA), Information Systems Management (ISM), Information on Demand (IOD), and IT Optimization (ITO), this strategy brought together major elements to help clients evolve to a more efficient and responsive model for IT service delivery.

The NEDC model has three stages of adoption: simplified, shared, and dynamic. In the simplified stage, IT organizations consolidate data centers and physical infrastructure such as servers, storage, and networks.

As the workload is consolidated, organizations can progress to the shared stage of adoption. To reap economies of scale, virtualization is used to place multiple workloads on the same physical piece of equipment, thereby improving cost, availability, and performance. It is typical in the shared stage to statically map virtual workloads to physical resources.

The dynamic stage of adoption provides policy-based system management that lets virtualized workloads move between physical resources without down time. Based on historical analyses of workload performance, automation functions are written and placed into the system management code to optimize the IT environment by moving the workload dynamically, in response to workload changes. This allows an IT organization to improve the utilization of its physical resources, as fewer excess resources are needed to respond to changes in workload.

The Dynamic Infrastructure Model

Even with the NEDC vision, additional progress was required as new technology continued to be developed. As of 2007, 85 percent of distributed capacity was still sitting idle. Consumer product and retail industries lost about $40 billion (or 3.5 percent of their sales) due to supply-chain inefficiencies. On average, 70 percent of IT budgets were spent maintaining current infrastructures, instead of adding new capability. Data explosion drove an increase of 54 percent in storage. Better security was also demanded, driven by the fact that 33 percent of consumers notified of a security breach terminate their relationship with the company, perceiving the company to be responsible.

In response to the continuing need to simultaneously improve service, reduce cost, and reduce risk, IBM announced the Dynamic Infrastructure model. The model consists of the elements shown in Figure 2.2.

Figure 2.2: The Dynamic Infrastructure model for continuous improvement.

As you can see, virtualization and energy efficiency are two of the elements of the model. Implementing virtualization through the Dynamic Infrastructure model enables organizations to do the following:

- *Reduce operating costs.* Virtualization can consolidate a workload onto fewer servers and accessories. The reduced number of devices, in turn, simplifies management of the infrastructure. The recaptured floor space from workload consolidation can either be used for growth or simply eliminated.
- *Improve service responsiveness.* Properly designed virtualization solutions improve system, network, and application performance. Processing more information in real time enables organizations to make better business decisions. Virtualization techniques also allow organizations to bring new services online quickly, as the wait for physical server installation decreases.
- *Manage availability in a 24-by-7 world.* By designing virtual solutions with high availability characteristics, organizations can increase availability and improve resiliency. They can also manage and secure data without negatively affecting its availability.
- *Dynamically adapt to the peaks of the business.* Virtualization allows organizations to dynamically deliver resources where they are most needed. If included in the virtualization solution, workload balancers can measure resource utilization and be directed through policy-based management to automatically optimize workload on the existing resources.

By implementing energy efficiency through the Dynamic Infrastructure model, organizations can do the following:

- *Reduce energy use.* As part of virtualizing the workload onto fewer physical resources, organizations can implement virtualization on more energy-efficient servers and storage. Improving the facilities infrastructure efficiency reduces the energy needed to supply power and cooling to the IT equipment, further reducing energy requirements.
- *Reduce capital and operating costs.* Improving facilities and IT efficiency extends the life of an existing data center and avoids or delays the capital costs of building new data centers. The reduction of energy usage reduces overall operating costs.
- *Measure and control energy usage.* By understanding energy consumption, organizations can determine the positive effects of such changes as virtualizing servers. This data can then be used to put in place policies to manage and control energy use via techniques such as dynamic image movement to minimize energy consumption.
- *Establish a green strategy.* Many governmental organizations have already unveiled voluntary programs for improving data center efficiency, such as the

European Union's Code of Conduct for Data Centers and the U.S. Environmental Protection Agency's (EPA's) Energy Star Rating for Data Centers. These voluntary programs are being extended by regulatory requirements for stricter controls over energy consumption, carbon footprints, and the disposal of hazardous substances. In response to these emerging requirements, companies are establishing green strategies to reduce energy usage, which also reduces costs.

Virtualization itself is a key tenet within the Dynamic Infrastructure model to improve service, reduce cost, and manage risk. Virtualization also improves the other tenets of asset management, information infrastructure, business resiliency, and security, as shown here with energy management.

The Smarter Planet Model

The world is getting smaller, flatter, and hotter as we integrate our global economy. The economic downturn requires us to do more with the same amount of resources. The effects of climate change are both a societal and a business concern. Meanwhile, energy use is rising at an unprecedented rate. The same IT techniques being used inside the data center can now be leveraged outside the data center, to reduce costs by eliminating waste in every industry.

This is the premise of the Smarter Planet model. Through the additional use of IT, an organization can become more instrumented, interconnected, and intelligent. Similar autonomic analysis can be performed on the data from each industry, and better decisions can be made not only to improve the quality of products produced but also to reduce their costs.

Smarter water use is produced by applying monitoring and management technologies to help reduce the use of water, as well as related energy and chemicals. Smarter traffic employs dynamic traffic prediction. This provides the basis for dynamic tolling, which leads to reducing congestion. Its byproducts positively improve customer traffic flow and conserve energy. Smarter energy conservation is promoted by analyzing customer usage patterns and providing customized products and services that boost efficiency from the source, through the grid, to the consumer.

Additional analytics produce a significant increase in productivity and reduced costs. These analytics increase the demand for IT resources. Virtualization is a major component in the Smarter Planet model to optimize the amount of IT resources required through higher utilization of physical resources.

The Five Building Blocks of Green Data Centers

There are five major building blocks for building and maintaining green data centers, summarized in Figure 2.3.

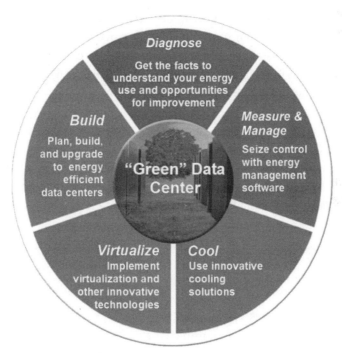

Figure 2.3: The five building blocks of a green data center.

Building Block 1: Diagnose

The first building task is to diagnose the data center, getting the facts so that you understand your energy use and opportunities for improvement. There are many metrics to use to diagnose the data center. At the highest level, the measure that has been most widely adopted is the ratio of power coming into a data center divided by the amount of power used by the data center's IT equipment. This metric has been further defined by the Green Grid, an industry organization formed to improve data center efficiency. The metric is called *Power Usage Effectiveness*, or *PUE*. In 2006, a survey showed that data centers typically had a PUE of 3 or higher, indicating that it took three watts of electrical energy coming into the data center for a piece of IT equipment to use one watt. The extra two watts were used to cool the IT equipment, or in power losses within the data center (from such things as charging emergency batteries, transforming to different voltage levels, and converting alternating current to direct current).

In addition to the PUE metric, organizations should also understand the facts around the major subsystems and components of the facilities and IT equipment. On the facilities side, this means keeping track of the utilization metrics for the power (utility, battery, and generator), three-dimensional space (how much space is left for IT equipment), and cooling (how many tons of cooling are required to keep equipment safe from overheating). On the IT side, this means keeping track of the utilization metrics for servers, storage, and network equipment.

At one time, these metrics were obtained manually. It was not uncommon for facilities personnel to walk around the data center periodically and record the metrics. In more recent times, the facilities and IT equipment have increased their instrumentation, interconnection, and intelligence (as indicated in the Smarter Planet model), so these metrics are now collected automatically.

Building Block 2: Build

There are three ways to improve the efficiency of a data center:

- Extend the life of an existing data center.
- Leverage the contributions of multiple data centers.
- Build a new data center.

Each of these ways involves a change of some sort (small or large), which for simplicity is called "build" here. This block includes the planning, building, and deployment of more efficient data centers. The result of the build should improve the PUE and utilization metrics obtained in the diagnose phase.

Extending the life of an existing data center starts by diagnosing which data center component is constrained. It is typical for older data centers to have developed different levels of capacity between major subsystems. For example, they might have 2 megawatts of Uninterruptible Power Supply (UPS, or batteries) and 2.4 megawatts of generators because they purchased UPS in 1-megawatt units and generators in 0.8-megawatt units. As both the UPS and generator capacity are needed for additional IT equipment, the UPS will become constrained before the generator. This mismatch is a source of optimization for data centers. In this example, adding 0.4 megawatts of UPS capacity uses up the excess capacity of the generator and postpones building a new data center.

Leveraging multiple data centers applies the same optimization concepts from a single data center to a collection of them. For example, there might be excess computing power in one data center, and excess storage in another. By understanding the constrained and surplus resources of the various data centers, an organization can move IT workload between them to better optimize its resources. Likewise, it might be possible to consolidate data centers. In many cases, they can be consolidated with a minimal amount of additional resources.

As is best practice for all major IT changes, a detailed business case should be prepared for any data center consolidation, so that you can understand the investments you would need to make and the returns that would be achieved.

Building Block 3: Virtualize

Most of the building blocks for green data centers apply to the physical facilities side of the data center. This block applies to the IT side. Although the primary focus of this book is the virtualization of servers, a number of other types of equipment—storage, network, and desktops—can also be virtualized to improve IT efficiency.

In the simplified adoption stage of the New Enterprise Data Center model, applications are dedicated to specific IT devices. Although this provides isolation and capacity planning at the application level, it is extremely inefficient, as excess capacity from one application cannot be used by another application. Virtualization removes that constraint, as it maintains isolation of server instances in the software, while logically partitioning the hardware in such a way that hardware resources can be shared between partitions when needed. This allows an IT organization to achieve economies of scale by pooling IT resources. It also decreases the amount of excess resources for a particular application, by making sure that sufficient resources are available in the pool.

Building Block 4: Cool

For the many data centers where the PUE is above two, more energy is being spent on cooling the data center than on IT equipment. Because this is the long pole in the tent, the IT industry has focused on improving cooling technology within data centers, both tactically and longer term. In many data centers, this is "low-hanging fruit" because they did not prioritize the management of airflow. Increases in the cost of cooling are causing them to take another look.

Many organizations can extend the life of their existing data centers by improving airflow. For instance, a best practice in the data center creates hot and cold aisles of IT equipment by facing the exhaust sides of the equipment toward each other, with cold air coming up through the floor via perforated tiles in the cold aisle.

Inefficiencies in airflow are created when hot air mixes with cold. This situation is all too common with cable cutouts in the floor, or racks of equipment with gaps in the rack that allow the air to mix. Low-cost solutions are now available to easily seal cable cutouts and install faceplates in racks of equipment. This improved airflow increases efficiency and reduces the amount of cooling needed. In turn, this efficiency translates to either lower energy costs or the ability to reuse the cooling capacity elsewhere in the data center.

Block 5: Measure and Manage

As mentioned earlier, initial metrics should be obtained as a baseline for any changes made to the data center. As changes are being made, the effects of these changes should be measured to ensure that they have the anticipated positive result.

As data centers continue to become more dynamic, the need to manage the environment becomes more important. An example is the implementation of the recent American Society of Heating, Refrigerating, and Air-Conditioning Engineers (ASHRAE) guidelines, which recommend that data centers can be operated at increased temperature and relative humidity. It has been suggested that temperatures be increased gradually up to the guideline, in order to understand the effects of the change in different locations in the data center and prevent any dangerous hot spots that might occur.

The latest release of the ITIL (version 3) includes a book devoted to the continuous improvement of IT. With this premise that IT constantly changes and never obtains a final state, you should continue to measure and manage your IT environment, to identify any problem situations or opportunities for improvement.

Data Center Transformation: A Global Case Study

This section demonstrates how the five building blocks of green data centers can be applied to an older data center. The data center in this example was built in the 1980s for the IT equipment that existed at that time. Its life was extended using the five building blocks.

Building Block 1: Diagnose

The PUE for the Lexington data center was measured at 2.0. This means that for every watt of energy used for IT equipment, an additional watt of energy was needed for cooling and power distribution. On the facilities subsystem level, 43,000 of the data center's 44,000 square feet were in use. The UPS system was at 92 percent utilization (2,227 kilowatts of 2,430 kilowatts), the generator system was at 85 percent utilization (4,229 kilowatts of 4,998 kilowatts installed, noting that additional equipment was installed on the generators that wasn't installed on the batteries), and the chiller system was at 94 percent (1,175 tons of 1,250 tons installed). On the IT level, 60 percent of the single processor servers were operating with a monthly utilization of less than 5 percent. (On average, there was 20 times more equipment on the floor than was needed.)

Building Block 2: Build

The data center was a leased facility, with little room for increases in facilities equipment. We were able to add 170 kilowatts of power to the data center. This created the equivalent of 4,250 square feet at the 40-watts-per-square-foot power density of the existing space. Because there was actually less than 1,000 square feet of physical space available, something had to be done to release some space so that the additional power could be used.

Building Block 3: Virtualize

The majority of the servers had a monthly utilization of less than 5 percent, so the opportunity existed to increase the utilization of each hardware server through virtualization. This would reduce the number of servers handling the current load and therefore create sufficient space to install the new servers enabled by the power upgrade. The net effect of virtualization allowed the data center to expand the IT server capacity by 800 percent, with less than 10 percent additional power capacity and no additional cooling capacity. The number of servers with less than 5 percent utilization was reduced from 60 to 14 percent over a period of two years.

Building Block 4: Cool

The cooling system at this data center was installed 20 years ago, when there were water-cooled mainframe computers. A data center energy-efficiency survey indicated that about a dozen Computer Room Air Conditioners (CRACs) could be turned off without adversely affecting cooling. By turning these off, the data center was able to reallocate almost 500k kilowatts of energy to other devices.

The survey also turned up several other tactical alterations that could increase the efficiency of the airflow. These included sealing cable cutouts, installing blanking plates in the racks of IT equipment, and rearranging some of the perforated tiles in the data center. The recommendations identified actions that resulted in a 10 percent savings of energy use.

Building Block 5: Measure and Manage

By implementing the suggestions from the energy study and virtualizing the IT workload, the data center was able to improve its PUE from 2.0 to 1.8, while increasing the IT capacity by a factor of eight.

By measuring the utilization of the newly virtualized servers, the capacity planning organization was able to create a utilization baseline that smoothed out, or "normalized," the workload on the larger servers. In essence, the workload in the virtual images did not all peak at the same time, allowing the overall utilization on a particular server to have less variability than when the workload images ran individually. The IT organization was able to "right size" the virtual servers based on this reduced variability. By rearranging virtual images and updating their size, the organization was able to reallocate six 16-way servers to other projects. This resulted in a savings of $2.4 million in equipment costs.

Metrics on equipment utilization are now reported automatically, and the IT organization looks for optimization projects as part of its continuous improvement program.

Why Virtualization Is Key
for Green IT and Data Center Transformations

There are many reasons why virtualization is key for green IT. We focus here on the top three: efficiency, economics, and transformation.

Promoting Efficiency

It wasn't that long ago when distributed workload was physically mapped to specific hardware. With a multi-tier application, it was common for the Web content to be on one server (or set of servers), the database to be on another, and the application business logic to be on a third. Application developers also needed a place to test fixes against the current production environment and a place to develop new functionality for the application. This often resulted in having nine servers per application: three per environment. As it was difficult to add physical resources to a running environment with minimal technology to share resources, the capacity planners often sized the workload for peak usage instead of average usage. This entire paradigm led to surprisingly low utilization. This was a reasonable approach until the physical data center became constrained and new equipment could no longer be added to it.

Virtualization reduces the waste of IT resources by putting multiple workloads on a single physical resource and sharing the equipment's excess resources. This reduces the amount of physical IT resources needed and its corresponding effect on facility resources. It is not uncommon to combine five older servers into the facility resources (power, space, and cooling) of one new server, increasing average single-digit utilization by a factor of five. This is further improved by the increased IT capacity of a new piece of IT equipment, as processors are faster (can do more work), memory is more compact, and the network bandwidth has improved. A five-to-one consolidation ratio, which is relatively modest, releases 80 percent of the facility's resources for additional growth. Reusing facilities resources makes the facilities more efficient as a byproduct of IT efficiencies.

Financial Impacts

Virtualization has a positive effect on financial capital and expenses. (A detailed analysis of the financial implications of virtualization is presented in Chapter 14.)

On the capital side, eliminating 80 percent of the servers, as indicated in the example, reduces the amount of capital needed for new equipment. Existing equipment can be reused for operations that would have required new investment. In a physically constrained data center, capital requirements for new facilities equipment is reduced, as virtualization provides the method to extend the life of an existing data center and grow IT capacity without the corresponding increase in facilities capacity.

On the expense side, the most obvious virtualization savings for green IT is associated with the reduction in the amount of energy needed to operate the data center. The energy reduction at the server level is multiplied by the PUE of the data center, which provides savings from not having the corresponding energy consumption of the facilities (power and cooling) equipment.

The reduction of IT resources due to virtualization also simplifies the environment, with a corresponding expense savings. An example is fewer network ports (connections) to maintain, with less cost associated with cabling installation and maintenance. The ability to dynamically move workloads between physical resources allows organizations to non-disruptively perform hardware microcode updates, preventing outages and saving the money associated with those outages.

Successive Transformations of the Data Center

Many managers considered virtualization predominantly as a way to reduce IT hardware costs through increased IT utilization. That is just the start. A reduction in servers lowers most other data center costs as well.

The next extension of transformation is the dynamic relocation of workloads without disruption. This is implemented not only to perform preventive maintenance on the physical equipment, but to respond to changes in capacity requirements of the workload. The addition of workload-balancing analysis at the image level provides policy management for dynamic image movement without human intervention. This policy management allows virtual workloads to run at even higher levels of utilization, further reducing IT hardware requirements.

The newest and most extensive transformation enabled by virtualization for green IT is the agility to position IT organizations for the future. An example of this is cloud computing. All of the public cloud computing implementations are based on some level of virtualization. This makes virtualization a prerequisite for those wanting to leverage cloud computing.

Summary

In this chapter, you learned about the forces driving the transformation of today's data centers. While you could consider these forces pessimistically, they provide the incentive for IT organizations to make the changes necessary to implement future IT requirements.

Virtualization technologies provide an excellent mitigation plan for green IT. In fact, virtualization was identified in the EPA's report to the U.S. Congress as the key IT technology that will improve data center efficiency in the next few years, decreasing the amount of energy consumption needed for the data centers of the future.

In this chapter, you learned the five building blocks for green data centers, examined a case study that applied those building blocks to a specific data center, and saw why virtualization is key for green IT. Although the majority of the building blocks are facilities-related, virtualization on the IT side is considered significant enough to be its own building block.

Green IT is as much about economics as the environment. In this chapter, you've looked at green IT in terms of optimization techniques implemented in the data center to integrate the facilities and IT components. This results in a lower carbon footprint with the same or higher functionality.

CHAPTER 3

The Lean Transformation System

Operations managers use the term *lean* to describe practices, principles, tools, and techniques that improve operational performance. It is a practical approach that identifies and simultaneously eliminates sources of loss from the whole value stream, by following a business process path and performing steps to deliver value that meets customer requirements. Lean principles can be applied to the business process to organize and manage product development, operations, suppliers, and customer relations. This increases value to the client faster, with less effort and less capital. The Toyota production system is a famous example commonly associated with a lean approach. (For more information about the Toyota system, see *The Toyota Way: 14 Management Principles from the World's Greatest Manufacturer* by Jeffrey K. Liker, McGraw-Hill, 2003.)

Lean techniques are applied to identify the sources of loss within a value stream. The primary sources of loss are as follows:

- *Waste*, which is activity that adds cost without adding value. There are eight common types of waste: overproduction, waiting, transportation, overprocessing, inventory, motion, rework, and intellectual resources. Later in this chapter, these types of waste are described in more detail.
- *Variability*, which is a deviation from standard operations designed to deliver quality service.
- *Inflexibility*, which is a reluctance to meet changes in customer requirements that could be provided without substantial additional cost.

Lean transformation is a holistic approach to simultaneously reduce waste, variability, and inflexibility. The benefits include the optimization of quality, productivity, cost, and delivery.

Lean History: The Toyota Production System

Japan's post-World War II economy was suffering, and Toyota faced the biggest strike in its history as the company struggled to even pay its employees. At the time, Toyota was small compared with American car companies. For example, in 1950, GM made 3,656,000 vehicles, versus Toyota's 11,000 vehicles.

At that time, W. Edwards Deming visited Japan and began to teach about variation and quality systems thinking, topics that he could not get American companies interested in. Toyota engineers such as Taiichii Ohno listened. In 1950, Ohno, chief engineer at Toyota, invented a radically new means of commerce and production incorporating Deming's ideas: the Toyota Production System (TPS).

The TPS embodies Toyota's management philosophy and practices in an integrated manner. It organizes manufacturing and logistics for the automobile manufacturer, including interaction with suppliers and customers. The system is based on the "lean manufacturing" concept championed by Taiichi Ohno, Shigeo Shingo, and Eiji Toyoda between 1948 and 1975. The founder of Toyota, Sakichi Toyoda, and his son, Kiichiro Toyoda, as well as Taiichi Ohno drew heavily on the work of Deming and the writings of Henry Ford.

When this delegation came to the United States to observe the assembly line and mass production that had made Ford rich, they were unimpressed. While shopping in a supermarket, they were inspired when they observed the simple idea of an automatic drink dispenser and how the supermarket reordered and restocked goods only as they were bought by customers. When the customer wanted a drink, he took one, and another drink replaced it. (The grocery store experience is recounted in *How Toyota Became #1: Leadership Lessons from the World's Greatest Car Company* by David Magee, Penguin Group, 2007.)

Toyota applied the lesson from the supermarket by reducing its inventory to a level that its employees would need for only a small period of time and then subsequently reorder.

This became the precursor of the now-famous Just-in-Time (JIT) inventory system, which preceded the Toyota Production System. Toyota was able to greatly reduce lead time and cost using the TPS, while improving quality. This enabled it to become one of the largest companies in the world.

In the 1970s, Toyota introduced TPS into the supply base to enhance the whole supplier chain, which could become the limiting factor to its performance capabilities. In the 1980s, Japanese companies in the United States and Europe achieved results similar to those in Asia. European and American companies realized that their successes were due to a systematic approach to operations. The effectiveness of the TPS was verified and documented in several books.

Since then, the lean system has been deployed in many manufacturing, production, and service environments. In health care, it has reinvented insurance claims processing and medical operations. More recently, IT companies have found lean practices beneficial in transforming their business. It has brought significant quality and productivity improvements. Figure 3.1 illustrates the penetration of lean techniques into other industries, since Toyota first used it for automobiles.

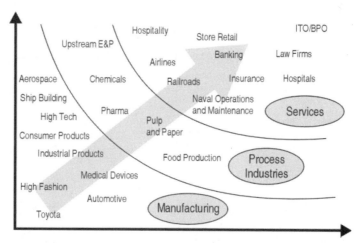

Figure 3.1: The lean system has been used in many different environments since its inception.

How Lean Methodologies Fit into the Field of IT

Infrastructure represents half or more of all IT costs. Labor represents half of all infrastructure costs. Therefore, the ability to introduce new technologies and applications that expand capacity and resolve problems efficiently is an increasingly important cost issue.

The past few years have witnessed a proliferation of distributed systems. As a result, IT infrastructures have turned into a heterogeneous mix of multiple platforms that often support thousands of customized and packaged applications. This leads to unprecedented levels of complexity and maintenance oversight.

Based on our work in IT service delivery, virtualization provides a way out of this dilemma. Lean principles offer an efficient way to implement virtualization transformation. Virtualization patterns based on lean levers (described later in this chapter) eliminate the major wastes of waiting, overproduction, inventory, rework, motion, and transport from a process, while improving quality and productivity.

A popular misconception is that lean is suited only for manufacturing. (See *Lean Thinking: Banish Waste and Create Wealth in Your Corporation*, 2nd ed., by James P. Womack and Daniel T. Jones, Free Press, 2003.) That is not true. The lean methodology applies to every business and every process. It is not a tactic or a cost reduction program, but a way of thinking and acting for an entire organization.

Lean proves to be applicable to IT infrastructure operations. IT infrastructure operations are comparable to industrial production when the data center is treated as a production system; software, hardware, and bandwidth are treated as raw materials; and application groups and end users are considered customers.

In fact, businesses in all industries and services, including healthcare, governments, insurance, and information technology, are using lean principles. Many organizations choose not to use the word "lean," but to label what they do as their own system, such as the Toyota Production System. Such a label establishes a commitment that lean is not a short-term sprint or a cost-reduction program, but the way the company operates.

The Elements of a Sustainable Lean Transformation

The term *lean transformation* is often used to characterize a company moving from an old way of thinking to lean thinking. The lean methodology requires a far-ranging business transformation but also facilitates such a transformation. It requires a long-term perspective and perseverance. The system must attain the transformation and sustain improved performance. If only a part of the system is implemented, the organization will fall back to its original state, forfeiting most of the progress achieved during the transformation.

As shown in Figure 3.2, an effective lean transformation addresses three major dimensions simultaneously: the operating system; the management system; and the mindsets, behavior, and capabilities, or MBC (John Drew, Blair McCallum, and Stefan Roggenhofer, *Journey to Lean: Making Operational Change Stick*, Palgrave Macmillan, 2004). These three dimensions are analogous to the legs of a three-legged stool; all must be securely installed for a stable, safe, and predictable performance.

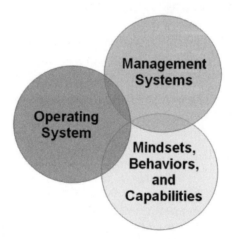

Figure 3.2: The three elements of a sustainable lean system.

The operating system organizes resources, processes, and assets to create and channel value to the customer. The management system monitors the effectiveness of the operating system and ensures its consistent use. Finally, the MBC encompasses the mindsets and behaviors that support the system.

Operating System Foundations

As mentioned earlier, the operating system in the lean methodology organizes your resources and processes to create and channel value to the customer. An optimized operating system structure lets the value flow to the customer with minimal losses.

In a manufacturing or production environment, the lean operating system consists of the standard operating procedures, process layout, production control methods, equipment utilization, inventory, and staffing levels. In the IT service industry, it includes the IT systems, information flow, operating procedures, office floor layout, organization structure, hardware, and software assets.

The operating system is the mechanism for adding value for the customer. Creating a new flow has benefits even without optimization, but eliminating losses from a current flow constitutes a major enhancement. Sometimes the first step is to create flow, and then to optimize by eliminating losses along the value stream path.

Operations flow should be flexible to accommodate changing customer requirements and customer demand. For example, the flow should be able to handle customer demand variations within a day, or seasonal variations within the year. The process should respond to customer's high or low demand within a day while maintaining the committed service levels of quality and productivity.

A lean operating system applies a few principles to channel value to the customer with minimal loss:

- Each value stream system must be analyzed and optimized from end to end. The value stream is analyzed to identify the value delivered to the customer and the sources of loss in the system.
- Once sources of loss are known, the appropriate lean tools and techniques are applied to eliminate the losses. Applying just one or a couple of lean techniques across the organization may yield only limited and temporary benefits. The proper method is to apply multiple tools and techniques at different levels, as determined by the value stream analysis. The tools must be applied to meet specific business objectives as part of a robust, coherent operating system.

Most organizations' operating systems evolve over time, as the business grows. The resources and people assigned to processes, on the other hand, evolve almost randomly. After a while, the operations are no longer conducted efficiently, and reasons for doing them a particular way are no longer clear. Some might assume the current method is a customer requirement; others might think it is the only imaginable way to deliver value to the customer.

Small and simple operations can become lean by accident; however, large, complex operations become lean only by design. As the business grows, the resources become complicated. Toyota is an example of a lean operation by design.

The first step to transforming operations is to design and deploy an effective operating system. However, the best operating system cannot be sustained unless it is aligned with a management system and with managers' and employees' mindsets and behaviors.

Map the value stream, identify value, define the value stream, and make value flow.

Management System Foundations

A proper management system supports, sustains, and enforces the operating system. For example, a complex process may require a small, agile front-line team with narrow span of control. The organization may vary from a dedicated team for complex processes to a shared team for cross-value streams that plan processes or carry out processes requiring specialized unique skills.

Performance management processes must have metrics with clear targets that are aligned to business objectives and are cascaded and visible to the entire organization. Cascaded metrics are interconnected across different levels of the organization. Actual performance is tracked and made transparent across the organization or even to the customer. Daily performance dialogs to review objectives and results should complement these metrics and targets. The dialogs are the conversations conducted frequently to discuss the impact of the metrics on the management system.

For an effective management system, the front line needs to have the skills and tools to track and manage the operating system. Front-line activities must be linked to business objectives to establish a feedback loop for the learning cycle that improves performance. Short, daily team meetings around the metrics and a visual performance board to start every shift make performance instantly visible.

Foundations for Mindset, Behavior, and Capabilities

MBC is the way people think of what they do: their attitude toward work and their goals, and how it influences their actions. It is important to engage people at all levels of the organization to support the lean transformation. They must understand the motivation, know where it is leading, and commit themselves to making the transformation successful.

Value Streams and Waste

A process adds value by producing goods or providing a service that a customer is willing to pay for. A process produces waste when more resources are consumed than are necessary to produce the goods or provide the service that the customer actually wants.

Viewing an entire value stream, instead of isolated points, as a target of waste elimination creates new processes that need less human effort, less resources, less space, less capital, and less time to make products and services at far less cost and with fewer defects, compared with traditional business systems. Companies are able to respond to changing customer desires with high variety, high quality, low cost, and fast throughput times.

One of the key steps in the lean methodology (explored deeply by Toyota in its TPS) is to identify which steps add value and which do not. By classifying all the process activities into these two categories, you can start focusing on value-adding steps and eliminating the non-value-adding steps. Once value-adding work has been identified, the rest of the work can be separated into incidental work—which does not directly add value but still needs to be done—and pure waste. The clear identification of incidental work, as distinct from waste on the one hand and the work that adds customer value on the other, is critical to identifying the assumptions and beliefs behind the current work processes, and to challenging them in due course.

As shown in Figure 3.3, there are eight generally accepted types of waste: overproduction, waiting, motion, transportation, inventory, rework, overprocessing, and intellect. We will describe each type and present some scenarios that demonstrate it. The lean levers discussed in the following section help eliminate these types of waste.

Figure 3.3: The eight types of waste.

Overproduction

Overproduction is the waste of producing your product or service in greater quantities, sooner, or faster than the customer needs. Overproduction occurs when too many parts are produced or when services are provided too early. In IT services, for example, overproduction occurs when lower-severity incidents get resolved sooner than necessary and take priority over higher-severity incidents.

With overproduction, some parts or services are produced faster, while others have long lead times or are delivered too late. To improve productivity, the organization starts to require operators to produce more than the customer needs. Extra parts will be stored and not sold.

Overproduction is the worst and most comprehensive form of waste because it hides or generates all other types of waste, especially inventory. Overproduction increases the amount of space needed for storing raw material as well as finished goods.

Overproduction could be a response to other problems in the environment. In a factory, for example, if the change over to a different product takes a long time, the tendency is to produce large quantities of the current product while the current line is set up, resulting in large batches of old product taking up space in the warehouse.

Large batches, poor scheduling, or unclear priorities could cause overproduction. Poor forecasting or unbalanced material flow could also trigger overproduction. Sometimes, in order to increase equipment or resources utilization, managers produce more than what is needed.

Just-in-time ordering, which includes tools such as continuous flow processing, cycle time management, pull system, and leveled production, help reduce overproduction. The reduction of time to implement changes helps eliminate overproduction because different products can be manufactured with minimum penalties between product changes.

The pull system produces parts or services as a response to a customer's request. Signals travel from the customer into the production environment to start the process. When the customer places an order or service request, it triggers a sequence of events to fulfill that order or request.

Waiting

Waiting is the idle time during which resources, people, or equipment perform no value-adding activities. This occurs when people are waiting for material or information to start performing value-adding work. For example, time spent watching machines run, waiting for an event to happen, waiting for others to approve decisions, or waiting to receive orders is a waste. This category also includes the time people wait for equipment to become available. Wait time causes the process to slow down and leads to production and delivery delays, resulting in productivity losses and longer lead times.

Large batch sizes upstream could cause material shortage and long wait times downstream. Suppliers not delivering the material in time for production results in staff waiting. If the approvals necessary for a process to start are not completed in time, resources could become idle. Poor maintenance of equipment causes downtime that results in resources waiting. Poor scheduling of the resources results in poor alignment of resource availability.

Typical causes for waiting in IT include waiting for customers to call to report incidents, waiting for changes to the environment to be approved before being able to execute them, waiting for equipment procurement to be completed and product to be delivered, waiting for outdated tools that fail to provide up-to-date information on the system, and waiting for the system to fail before taking actions to prevent the problem.

Lean levers such as a flexible staffing system and standardized work minimize waiting. For IT equipment, better maintenance helps reduce the waiting time and improve availability.

Motion

Any superfluous movement of resources, material, or product in a process constitutes wasted motion. Examples include excessive walking by the operators, searching for parts, searching for tools, launching applications or databases, misrouting work, and customer requests jumping around the organization without being completed.

Motion waste may be attributed to poor workplace layout, lack of clear demarcation of roles and responsibilities, and the absence of visual management. All of these can affect IT as frequently as any other organization.

Pay particular attention to the situation where a product is wandering around the process with little or no value added. It might do so to meet misguided organizational needs rather than to benefit the customer.

Transportation

While motion waste concerns movement within a process, transportation waste encompasses movement between processes. Transportation waste includes the multiple handling of a product, product travel over long distances between processes, and the travel required to handle damage or delays. Long lead times and higher costs are common symptoms of excessive transportation. This waste can be introduced into the process when sequential processes are physically separated, material inventories are scattered, or work resources are not co-located. It can also occur through poor workplace layout or process fragmentation.

A specific example of IT transportation waste is the misrouting of incident tickets. These could bounce around from department to department without being resolved.

Continuous flow and workplace structuring help reduce transportation waste. Avoid sending a product or activity long distances, consuming long times from resource to resource or site to site, without significant value being added.

Inventory

Inventory waste is any excess product above the minimum required to deliver what the customers want when they want it. Inventory can be the buildup of completed tasks ahead of time, or the buildup of tasks in a queue to be done by the next resource. It can be in the form of raw materials, work-in-progress (WIP), or finished goods. Inventory waste represents a capital outlay that has not yet produced an income either by the producer or for the consumer. Overproduction waste can cause inventory waste.

If the technology is progressing quickly, excess inventory may become obsolete. Inventory causes cash flow problems, as it locks assets in unproductive parts. Inventory also wastes space, either physical floor space in a production environment or computer storage space (along with related costs, such as backup time) in an IT service environment. While the inventory is being produced, parts really needed by the customer could suffer long lead times. When a quality issue is identified in any of the inventory parts, a huge rework could be triggered.

Overproduction, poor forecasting, poor scheduling, poor quality, unreliable suppliers, shortsighted procurement policies, and overly large batch sizes commonly result in excess inventory. Lean tools, such as just-in-time, continuous flow, pull system, production leveling, standardized work, supplier development, proper maintenance, and effective management system help eliminate inventory waste.

Rework

Rework is redoing a task due to an incorrect or incomplete operation. Some operations have dedicated resources and processes to perform rework activities as a reaction to high defect rates. Often, rework is treated as an expected part of the process.

Rework is pervasive in environments with low-quality materials, poor machine conditions, poor forecasting, unpredictable processes, low skills, or unclear customer requirements.

For example, if customer requirements are not clear or not forecasted correctly, products that are built to these requirements will need to be reworked to meet updated customer needs. This is an obvious risk in IT.

Overprocessing

Overprocessing is any effort that isn't required by the customer and does not add value. This includes using tools that are more precise, complex, or expensive than absolutely necessary. Over-engineered processes, unclear customer requirements, inappropriate policies, outdated procedures, and lack of standard operations can result in overprocessing. All too often, IT adds bells and whistles that no one uses and that just weigh down an application.

Intellect

It is a waste of intellectual resources to apply a higher skill or capability to a task than it requires to meet customer requirements. In labor, this waste involves applying higher-skilled or higher-cost personnel to perform a task that can be done by a lower-skilled person. In hardware, it is wasteful to use high-performance hardware to perform simple functions. High-performance resources are wasted because they idle the majority of the time. Therefore, low hardware utilization is evidence of a waste of intellectual resources.

In software, calling up a complicated application to perform simple functions that simple applications can perform as quickly with the same level of accuracy is a form of waste. Complicated software may require higher performance hardware, which compounds the waste.

Organizations employ their staff for specific skills. However, these employees have other skills, too, and it is wasteful not to take advantage of these skills.

Lean Levers

Lean levers are applied by organizations to reduce waste, improve processes, and increase flexibility. In this section, seven lean levers, shown in Figure 3.4, are described from a generic perspective. These levers correspond to the seven virtualization patterns discussed later in this book. Each pattern applies the lever principle to optimize a virtualization approach.

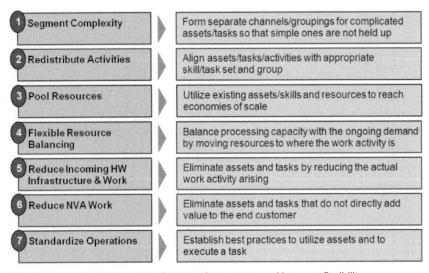

Figure 3.4: Lean levers to reduce waste, improve the process, and increase flexibility.

Segmenting Complexity

Segmenting complexity refers to the separation of tasks by their complexity, which can be measured by the task's difficulty or the time it requires to complete.

Mixing time-consuming tasks, such as change packages that involve many cross-technical elements, with simpler tasks, such as a simple software procedure, can break the cadence of work activity. This holds up the simpler tasks, leads to overprocessing and unnecessary transport (because lower-skilled resources spend time before routing to higher-skilled resources), and adds further delays. Preprocessing the work to segment out more complex activities and route them to groups of more skilled resources consistently tends to increase throughput and lower costs per activity.

Each complexity level has its own value stream path. This allows the simple tasks to start on their own and not to wait for the complicated tasks to complete. For example, preprocessing incident tickets in work queues to segment out more complex tickets and route them to groups of more skilled resources consistently increases throughput, decreases resolution time, and lowers costs per ticket.

Simple tasks can be batched together and channeled to specific resources to be performed as a group. The grouping of tasks allows a set of preparation steps to be performed once for the whole group, rather than for each task. Therefore, the average time per task is reduced. When batching, batch formation should not be allowed to exceed the customer-required time. If similar tasks occur frequently, the customer requirements will not suffer.

Similar complexities are assigned to the appropriate resources based on skill, capability, or availability to handle that task with highest efficiency and quality. The actual operating procedures to perform the various complexities could be different, too. Different complexities may require different value streams to complete. For example, a complex design change may follow a longer value stream path, while a simple change may follow an expedited path.

Redistributing Activities

The objective of redistributing activities is to channel work to the right resources with the lowest cost, pay, and skill set needed to meet the customer requirement. For example, infrastructure services personnel tend to work on a variety of activities that range from shift work and day-to-day "firefighting"—taking inquiries, responding to incidents, and solving problems—to activities with a more project-like nature, such as upgrading an operating system. Often, the same individuals do a mix of these types of activities, which tends to lower task productivity and complicate performance management. Work redesigns, such as concentrating call-handling in specific roles, creates focus and enhances repetitive learning.

Pooling Resources

Pooling is the process of combining resources to gain economies of scale. Pooling allows the leveling of workload among the resources in the pool. It improves capacity utilization, allowing dynamic resource allocation. If a specific resource is not available, other properly trained or configured pool resources are able to handle the workload. In a data center, pooling can be applied to hardware resources or labor resources.

Pooling similar labor skills lets an organization apply them across multiple customers who use the center. Further, the pool can be divided into groups that have different levels of the same skill to handle the segmented work through the segmenting complexity lever. These groups are normally called "Rhythm and Blues." Rhythm performs simpler activities, while the Blues perform activities that are more complex.

The lower-skill grouping allows staff to be trained effectively, gaining skill in performing lower-complexity tasks and increasing their capability level by performing a variety of tasks. Higher-skill resources are used for high-complexity activities that require specific knowledge, uncommon tasks, or tasks that warrant more time or special attention. Higher-skill or higher-capability resources are shifted to assist lower-skill resources if the workload volume requires it.

The advantages of pooling are many, including workload leveling, capacity improvement and management, cross training, better resource utilization, and productivity improvement.

Flexible Resource Balancing

Reducing inflexibility is the key to unlocking structural under-utilization in infrastructure environments, where it is not uncommon to find groups spending 80 percent of their time on low-value tasks. Flexible resource allocation assures that the right resources are available when needed. This requires the monitoring or logging of the workload history so you can predict upcoming workloads and make sure the resources are available when required.

One method of achieving dynamic resource allocation is to direct excess time-sensitive workloads to available people or machines that are performing non-time-critical tasks. These resources (who must have the appropriate skills and capabilities) are placed on standby for the overflow workload. When the excess workload dissipates, these resources go back to their non-time-critical tasks. Hence, redirection does not negatively interrupt their workflow or customer commitment.

Proper utilization prevents the resources from idling while waiting for work to arrive. In labor, for example, resources are shifted between real-time and back-office work. The equivalent shift in software is between real-time and batch workload.

To be lean, we must create an operating system that is self-correcting and can adapt to customer requirements with the minimum allocation of cost and resources. We must deliver customer value without additional non-value-add activities, which in turn requires an understanding of the true customer requirements and the capability to flex the scale and pace of the operation in order to follow the customer needs.

Flexible operating systems manage the pace at which customer requirements are being met. When customer requirements increase, assets and resources have to be organized and optimized to complete each operation in less time. If the customer demand decreases, the assets and resources must be reconfigured to reflect the new reality, while minimizing waste such as waiting and inventory.

Often, customer demand changes due to seasonal variations. In these cases, you have a few options to meet the customer requirements. For example, you can allow staff to work overtime or accumulate extra off-time hours. Accommodating intra-day variations that create workload peaks during a single day may require multi-skilled members of staff to play customer-facing roles during peak hours and then revert to their back-office roles at slower times.

Flexible resource management can be supported by standardization, a topic discussed later in this chapter. Standardization ensures quality and enables labor flexibility by making it easier to switch from one task or workgroup to another. This, in turn, allows quicker responses to customer demands and maximum staff productivity.

Flexible staffing can be achieved by encouraging front-line personnel to train and work on a variety of tasks across technical disciplines. This allows better matching of production capacity to incoming demand and creates personnel who are better at cross-technology and problem-solving.

Eliminating Incoming Work and Hardware Infrastructure

Perhaps the best source of efficiency is to eliminate incoming requests for work that does not add value or revenue. This work is typically generated by external sources. For example, if you provide a customer with a reliable delivery schedule when he or she places an order, the customer will find it unnecessary to call back to check its status. However, if the schedule is not provided or not reliable, additional customer queries are generated. This takes the staff's attention away from real work.

Hardware infrastructure can be reduced by holding off on building resources for applications that can be absorbed by the current infrastructure. This reduces both the cost and the complexity of your infrastructure. For instance, in Chapter 5, you will learn how adding a cache can eliminate redundant database requests as well as the network resources required for them.

Reducing Non-Value-Adding Work

As mentioned earlier, the lean methodology breaks work into three types: value-adding work, incidental work, and waste.

Value-adding work meets the customer's needs. Customers are willing and happy to pay for this work because it contributes to their success. Without this work, they are not able to deliver their own products or services, and unsatisfactory performance in the delivery of this work negatively affects the customers' ability to run their businesses. It is important to view each activity from the customer perspective, not from the perspective of the provider. Value-adding work adds value to the customer, not the provider organization. To determine what is value-adding, customer requirements must be clear to the delivery team.

Incidental activities are performed to support value-adding work. By themselves, they are not part of the customer requirements or specifications. However, delivery of customer requirements is not possible without these tasks. For example, if the customer places an order for a product, the product is the value-add. Placing the order into the tracking system, transmitting it to the factory, and shipping it to the customer are incidental activities. Although the customer does not receive direct value from order entry or shipping, the delivery of the product is not possible if these activities are not performed. It is always worthwhile to minimize incidental work.

Waste provides no value to the customer and frequently is frustrating for the provider to perform. This kind of work is performed because the process is not working as intended or is defective. For example, a follow-up with the factory to check on the order status if the delivery is delayed is a waste. If the process worked properly, the customer would have a precise time for product delivery, making follow-up unnecessary. A key goal of the lean methodology is the total elimination of this type of work.

It is essential to break down all activities performed into these three types. For each activity, determine the time it takes to complete. Then, sum up the time for each of the three types of activities to find the proportion of time spent. You can then devise a project plan that offers the most benefit in eliminating the non-value-adding activities and maximizing the proportion of time spent delivering value to the customer. To help visualize the tasks, teams usually generate a graph that shows the percentage of each activity type.

Standardizing Operations

Standardization is an essential step for efficiency, by discovering best practices and deploying them in all relevant processes. It is also necessary for the related lean goal of flexibility. Standardization promotes flexibility by providing opportunities for employees to enhance their skills and learn new ones, which also improves job satisfaction.

Standard operating procedures specify the most efficient, consistent, safe, and repeatable way of performing the activity. The customer receives better and more consistent quality. Operations become more efficient, and the staff has a clear and safe procedure to follow. Standards reduce risk during the introduction of new products or services and ensure that tasks are performed in the same way regardless of who is performing them. They also greatly facilitate training and provide a common base for process improvement.

For standards to create flexibility, people have to be trained, and standards need to be properly maintained. Standards warrant intelligent interpretation, without which they can be constricting. A particular standard may apply slightly differently to a specific customer, for instance. The standard and the process must allow these differentiations.

Standards should be living documents that are updated and improved frequently by the teams applying them. When the process is improved, the standards must be updated to reflect the changes. The new process is the new baseline for future improvements.

Standards ensure quality and provide labor flexibility by making it easier to switch from one task or workgroup to another. This allows quicker response to customer demand and maximum staff productivity.

Standardization of the workplace's look and feel makes it easier to transfer staff or resources from one work location to another. The visual management of the workplace, which includes the appearance of the work area, the labeling of resource roles, and performance metrics on visual boards, should be standardized. A standard layout adds flexibility to the operating system, as it allows a common platform for work to be performed and allows resource movement with minimum cross-training.

Summary

This chapter introduced lean concepts and discussed ways to identify waste and banish it using the seven lean levers. You learned the eight commonly known types of waste: overproduction, waiting, motion, transportation, inventory, rework, overprocessing, and intellectual resources. You also learned the seven lean levers used in the virtualization patterns: segmenting complexity, redistributing activities, pooling resources, flexibly balancing resources, reducing incoming hardware infrastructure and work, reducing non-value-adding work, and standardizing operations.

CHAPTER 4

A Template for Virtualization Patterns

Before taking on decisions that involve substantial uncertainty, complexity, and risk—all of which certainly apply to virtualizing a computing environment—people like to hear what has worked for others in similar situations. To share such experiences, organizations in many industries have used the concept of *patterns* to identify and document best practices, opportunities, and common pitfalls. These patterns have been developed over multiple projects in different environments, are thoroughly documented, and can lead to relatively predictable successes. Many excellent examples of such patterns can be found in diverse fields such as architecture, gardening, sewing, engineering, IT, and organizational management.

We have led IBM's efforts in developing leading-edge technologies and methodologies for virtualization in the mainframe and midrange space over several decades and have led virtualization transformation projects around the globe. These projects have ranged from very large-scale multi-data center relocation projects to smaller departmental server projects, and from very large multi-national enterprises to small and medium businesses.

While implementing server virtualization for tens of thousands of servers in a distributed systems environment, we have assembled a vast set of lessons related to what has worked and what has not worked well during virtualization transformations. We have captured these experiences and our guidance as patterns for virtualization transformations. The remaining chapters of this book describe these patterns.

If you understand exactly what is provided by each section of our pattern descriptions, and how you can apply that section to your particular organization, you will be able to choose and apply the patterns productively. We consider that understanding important enough to devote this chapter to illustrating and explaining the template used in the rest of the book for our patterns.

Elements of a Well-Documented Pattern

A pattern is a reusable solution to a problem within a specific context. The *problem statement* includes the goals and objectives to be achieved. The *context* specifies the preconditions under which the problem seems to recur, and for which the *solution* is attractive.

Although the context tells us about the pattern's applicability, and the solution describes how the problem is solved, a pattern is more than a battle-proven remedy to a problem. Typically, numerous and sometimes competing sets of issues, or *forces*, have to be reconciled when solving a problem. The solution provided by a pattern balances these forces in the best way for the given context.

The Pattern Specification

A template for describing a pattern helps both the author and the reader. It ensures that the author includes all the knowledge that is useful and relevant. After studying a few patterns, the reader knows where to look for information that is useful at each stage, such as identifying the need for a pattern and determining how many resources it will require.

Thus, we have developed a specification for virtualization patterns, based upon prior work done by the IBM Software Group Architecture Board (Thomas Jobson, Jr., Gang Chen, Kyle Brown, Alexandre Polozoff, Bobby Woolf, Paul Verschueren, Pieter Lindeque, and Peter Bahrs). The sections of the pattern specification are as follows:

- *Name*—A noun or short noun phrase describing the pattern, convenient for citation
- *Value Statement*—A summary of what the pattern is meant to accomplish
- *Context*—The conditions under which organizations are likely to encounter the problem
- *Problem*—A statement of the difficulty or need encountered
- *Selection Guidance*—Information on when to select this pattern
- *Forces*—Constraints that commonly make the problem difficult to solve
- *Solution*—The steps to successfully resolve the problem

The solution itself is also divided into several sections:

- *Sketch*—An illustration, usually graphical, of the solution
- *Results and Next*—An expanded explanation of the solution that details its application and how it resolves the forces, the other problems it introduces, and what patterns are used to address those problems
- *Sidebars*—More detailed technical issues or variations of the pattern (optional)
- *Examples*—Simple examples of applying the pattern
- *Known Uses*—Brief case studies where the pattern has been applied

A good pattern specification should not be product-specific. Instead, it should focus on a common dilemma that appears in many organizations, regardless of the hardware and software in use. The solution can be implemented by an expert using tools crafted for this particular purpose, or by using a feature already built into a product. Whether a particular product includes an implementation of the solution is not relevant to the pattern, although it could be an important part of the value statement section for the pattern.

The Name Section

The name provides a convenient handle for talking about the pattern. It is a noun phrase that captures the essence of the pattern. It can be used in sentences, such as "We will use a Requestor Side Cache here." It can also help you quickly determine whether to read the pattern's description.

The Value Statement Section

The value statement explains what the pattern offers to the reader—what it is intended to accomplish. It helps you decide whether this pattern is applicable to your current needs.

The Context Section

The context is a short introduction to the scenarios in which this pattern may be expected to deliver value. It describes when the problem is encountered and who encounters it. The context describes the activity you might typically be performing that would lead you to encounter the problem this pattern solves. Outside of this set of circumstances, it is less likely that applying the pattern will be successful.

Often, the successful application of other patterns leads to a new problem for which the current pattern should be applied. If so, the patterns likely to lead to this point are referenced in this context.

The Problem Section

Each pattern solves a specific, common problem. The problem section of the specification states the dilemma to be resolved.

The Selection Guidance Section

The pattern should be applied only if the current situation meets certain criteria. This section describes the key criteria that are necessary for this pattern to be successful. This section differs from the context. The context outlines conditions under which organizations are likely to encounter the problem, while this section specifies when to select this pattern.

Some of the issues addressed in this section include the following:

- What selection criteria should the reader use?
- What are non-obvious prerequisites?
- What goals distinguish this pattern from others that look similar?

The Forces Section

A pattern documents a problem that is difficult to solve; otherwise, it wouldn't be worth documenting and teaching. The forces section explains why the problem is difficult to solve and leads the reader to the solution.

Forces provide additional details about the problem that help you decide whether this pattern is the most appropriate solution for the problem. This section can also be used to describe the constraints that a good solution must meet and balance. A novice most likely doesn't know or understand these constraints, so the author must list them and identify any constraints that might oppose each other, thus making the solution more difficult to implement.

The Solution Section

Having described a problem and why it's difficult to solve, the pattern then has to tell the reader how to solve it. Most readers would like to see the solution first in the pattern, but it should be withheld until after the discussion of the context, selection criteria, forces, and so on. Otherwise, the reader might make a hasty choice or apply the solution incorrectly.

The solution section is accompanied by sketches or illustrations, examples, optional sidebars, and areas of known use. It shows how a pattern solves the problem and resolves the forces facing the reader. It also addresses new challenges that might arise as a result of applying this pattern. Many solutions lead to new problems that require other patterns. Thus, as the solution discusses the new challenges, it lists other patterns to be considered after applying the current one. It answers the question, "What are the likely next steps and patterns I should consider?"

A pattern should not just *tell* you what to do, but also show you. Therefore, illustrations and examples are an important part of the solution. In many cases, just by looking at the pattern name and the sketch, you should be able to grasp the essence of the pattern.

Often, discussing a pattern leads to tangential topics. These are not necessarily part of solving the problem but provide additional pieces of information related to the pattern that might be useful. These topics go into sidebars, which are set apart visually. Sidebars may discuss more detailed technical issues or variations of the pattern.

A pattern is most useful if it has already been applied successfully in a real-life situation. Case studies demonstrate that the pattern is not just the author's theoretical invention but a best practice in wide use. In addition, readers who have difficulty thinking about the problem abstractly can often understand the pattern by finding the commonality between their scenarios and the examples described for the pattern.

Based on our wide array of experiences with multiple clients, we have leveraged client scenarios to help explain the problem, context, forces, and solution for each of our patterns for virtualization.

A Sample Pattern

Some patterns involve small processes that can be implemented within a team. Others describe much more abstract processes and span large parts of an organization, threading together multiple units of work and their recommended methodologies. An example of a higher-level pattern might be one for "estimation of cost related to setting up a new IT infrastructure."

This section of the chapter provides a straightforward example of a simple pattern, the Requestor Side Cache. It is documented using the pattern template specification just described, which serves as an example of the structure for all the virtualization patterns in the rest of this book.

Name

The name of this pattern is Requestor Side Cache.

Value Statement

This pattern helps to improve read response time, and reduce server and network load, when clients read the same data multiple times. It is particularly valuable when the middleware or central application is not a suitable location for a caching service.

Context

A client needs to read some data. The performance of the read is slow, perhaps because the data must be accessed from a database or over a network connection. Alternatively, the performance creates significant load, perhaps because the data set is large.

When data travels over a network, this pattern applies when an analysis of application behavior and the layout of servers has demonstrated that the same data is being read repeatedly and traveling over a saturated network.

Problem

How can a client improve the performance of a read request that it makes repeatedly? Bottlenecks vary, depending on how the data gets from storage to the processor:

- If data is passed between functions in a single process, the problem may simply lie in passing data by value instead of by reference. (Within a process, you can pass data by reference, which requires extra memory only for a pointer.)
  If possible, rewrite the application to pass the data by reference.

- If the data is retrieved from another process on the same server, it must be passed by value. This could cause bottlenecks.

  Solutions involve reducing the amount of data that has to be passed between processes or rewriting the application to combine the operations in a single process. Both of these solutions lie beyond the scope of this book.

- If the bottleneck is caused by retrieving data from an underpowered database server or storage area network, you can invest resources in these areas. The investment will improve performance on all transactions, not just the repeated reads covered in this pattern. Possibilities include the following:

  » Tuning the database storage engine or buying faster hardware, if the database itself takes a long time to resolve a query.

  » Speeding up the network by installing faster I/O cards or dedicating some storage to a machine that is only one hop away from the application that needs the data, if the network is a bottleneck.

  » Reducing the amount of data being read. For instance, optimize the query to return only the specific columns needed by the application. Return just 10 or 20 rows, and let the application's user decide whether to request more rows.

If the remedies in the previous list have been tried or have been rejected, the Requestor Side Cache pattern might be the solution. A cache can bring data closer to the process reading it, without major changes to the application or network.

Selection Guidance

Use this pattern when the following are true:

1. A client is reading data and the read is expensive to perform.
2. The read has been made as efficient as possible.
3. The read comes from another system.
4. The read is slow because of network bandwidth constraints.
5. The client performs the read repeatedly.
6. The data does not change between the repeated reads.

Forces

The majority of inter-application requests involve the retrieval of information, as opposed to updating the information. A ratio commonly associated with online shopping, for example, is 60 information requests to one update. In stock trading, the ratio can be well over 100 to one. Even in applications such as customer self-service, it is common to find ratios in excess of 10 to one. It is common for these information requests to play a major, or even dominant, role in overall application performance.

Solution

If the client needs a significant amount of data, and the data store and network are as fast as possible, each read is going to have a significant amount of overhead. There's nothing more you can do to change that. However, if the data is going to be read repeatedly, the client can store it locally, to avoid having to retrieve it repeatedly. Subsequent reads use the local store and avoid the remote retrieval.

One implementation of this pattern is to introduce a caching proxy into the requestor process. The caching proxy has the same interface as the target service, runs in the requestor process, and is used by the requestor as if it were the target. When the requestor invokes the service and the cache is empty, the proxy invokes the target service, stores the result, and returns the result to the requestor. In subsequent invocations, the proxy simply returns the stored result, without invoking the target service.

The requester component is not aware that a cache is present because it is not exposed to any caching APIs. From the requester's point of view, the proxy is the target, and the target component just got much faster. From the target component's point of view, the number of requests it is receiving from the requestor just went way down. Thus, caching to accelerate requests to a component has minimal impact on application logic and is quite simple (actually transparent) to use.

Sketches

Figure 4.1 shows typical programming classes for a requestor side cache. The IService interface uses the CachedServiceImpl whenever possible to retrieve data and resorts to ServiceImpl when the data changes.

A client can make a read request either synchronously or asynchronously, as shown in Figure 4.2. In a synchronous request, a single thread blocks while the data is retrieved. Asynchronously, one thread sends the request, and a separate thread retrieves it when it is available. Either way, this pattern still applies: cache the data in the client to avoid repeated retrievals. However, the implementation differs in the asynchronous case.

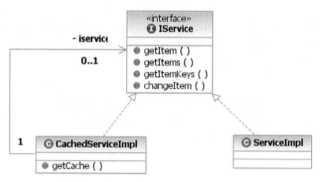

Figure 4.1: Sample classes for a requestor side cache.

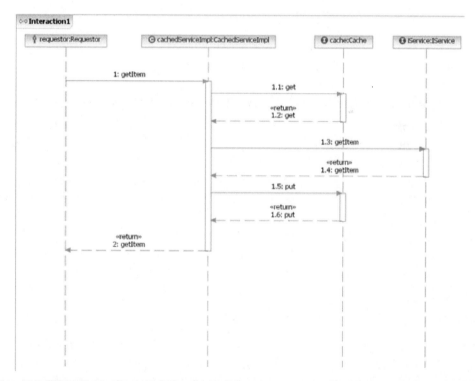

Figure 4.2: Transactions using a requestor side cache.

Results and Next

The Requestor Side Cache pattern can be used to implement a requestor side cache in a requesting process. In the simplest case, this pattern assumes that the data being read is static and does not change after the initial request. In reality, unless the data is read-only for all clients, it can change. If the data can be changed, clients implementing this pattern to read that data should also implement a Cache Invalidator pattern that will flush the cache (and optionally repopulate it) when the data changes.

Over time, a client may cache so many different sets of data that the cache becomes too big or runs out of space. Clients implementing this pattern should also implement a Cache Scavenger pattern to manage the cache's size.

Examples/Known Uses

Here are two examples/known uses of this pattern:

- A Web browser caches artifacts such as static HTML documents and GIFs, so that they don't have to be retrieved from the Website repeatedly. Each artifact is accompanied by meta-information, such as an expiry time or a version identifier. This tells the browser when the artifact has changed and therefore must be downloaded again.

    This pattern is implemented by WebSphere Application Server's client-side Web Services cache (which uses Dynacache) as the supported caching mechanism. In non-WebSphere environments, and in situations where a custom in-memory cache may be preferable to Dynacache, a Java Requester Side Implementation is available at RSCImplementation.
- The ObjectGrid feature, available separately or as part of WebSphere Extended Deployment, is a sophisticated caching runtime that stores frequently used data in the application so that it doesn't have to be retrieved repeatedly from the data store.

Classifying Patterns Along the Lean Levers

The patterns in this book are organized around the lean methodology described in Chapter 3. This classification will help guide you in choosing which patterns are most valuable to your organization. It will also help you pull together the people who can implement the pattern. Each of the next seven chapters encompasses patterns that move forward one of the lean levers.

In defining the seven lean levers, we used the following criteria:

- We kept the number down to seven to help you grasp all the categories, without feeling like you're trying to "boil the ocean."
- Patterns should selectively address those aspects of People, Process, and Technology that either significantly impede the success of virtualization transformations or significantly enhance the likelihood of success—hence addressing both threats and opportunities.
- Patterns should be classified in a way that facilitates their easy and consistent reuse across several small or large engagements.
- Patterns should be classified so that they can be executed within the discipline of a well-established and proven methodology that has been successfully adopted for optimizing work efforts across several industry sectors.

The left side of Figure 4.3 illustrates the high-level phases of a project to virtualize an environment:

- Solution framing
- Planning and design
- Implementation

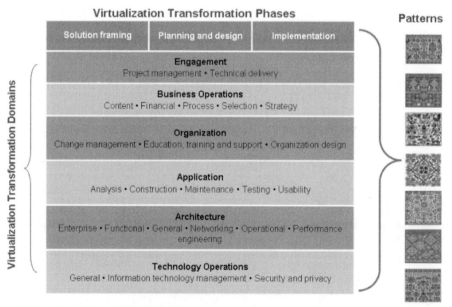

Figure 4.3: The abstraction of virtualization patterns.

Each of these three phases must be carried out within several domains, which represent different types of people or expertise. We have picked the following domains as the ones required to make each phase a success:

- Engagement
- Business Operations
- Organization
- Application
- Architecture
- Technology Operations

Based on our experience, a well-orchestrated interplay among these domains is required to achieve success in each phase of the virtualization transformation. We have also found that there are literally hundreds of patterns, members of the universal set of patterns, defined by the intersection of phases and domains involved within a virtualization transformation. To stay true to the classification goals stated above, we have abstracted and selected seven patterns for virtualization from this overall universal set.

Figure 4.4 shows the icon for each of the seven lean levers. Note that we have expanded the fifth lever to include reduction in hardware and infrastructure, both of which are significant targets of optimization through virtualization.

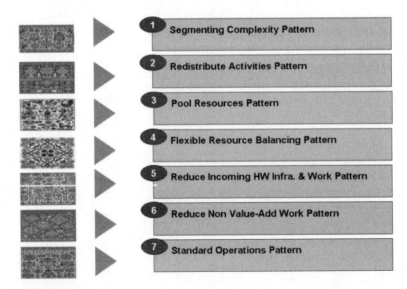

Figure 4.4: Icons denoting lean levers.

Example of Lean Levers in an IT Pattern

This section discusses the wastes and lean levers applicable to the Requestor Side Cache pattern.

Wastes

This section tallies the wastes in the pattern based on the original design, without the side cache.

Waiting

These waits occur every time the data is requested (following the first request, which cannot be eliminated, even with a cache):

The application waits for its request to be transmitted to the remote database server.

1. The application and database server wait for a database query.
2. The application and database server wait for the data to be extracted from the database.
3. The application waits for extracted data to transmit from the remote database system to the application system.
4. Other processes wait for this application data and requests to be transmitted.

Motion and Transport Waste

The following motion and transport wastes occur in the original design:

1. The request is transported from the application system to the remote database server.
2. Data is transported from the remote database system to the application server.
3. The transport is repeated for every data request.

Rework

All requests for the same data require the following rework:

1. Additional network requests
2. Repeated transmissions of requests and data
3. Repeated database queries

Intellectual Resources

If the application is the only source for changes, the application might be capable of determining whether the data has changed. Repeated queries do not use this capability and reuse of previously acquired data.

Lean Levers

This section discusses a few lean levers that can be applied to this simple example.

Segmenting Complexity

Most applications perform far more reads than writes. That means the data flow is mostly from the remote database storage to the application. Also, most applications frequently reuse a significant proportion of the data. These facts help us eliminate waste in data acquisition. The solution is to cache a local copy of the data at the application server, or close to it. The closer the data to the application, the faster the acquisition time and the less delay introduced in the process.

This lever is applied as follows:

1. Data requests are segmented into two types: repeated requests for data in the cache, and requests whose data is not in the cache.
2. When the requested data is available in the local cache, data can be retrieved from the local cached copy, making remote server requests unnecessary.
3. When requested data is not in the local cache because it has been requested for the first time or has changed since the previous request, it has to be retrieved from a remote server.
4. Requested data that is frequently updated by other applications must be sent by the server and cannot be cached, unless the cache has information about the change status of the requested data. This information must be acquired from a remote server.

Distributing Activities

This lever is applied as follows:

- Data is retrieved from appropriate data stores depending on its utilization or frequency of updates.
- Data stores are distributed or duplicated, in some cases, to provide faster access, eliminating some wastes types.

Eliminating Non-Value-Adding and Incoming Work

This lever is applied as follows:

- Reduce network traffic by eliminating repeated data transfers.
- Eliminate the remote database query and retrieval.

Summary

This chapter introduced the notion of patterns, their significance in the business world, and how they describe the best practices, opportunities, and common pitfalls in the move to virtualization. It also provided the template used to describe patterns in this book, along with a simple example illustrating the use of this template. Finally, it defined seven high-level patterns that summarize the lean methodology. These patterns are the basis for the next seven chapters of this book.

CHAPTER 5

Segmenting Complexity

Virtualizing IT resources can lead to savings of over 50 percent in hardware, maintenance, and energy costs in a data center. The transitional cost of virtualizing large-scale IT infrastructures is hard to estimate, however. If not planned correctly, it can often outweigh the benefits of virtualization for several years. This chapter outlines a "divide and conquer" approach to planning and cost estimation for virtualization transformations. This enables an organization to plan and execute complex virtualization transformations while maximizing its return on investment (ROI) within a favorable payback period.

Barriers to Cost-Effective Virtualization

This section offers a bit of background to support the detailed discussions of organizational environments that come later in this chapter. It also summarizes the approach to virtualization we'll lay out in a virtualization pattern.

IT infrastructures in large organizations are highly complex. They tend to have thousands of servers running hundreds of applications on a diverse set of hardware, operating systems, commercial off-the-shelf (COTS) software components, and homegrown applications in a multi-vendor, multi-version environment. Similar applications might have been developed at different times for different parts of the organization, especially when the organization has been created through corporate mergers. Combining similar applications might prove difficult because they are running on different hardware and operating systems. The complexity is further increased by business rules and constraints that are imposed by an organization's environment.

Given that 80 percent of the world's data centers were built before 2001, many of their hardware, operating systems, applications, network, middleware, and data center facilities are outdated or near end of support from their original manufacturers and providers. Many of these components were also designed with earlier business requirements in mind and are not able to scale up or out readily to meet the future computing demands of the business.

Virtualization of the IT infrastructure provides an organization with the opportunity to upgrade and consolidate these components to better address and manage future strategic, tactical, and operational business goals and IT requirements. The virtualization effort, however, also depends on the particular components and their uses by the organization in a deep and detailed way. For instance, management might forbid a major upgrade to some critical component, such as a payment system, because any disruption could be fatal to the corporation. However, the organization might desperately desire a major upgrade to some other component that has dependencies on the critical system.

Thus, revamping the IT infrastructure and data center facilities via a virtualization transformation can be a very complicated and expensive endeavor. Without careful design, planning, and execution, it can end in unaffordable costs, or even disaster.

As a reader of this book, you are probably involved with preparing proposals and budgets for virtualization transformations. You might be used to doing migrations on a small, local basis through direct source-to-target mapping and ground-up cost estimation. These straightforward planning techniques break down during a large virtualization transformation because of large combinations of servers and applications that have interdependencies. In fact, if you stick to traditional techniques, you might not even have time to generate a proposal covering a project of such a large scope. Furthermore, sticking to these traditional estimation approaches deprives you of optimization opportunities in planning and execution, by failing to fully realize the economies that present themselves in large-scale transformation programs.

Achieving an optimal transformation in such an environment requires the assessment of a large number of decision variables and transformation parameters and the evaluation of multiple possible paths. We recommend that IT virtualization transformation be managed in a phased approach, with the goal of minimizing risk while maximizing ROI. This requires a meticulous approach to planning and cost estimates, along with comprehensive program management to set up and achieve the results in the plan.

The pattern in this chapter segments the enormous task of virtualization among both resources and time:

- By segmenting the task among your resources—servers, applications, and data stores—you can group your staff's efforts efficiently and apply a single project to multiple resources.
- By segmenting the task in time—among multiple independent projects—you can budget for each project separately and execute the ones with the best chance of success and ROI first.

The scope of each project is determined by examining a number of business and technical variables and objectives. It is managed as an independent end-to-end program, governed by rigorous program management. Each project contributes to the efficiency and progress of the organization as the virtualization transformation continues.

Scenario

To give a sense of the forces affecting a large virtualization project, this section provides a typical client scenario.

The CIO of a financial firm that manages global financial assets is driven by business pressures from her stakeholders to optimize IT infrastructure and data center costs while continuing to support the company's strategic business goals. These strategic goals are revenue growth, expanding margins, and competitive differentiation via better alignment of business and IT models. The firm has grown over the decades, via an aggressive acquisition strategy. This has created several islands of technology, in the form of data centers with a heterogeneous mix of hardware, software platforms, and applications.

The firm's IT infrastructure includes over 1,500 applications, hosted on 5,000 servers that are a heterogeneous mix of distributed servers and a handful of old mainframes. Some of the factors weighing down the data centers include the following:

- In addition to the presence of operating systems and hardware from almost every major vendor in the industry, the company's IT portfolio also includes a diverse mix of applications, ranging from COTS applications to those with specific major customizations, as well as those developed in-house.

- The demand at this firm's seven data centers reached maximum power capacity this year. Fifty percent of these data centers cannot be upgraded to increase power density.
- The currently designed data center capacity is not suited for the varied requirements of production servers, versus those of development and test servers.
- The data center landscape has a high degree of fragmentation, with four medium/large locations, three small locations, and many additional "data rooms." This fragmentation also contributes to higher data center personnel costs and facilities management costs.
- The layout of the existing data centers also results in unnecessary operational risks (e.g., dependence on multiple lower-tier data centers), an inefficient disaster recovery model (e.g., requiring additional equipment to replicate data), and a very expensive storage environment (e.g., most of the data resides on expensive tier-1 storage without an effective information lifecycle and data management policy).
- The production infrastructure for individual applications is spread across the multiple data center facilities. The impact of planned shutdowns and maintenance or unplanned outages is high because the staff members don't understand the interdependencies with other facilities well. The dependency of application chains on multiple data centers multiplies the risk of failure and complicates recovery.

Although the IT staff has some projects to address the complexity of maintaining and recovering applications across all data centers, the CIO has recognized that a critical enabler will be the larger job of creating a much simpler data center landscape. Hence, the firm's executive management has given the CIO the charter to consolidate the firm's fragmented islands of technology into three state-of-the-art data centers over a period of two years.

The CIO has decided to leverage virtualization technology to rationalize and optimize IT infrastructure. She has set out to develop a plan for an IT infrastructure transformation with the following strategic objectives (SOs), critical success factors (CSFs), and key performance indicators (KPIs) in mind.

Strategic Objective 1: Reduce Annual Server Operating Expenses

The objective to reduce annual server operating expenses by $8 million and capital expenditures by $40 million will be met using the following CSFs and KPIs:

- CSF 1.1: Reduce the server count and associated maintenance/license costs for distributed servers.

  » KPI 1.1.1: Reduce the number of physical servers by more than 80 percent.
  » KPI 1.1.2: Reduce the number of operating system instances by more than 20 percent.

- CSF 1.2: Reduce the IT labor costs needed to support the target state for distributed servers.

  » KPI 1.2.1: Reduce server administration staff by more than 20 percent.
  » KPI 1.2.2: Reduce the average server burden on administrators by more than 30 percent, through simplification and automation.

Strategic Objective 2: Align IT to Service Level Expectations

The objective to align IT to service level expectations will be met using the following CSF and KPIs:

- CSF 2.1: Business platforms will have a business-driven Service Level Agreement (SLA) and cost breakdown.

  » KPI 2.1.1: Service level managers will assign Service Level Objectives (SLOs) to all servers and publish compliance reports.
  » KPI 2.1.2: Cost transparency will be accomplished by applying unit costs to all consumed server resources.

Strategic Objective 3: Simplify the IT Environment

The objective to simplify and standardize the IT environment will be met using the following CSF and KPIs:

- CSF 3.1: Leverage repeatable processes, procedures, and technology standards.

  » KPI 3.1.1: Post all of the organization's standard technology and services in its IT service catalog.
  » KPI 3.1.2: Require explicit approval of all nonstandard technology from the Change Control Board.

Strategic Objective 4: Increase the Agility of IT

The objective to increase the agility of IT to respond to business needs will be met using the following CSF and KPI:

- CSF 4.1: Automate and accelerate the operational readiness of new or modified servers.

    » KPI 4.1.1: Keep the average request-to-readiness time for new OS images to less than four days.

Strategic Objective 5: Optimize the Use of IT Resources

The objective to optimize the use of IT resources will be met using the following CSF and KPIs:

- CSF 5.1: Increase the average utilization of servers.

    » KPI 5.1.1: Keep the average CPU utilization across the entire production server landscape at more than 60 percent.
    » KPI 5.1.2: Complete provisioning and application readiness of standard offerings in less than five days.

The CIO understands that the virtualization transformation of the server infrastructure will be critical to achieving the strategic objectives. However, she is quite concerned about the cost, complexity, risks, and scheduling of the transformation. Her team has never undertaken a complex IT infrastructure transformation of this nature.

The Segmenting Complexity Pattern

In the scenario outlined above, the Segmenting Complexity pattern can lead to a robust plan in a reasonable amount of time. The plan mitigates risks to scope, schedule, and costs, while providing the foundation for managing the transformation in phases.

Name

The name of this pattern is Segmenting Complexity.

Value Statement

This pattern allows you to break down the complexity of the IT environment into manageable components. It enables you to generate optimal plans and schedules for a server virtualization transformation project, while minimizing cost overruns and maximizing the return on your transformation investment.

This pattern focuses specific operations-management techniques on the goal of server consolidation and virtualization. The implementation selects subsets of the server and application workload components and then prioritizes them to identify the most and least likely candidates for a virtualization transformation. The prioritized virtualization candidates are then categorized into clusters and assigned to different phases of the transformation. The first phase (and cluster) comprises servers and applications that offer a "sweet spot," in the sense that they are the easiest (in terms of migration complexity) and the most economical (in terms of costs and schedule) to migrate to a virtualized environment. The degree of difficulty, costs, and risk involved in virtualizing the IT infrastructure increases with each subsequent phase.

The segmentation provided by this pattern is very extensive. Each phase can be scoped, scheduled, and managed as an independent project, with its own financials, earned value analysis, and return on investment. The last attribute allows implementers to demonstrate tangible incremental value and ROI for the organization undertaking the virtualization transformation, as each phase is completed.

Context

This pattern should be explored near the beginning of a transformation. It is appropriate for any organization with a large number of heterogeneous servers and applications. Typical sites that benefit from this pattern have thousands of servers and hundreds of applications.

Problem

Migrating an IT infrastructure to virtual systems requires a great deal of specialized planning and technical effort. Most virtualization transformations are very complex, so it's hard to anticipate their costs. While there's a great potential for cost savings by combining the migration efforts of many servers or applications with similar characteristics, many sites haven't kept track of the data that would help them combine related migrations. This is particularly true for organizations that have undergone mergers or developed similar systems to meet the needs of different departments over a long period of time.

In short, virtualizing a large site usually requires a specifically tailored plan. The plan makes the most of the efficiencies and cost savings available to that site's particular configuration of systems and applications, taking into account the training and expertise of the staff. It also requires firm governance at a high level. Sites that bypass this planning stage often fail to generate a positive ROI, due to cost and schedule overruns.

Forces

The difficulty of carrying out a large-scale transformation can be explained by the large number of variables and constraints involved. The main ones we've found include the following:

- Heterogeneity of IT infrastructure components, including diversity of hardware and operating system platforms, applications, software, and storage environment components
- Requirements to demonstrate positive financial returns during and after a virtualization transformation project
- Varying characteristics of applications, some being I/O intensive, others being CPU intensive or memory intensive, and so on
- Dependencies on legacy infrastructure
- Data sharing among applications that makes it hard to migrate them individually
- Security and compliance (regulatory) considerations
- Availability of technical skills and resources, along with the difficulty of balancing the workforce to accomplish the transformation, which is often very labor-intensive
- Aging data center and facilities infrastructure with constraints on power, cooling, and floor space
- Dependencies on third-party application vendors for certifications of applications to move to a virtualized state
- Dependencies on business reliance, high availability, and disaster recovery objectives and requirements
- Dependencies on IT systems management to meet or exceed required IT infrastructure-related SLAs in the to-be-virtualized state

The Segmenting Complexity pattern provides a structure for considering all these pressures, so planning can be approached in an orderly and predictable manner.

Selection Guidance

Use this pattern when your organization meets many of the following characteristics:

- The scope of your virtualization transformation includes a mix of heterogeneous server hardware, operating systems, middleware, applications, and storage environments.
- The number of servers being migrated is in the hundreds or thousands, and the number of applications they run is in the hundreds.
- You are relocating IT infrastructure components to different data centers.
- You are running a refresh project on large-scale IT infrastructure technology or data center facilities.
- You are required to generate costs and schedule estimates for the transformation.
- Your transformation includes capacity and performance optimization of servers, applications, or storage environments.
- You are developing green IT solutions.
- You have the skills for sophisticated project planning and cost modeling.

Solution

This pattern's solution consists of three stages, which might be summarized as what to do, how to do it, and whether to do each part:

1. *Determining individual transformations*—In this stage, you decide on a server-by-server basis whether a server can be migrated, and how to do so. For instance, it might be done through a "lift and load" move to a binary-compatible platform or through a "platform refresh" that involves recompilation and sometimes recoding. We provide a list of attributes that you should check for each server and a decision tree for choosing the migration type.
2. *Grouping transformations*—In this stage, you identify servers and applications with similar characteristics that can be handled as a group to generate economies. We call this a *factory model* for performing transformations.

    The benefit of grouping your efforts for different servers and applications is incalculable. It not only saves money and time but provides input to the next stage, where you define phases and determine how much each is worth to your organization. Each group undergoing a transformation should be a separate project within the organization.

3. *Cost analysis*—Finally, you can use a predictive model to estimate costs for each transformation defined in the previous step. Time and cost estimates help you define independent phases and schedule them in a way your staff and budget can support. Most organizations perform the simpler phases with lower costs and faster schedules before the more complex and costly phases, to maximize their ROI from virtualization. Cost estimates can be refined during the project, using new data on transformations as input.

Determining Individual Transformations

In the first phase of the pattern, you examine each server to determine its prospects for migration to a virtual environment and the best way to do it. To complete this task for each server, the technical staff must assess its hardware, operating systems, applications, linkages to other servers, storage systems, and applications in the existing environment. The possible hardware, operating systems, and applications available in the new environment you want to offer for virtualization must also be assessed.

There are many ways to migrate from your source environment to a virtual environment. For instance, the virtual environment may or may not use the same hardware and operating system as the original. Third-party COTS components may also change. When the platform remains the same, the migration can be a "lift and load" approach, where the original binary runs on the new server. (This should not be assumed, of course; it must be tested.) A change in platform requires a "refresh and rebuild," which also offers opportunities to upgrade the application.

In addition, migration plans must take into account such business considerations as how critical each application is to the functioning of the organization. In short, this stage involves both determining the target environment (such as Windows or Linux) and determining how to move the server and its applications.

One of the major goals of the virtualization transformation is to realize cost savings by creating a more uniform operating environment. However, it would be cost prohibitive to do all the recoding and recompiling necessary to implement a completely homogenous environment. Typically, the target environment will have a few virtual systems reflecting the predominant operating systems present in the legacy environment. In one example, where there was a mix of Sun OS, AIX, HP-UX, and Windows, the target environment was constructed from virtualized AIX, Solaris, and Windows systems. The systems based on HP-UX were migrated to AIX.

Different source-to-target mappings present different degrees of risk and have different cost characteristics. The optimal transformation path depends on the customer's risk tolerance, the amount of staff time available for rebuilding applications, and the diversity of both the legacy environment and the target environment. There are three major types of migration, summarized in Table 5.1:

Table 5.1: Transformation Options			
	Application Characteristics	**Pros**	**Cons**
Binary	• Little enhancement activity • Legacy software or retirement candidate • Not mission-critical • Compatible with target in hardware, OS, and third-party software	• Lower cost • Addresses hardware end-of-life issues • Easier and fastest OS upgrade path • Viable in spite of missing code	• Risk of failure, leading to more expensive path • Does not address COTS software end-of-life issues • Limits ability to make functional changes to the application • Does not address gaps in nonfunctional requirements • Does not enhance application maintainability and supportability • Does not take full advantage of OS performance improvements
Like-for-like	• High enhancement activity • Mission-critical • Platform software and COTS nearing or at end-of-life • Compatible with target (once recompiled) in hardware, OS, and third-party software • Architecture remediation is required	• Relatively predictable upgrade path and costs • Refreshes third-party software and addresses end-of-life issues • Potential to address gaps in nonfunctional requirements • Enhances application maintainability and supportability	• Higher cost and longer upgrade time than binary migration
Custom	• Similar characteristics as like-for-like, but on a larger scale • Missing code or known problematic areas require code rewrite • No upgrade path for current OS or third-party software	• Enables future application enhancements • Restores application maintainability and supportability • Solves software and language issues	• Additional remediation costs to address code, language, and third-party software gaps • Highest cost and longest time

- Binary migration
- Like-for-like migration
- Custom migration

Binary Migration

Binary migration is possible when the legacy chipset, hardware, and operating system are the same as the target or when the target offers emulation for the legacy environment. When binary migration is successful, the binary executable code for the application and any third-party software it depends on is installed on newer, supported hardware. There are two subpaths within binary migration:

- *Binary with OS upgrade*—This option is feasible where the current legacy binary code is able to run on new the OS version; that is, where the OS and COTS vendors support "binary compatibility mode" operation. To be successful, the version gap between the source and target should be very small.
- *Binary without OS upgrade*—This path provides a low-cost way to address hardware end-of-life issues in legacy systems or to realize server consolidation/virtualization without having to do a software refresh.

Binary migration is the strategy of choice for applications that are in maintenance mode and not seeing much enhancement activity. These applications are needed for running the current business but are not part of the organization's long-term strategy and are slated to be retired soon. Due to maintenance-mode operation and lack of new investment in these applications, the organization often faces a lack of application expertise, and sometimes even missing source code. The objective is to get these applications migrated to the target environment at the lowest possible cost and to keep them running until they can be retired and replaced.

Even when the target environment appears to permit binary migration, however, some risk remains. The larger the gap between the legacy and target OS versions, the greater the chance that the binary will not run. In the worst case, problems with binary compatibility mode may force a like-for-like or custom migration.

Like-for-Like Migration

Like-for-like migration entails recompiling the application and upgrading COTS components to a new version of the same vendor OS. This migration option requires more effort than binary migration, but much less than custom migration. This path requires the target to have both a version of the legacy OS and the COTS components on which the application depends.

This is the suggested option for applications that are part of the corporate strategy and are candidates for new investment and enhancement. This migration path refreshes the application and COTS components and provides an opportunity to address performance, availability, reliability, security, and capacity issues. Like-for-like migration should be considered for all applications where continuing support is important.

In the example of operating system migrations given earlier, the legacy, older versions of Sun OS systems were migrated to Solaris 9 in the target environment. Because the operating systems were in the same family, application migration required a simple recompilation.

Custom Migration

Custom migration is the most time-consuming path, but it is necessary when the organization's strategy calls for new hardware and operating systems, and emulation of the legacy systems is not possible. It might also be necessary when an application is being upgraded and no longer runs on the old system, or when third-party components cannot be migrated to the new platform.

This is the only viable option when there is no upgrade path for the current OS and COTS components to the target environment. You also need a custom migration when you need to rewrite application code because missing source code makes recompilation impossible, or when the application has other problems. This option will incur additional costs over like-for-like migration to address OS, COTS, and language gaps, as well as to restore missing functionality left by missing code.

The example migration mentioned earlier moved legacy HP-UX systems to AIX in the target virtual environment. It also replaced several COTS components with new COTS components that provided similar functionality. One example of a COTS component change was to migrate from proprietary communications middleware to a standard WebSphere Enterprise Services Bus running under AIX.

Choosing a Migration Path

This section presents decision-support tools that help determine the best migration for each server. There are two components of this approach: application surveys and decision trees.

Application surveys collect critical application data, which are scored and weighted to come up with a single quantitative score. This score helps you determine at the start of the process whether the application is a good candidate for binary migration. Parts of decision surveys can be automated by implementing discovery tools such as IBM's Tivoli® Application Dependency Discovery Manager (TADDM) software.

A *decision tree* is a visual guide that helps you progressively evaluate the requirements of the migration and choose the best path. It incorporates various technical, business, and risk parameters in the decision-making process, to find the best transformation path from a cost and risk perspective.

We incorporate the following attributes into the binary migration decision:

- Business factors
- Application factors
- Technical factors

Business factors weigh the application in terms of the following:

- *Application activity*—Past and planned investment
- *Mission criticality*—The impact if the application were not available
- *Retirement status*—The prospects for using the application over the long term

Application factors weigh the application in terms of the following:

- *Application codependency*—The degree of interaction with other applications in the infrastructure
- *Nonfunctional requirements gaps*—How well the application is meeting the organization's goals for performance and robustness

Finally, technical factors weigh the application in terms of the following:

- *OS gap*—How well the application is expected to make the move to the target OS
- *OS vendor support*—How well the OS vendor supports upward migration of applications to new versions of the OS
- *Third-party software gap*—Whether third-party software can be migrated to the target
- *Third-party vendor support*—Whether support from the vendor of third-party software can be expected during and after the migration

Our approach is extensible. It can be easily customized and augmented to include other factors, or to vary the weightings of the factors based on your specific needs.

The decision tree, shown in Figure 5.1, offers a series of gates that guide the decision-making process for application migration. It is evaluated from left to right. Each decision node is determined by a combination of factors that were gathered during the application survey. The endpoint nodes are the migration choices described in the previous sections (binary, like-for-like, or custom).

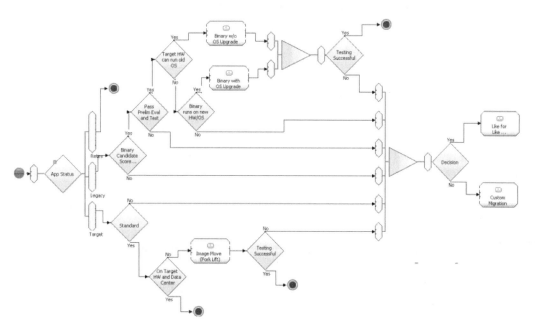

Figure 5.1: The decision tree for determining migration paths.

The decision tree model first considers the application's mission criticality and retirement status:

- Critical applications will need enhancements and therefore should undergo like-for-like or custom migration. On the other hand, legacy applications are good candidates for binary migration.
- Applications that are already planned for retirement need not be brought into the transformation and require no further consideration.

The candidate applications for binary migration undergo a binary candidate survey that scores the application characteristics on a number of business, technical, and application factors and enumerates an aggregate score. You'll see this process later in the chapter.

If an application passes the threshold for binary migration based on its score, the environment then undergoes an evaluation. If the target hardware can run the current OS, the application becomes a candidate for binary migration without an OS upgrade. If the target hardware needs a newer version of the OS, the application becomes a candidate for a binary migration with an OS upgrade.

Since binary compatibility is assured only for "well-behaved" applications, we take the binary candidate application through testing in the target environment. If problems turn up during testing, we revert to like-for-like or custom migration.

The enterprise target architecture applications are slated for platform refresh if they are not already on the target platform. If the applications are already on the target platform, a binary load is performed. Otherwise, a like-for-like or custom migration is performed.

Application Surveys

An application survey produces a scorecard that helps you determine what migration path is most suitable for each application. Tables 5.2, 5.3, and 5.4 show the business, application, and technical attributes we used to determine binary migration candidates.

Table 5.2: Scoring Business Attributes			
Metric	**Attribute Definition**	**Attribute Weight**	**Attribute Score**
Application activity	Functional releases in the past 24 months or planned in the future • *High:* Active application with regular quarterly releases, medium to large (more than 20 FTE) • *Medium:* Application with irregular or smaller quarterly releases (fewer than 20 FTE) • *Low:* Application in maintenance mode, with few to no functional releases	1	High: 11 pts Medium: 6 pts Low: 2 pts
Mission criticality	Severity and extent of business impact due to application unavailability • *High:* Touches on multiple business functions with widespread business impacts • *Medium:* Limited impact—business transactions can be rerun and recovered when application is restored • *Low:* Limited impact—workarounds and manual processes provide business continuity	1	High: 11 pts Medium: 6 pts Low: 2 pts
Retirement status	Retirement plans and funding commitment • *High:* Target retirement date not established or over 3 years away • *Medium:* Target retirement date established, with funding being worked on • *Low:* Target retirement date established, with funding commitment in place	1	High: 11 pts Medium: 6 pts Low: 2 pts

Table 5.3: Scoring Application Attributes			
Metric	**Attribute Definition**	**Attribute Weight**	**Attribute Score**
Application codependency	Real-time interfaces that this application has with other applications • *High:* More than 15 interfaces • *Medium:* Between 5 and 15 interfaces • *Low:* Fewer than 5 interfaces	1	High: 11 pts Medium: 6 pts Low: 2 pts
Nonfunctional requirement gaps	Application's ability to meet present and projected nonfunctional requirements • *High:* Application not meeting requirements in performance, volume, availability, or maintainability; application architecture changes or enhancements needed to address current gaps • *Medium:* Application meeting current nonfunctional requirements but requiring architectural changes to meet projected requirements in 12–18 months • *Low:* Application meeting current nonfunctional requirements; no changes foreseen	1	High: 11 pts Medium: 6 pts Low: 2 pts

Table 5.4: Scoring Technical Attributes			
Metric	**Attribute Definition**	**Attribute Weight**	**Attribute Score**
OS gap	• *High:* Application's current OS version over 5 versions behind target OS • *Medium:* Current OS 3–4 versions behind target • *Low:* Current OS version same as target, or only 1–2 versions behind	1	High: 11 pts Medium: 6 pts Low: 2 pts
OS vendor support	• *High:* Limited support/guarantee for source-to-target migration, involves restrictions and exclusions, or requires newer versions of third-party software to be compiled on target OS • *Medium:* Vendor supports binary compatibility mode with modest restrictions and exclusions • *Low:* Vendor guarantees binary compatibility mode with few or no restrictions or exclusions	1	High:11 pts Medium: 6 pts Low: 2 pts
Third-party software support	• *High:* Critical components not supported on target platform • *Medium:* Majority of critical components supported on target platform • *Low:* All components supported on target platform in binary compatibility mode	1	High: 11 pts Medium: 6 pts Low: 2 pts

Simply add all the scores for the attributes in the three tables. The lower the score, the more likely the application is a good candidate for binary migration. The exact cutoff point should be set by each organization based on its risk tolerance, but we find the following rough cutoff points widely applicable:

- For an application score of less than 30, binary migration is recommended.
- For an application score between 30 and 60, binary migration is worth considering.
- For an application score greater than 60, use like-for-like or custom migration.

Application Scorecard Examples

This section illustrates the use of the application scorecard in two example applications. Application A is a legacy application in maintenance mode, which is slated for retirement in the next three to five years. There has not been much enhancement work on the application in recent years, and the business has limited the funding on this application to critical bug fixes only. The application is running on Solaris 8, which is two versions behind the current Solaris 10. All the COTS component versions are supported by vendors, and most are supported in binary compatibility mode.

Table 5.5 shows the application survey results and scores for this application:

- Low on application activity and mission criticality.
- Medium on retirement status, since it is identified as a retirement candidate, but no retirement date has been established.
- Low on application codependency because the application has only three interfaces to external applications.
- Medium on nonfunctional requirement gaps. It is currently meeting the requirements, but new user migrations are planned for this application next year, which might require support for additional capacity.
- Low on the OS and third-party software gaps. The application is only two versions behind on the OS level, and the third-party vendors are supporting the versions of their software that are deployed.
- Medium on third-party software support, since a few vendors would not support the binary compatibility mode operation.

The overall score for this application is calculated to be 30, which suggests a binary migration path.

Table 5.5: Application Survey Results for Application A		
Application Characteristic	**Survey Result**	**Score**
Application activity	Low	2
Mission criticality	Low	2
Retirement status	Medium	6
Application codependency	Low	2
NFR gap	Medium	6
OS gap	Low	2
COTS gap	Low	2
OS vendor support	Medium	6
COTS support	Low	2

Application B is a legacy application that is undergoing regular enhancements and has been deemed mission-critical by the business. The application is not part of planned future operations, but no retirement target has been set. This application has interfaces with ten other applications and thus has been rated medium on codependency. The application is meeting current performance and availability requirements, but additional transaction volumes expected in the next 12 to 18 months will exceed the current capacity on the system. The OS is only two versions behind the current version, so the OS gap is scored low. The OS vendor assures binary compatibility mode operation, with a few restrictions. Communications middleware on the application is now out of support; a version upgrade would be required to migrate to the supported version.

Table 5.6 shows the survey results for this application. The score comes to 60, so this application is only a marginal candidate for binary migration.

Table 5.6: Application Survey Results for Application B		
Application Characteristic	**Survey Result**	**Score**
Application activity	High	11
Mission criticality	High	11
Retirement status	Medium	6
Application codependency	Medium	6
NFR gap	Medium	6
OS gap	Low	2
COTS gap	Low	6
OS vendor support	Medium	6
COTS support	Medium	6

Grouping Transformations

The first stage of the Segmenting Complexity pattern determined the path for each server you are considering for virtualization. The goal in the next stage is to find common elements that allow your staff to process several servers or applications at once. Large-scale transformation projects present many opportunities for organizing and timing transformations so you can exploit the following efficiencies:

- Economies of scale based on sheer repetition of tasks
- Reuse of your staff's expertise and their knowledge of resources
- Reuse of tools developed along the way
- Organizational structures mapped to dependencies within the applications being transformed

The Factory Approach

A factory approach, developed in this section, leads to the following economies:

- *Economies of reuse* are realized when the same or similar transformations are performed repeatedly. You can achieve these economies by capturing knowledge and experience gained from the first set of transformations in a knowledge base. The factory model retains tools and personnel during multiple transformations.
- *Economies of organization* are realized by organizing the factory around Centers of Excellence, by target. This allows for critical expertise to be developed, enhanced, and retained in focused organizational units.
- *Economies of integration* are realized by identifying clusters of dependent applications that need to be transformed, and by placing codependent applications in the same transformation bundle. Such clustering allows integration testing on all the members of the cluster in the target environment, instead of repeating the same integration points multiple times.

This section presents the criteria that help you make the best choices for grouping servers as well as applications and lays out the migration process at a high level. We recommend that you catalog applications and apply analytical tools to generate quantitative scores that determine the most optimal transformation path. The Redistribute Activities pattern, described in the next chapter, discusses the redistribution of workforce skills within an organizational structure and management system in more detail. That pattern will help you realize the potential savings that your planning at this stage makes possible.

Figure 5.2 shows the process for grouping servers. As you can see, the factory process starts with an analysis of the existing code. Here, you want to be assured that all of the source code is available and can be built in the source environment. After a successful build, you install the code in the test environment and run some broad sanity checks on it. This gives you an idea how many changes to the code you will need to migrate the application.

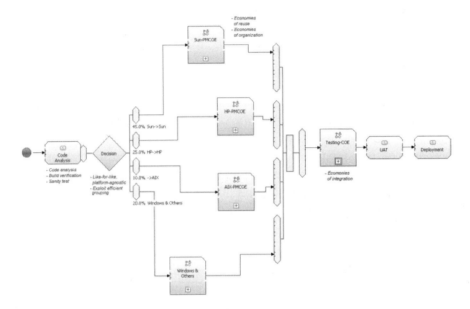

Figure 5.2: The transformation-factory decision tree for grouping servers.

If these two steps are successful, you can move forward with the application transformation. We recommend establishing a Center of Excellence (CoE) in your IT organization for each guest OS you are considering in your virtual environment. Each CoE is responsible for taking the application code from the source environment to the target environment and making the code changes needed to run the application in the target environment with the new OS and third-party components.

CoEs also perform system testing on the migrated application, to verify its operations in the target environment. By concentrating OS and third-party software expertise in the CoE structure, you ensure continuity and retention of knowledge and experience, as well as the reuse of tools and other assets.

After the system testing has been completed, the applications move to the integration and user testing phases. Integration testing is centralized in an Integration Test CoE.

This ensures the retention of test expertise, as well as making integration efficient by performing it on codependent applications as a group.

Application Clustering

One of the key enablers to realizing the economies of scale, organization, and integration is properly coordinating the work that flows through the factory. Work should be organized into separate application clusters. Each cluster should be managed as a discrete end-to-end project, with its own budget, ROI targets, and payback period.

You have many options for how you form application clusters. You should make the decision based on the most pressing tasks you need to perform and the characteristics of your software and IT team. The most efficient clusters contain applications that:

- Share similarities in design and construction (e.g., common languages, common third-party components, and common libraries)
- Are highly cohesive, internally
- Conversely, have loose dependencies on applications not in the cluster

Other considerations for choosing clusters include the following:

- Similarities in the transformation effort required (e.g., one cluster for applications that are easy to migrate, another for those where the effort is more complex, and another for those where the effort is very complex), staffed with people whose expertise you can trust at that level of complexity
- Similarities in the dependencies on other applications; for example, clustering all applications migrating from Sun's JVM to IBM's JVM
- Business constraints and larger organizational goals, such as determining that all marketing applications need to be transformed before finance applications

Organizing work in these types of application clusters ensures that economies of scale, organization, and integration are exploited fully.

This stage is where automated analytical tools can help you choose the best application clusters. Tools can find and weight the commonality and variability among applications, taking into account the OS and third-party components used. Typically, the various criteria can be visualized as vectors, and the applications can be placed near the relevant criteria based on how important each criterion is for migration. This is illustrated in Figure 5.3. Clustering analysis finds the applications that are closest in this multi-dimensional space.

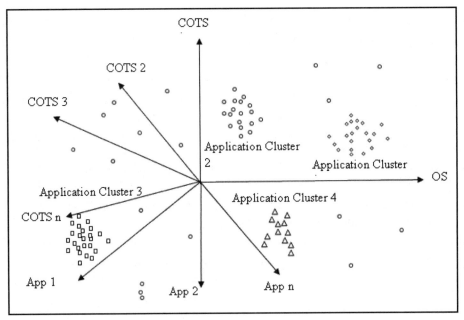

Figure 5.3: Visualizing application clusters for project scheduling.

Having formed clusters, you need to consider scheduling carefully. Your plan needs to ensure the availability of critical expertise in OS and third-party software in the CoE, as well as your release planning cycles. Migration should be scheduled around major functionality releases.

We recommend that IT infrastructure virtualization transformation be managed in a phased approach, with the goal of minimizing the risk for the organization while maximizing the return on the organization's investment. Therefore, each of the clusters should be prioritized and assigned to project phases based on migration effort.

Focus first on the clusters that are easiest and most economical to transform to a virtualized state, and which offer the quickest and largest ROI. We refer to these prioritized clusters as the "sweet spot" of workloads for virtualized transformations. The clusters that are more difficult to virtualize and that offer long-term ROI should also be organized into separate, discrete project phases.

Each project phase should be managed as a discrete project, with its own ROI, set of costs, and completion criteria. The cost analysis in the next section will be invaluable for your planning.

Cost Analysis

The business aspects of cost estimation and proposal generation are just as complex as the technical complexity of planning and implementing large-scale virtualization transformations. When dealing with thousands of servers and hundreds of applications, traditional cost estimation approaches based on direct effort-based cost are impractical.

This section presents an approach for building cost estimates based on measuring key characteristics of the applications and servers you need to migrate: code size, OS gaps, and so on. We recommend you perform a migration on a small, representative set of applications and servers, measuring the staff time required. From this data, you can predict the costs of the full migration for each phase you defined in the previous sections, using a multivariate analysis.

Figure 5.4 shows the process. The application characteristics are gathered partly through surveys, and partly through your sample migration. Various coefficients, which we'll illustrate later in this section, are applied to produce the cost estimate. Finally, the data

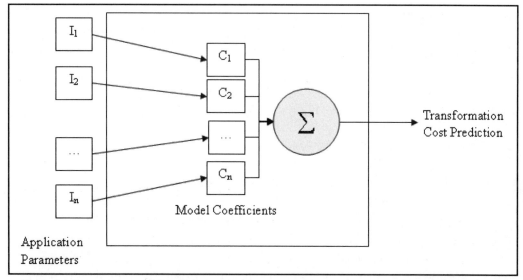

Figure 5.4: A model for predictive analysis.

you gather about time and effort during early phases can help you refine your predictions for later phases.

Building the Model

The accuracy of your model depends on choosing the following:

- A small set of applications that you trust to be representative of the transformation efforts as a whole
- A set of coefficients that you trust to reflect the real effect of each input parameter

Where application parameters are not independent (i.e., one application parameter is related to another), you can use factor analysis to cull input parameters. Alternatively, you can simply assign a large coefficient to one of the codependent parameters and a low coefficient to the other. When there is a very high dependency, you can exclude the dependent parameter from the model and rerun the analysis to re-estimate coefficients.

We have found that some combination of the following parameters is useful for predicting costs:

- Application size, measured in thousands of lines of code (KLOC)
- Number of system interfaces (SI)
- Number of third-party packages (TH)
- Number of versions in the gap between source OS and target OS (gap)
- Number of nodes (ND)

Thus, the staff effort, measured in full-time employees (FTE), will be a function calculated from your coefficients and an extra fixed cost component, as follows:

$$\text{Effort (FTE)} = \Sigma \, (C_i \times KLOC) + (C_s \times \text{System Interfaces}) + (C_c \times COTS) + (C_o \times \text{OS Gap Factor}) + (C_n \times \text{Nodes}) + K$$

Test the model against available data to validate its accuracy at estimating costs. You can perform this test by performing a correlation analysis between the model's predictions and ground-up estimates. A high degree of correlation indicates a sound model and confirms that you have included all the significant application parameters. Conversely, a poor correlation suggests that a significant application parameter is missing from the input. In such cases, review the cost drivers in the ground-up estimation model to identify the missing application characteristic that is driving the cost.

Applying the Model

Once you have built the model and chosen coefficients that you have demonstrated to produce accurate results in tests, you can conduct application surveys and analyses to quantify the input parameters for estimating the cost of your virtualization transformation. Plug the parameters into the model to calculate the predicted cost.

Cost predictions from the model should be at the project level, not for individual applications. Each application presents unpredictable variations, but these tend to cancel each other out when the model is applied at higher levels. Therefore, we have found that our model, given well-tested parameters and a valid sample of applications, provides an excellent estimate for transformation projects.

Maintaining the Model

Another aspect of our approach is continuous improvement, generated by calibrating the model against actual performance data. As applications move through the transformation factory, you should collect actual cost data and feed it into the model. This is illustrated in Figure 5.5, which extends the earlier Figure 5.4 with a feedback loop.

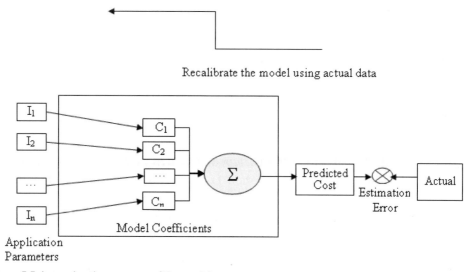

Figure 5.5: Improving the accuracy of the model.

An Example of Predictive Cost Estimation

This section applies the cost estimation model to the large-scale virtualization transformation project described earlier in the client scenario. We built the model using ground-up estimation data from a representative sample consisting of roughly 20 percent of the applications to be migrated, attempting to find a diverse cross-section. We started by identifying key application parameters and then used correlation analysis to choose the parameters for the model.

Table 5.7 shows the statistics collected for 14 representative applications, along with the characteristic parameters (KLOC, system interfaces, third-party components, OS gap, and nodes). The model produced the results in the "Prediction" column, which correlated quite well to the actual ground-up estimates for these applications shown in the "Estimate" column.

Table 5.7: Sample Results for the Model's Input Parameters							
Application	KLOC	SI	TH	Gap	ND	Prediction	Estimate
1	780	10	8	2	8	33.29997	35
2	1020	15	12	3	10	42.88751	45
3	4500	20	15	6	14	147.0191	150
4	2350	20	12	2	15	81.53557	80
5	400	10	6	1	8	21.13678	20
6	340	8	8	3	6	21.07582	20
7	840	14	9	4	7	37.41194	40
8	5045	30	20	2	12	159.7783	160
9	460	15	7	2	4	23.53707	25
10	530	20	5	1	6	25.24548	25
11	3100	20	12	5	10	104.64	100
12	1050	18	10	3	12	44.27054	45
13	600	12	8	4	6	29.94128	30

We ran a statistical analysis—the LINEST function offered by the Excel spreadsheet program—on the data set to estimate our model coefficients. Here is the resulting model:

$$\text{Effort (FTE)} = \Sigma \, (0.284 \, KLOC) + (0.11 \, System \, Interfaces) + (0.164 \, COTS) +$$
$$(1.03OS \, Gap \, Factor) + (0.263 \, Nodes) + 4.54$$

After estimating the costs for the representative set, we validated the model's accuracy by comparing ground-up estimates against model predictions, as shown in the preceding table. Having validated the model coefficients, we could apply the model to estimate costs for other applications in the transformation set and check it as further results came in.

We have applied the approach in this section successfully to several virtualization transformation projects. Figure 5.6 compares the actual and predicted costs for the project described in the client scenario at the beginning of this chapter. For this project, there was a high degree of correlation, confirming the validity of the model. The total costs predicted by the model were within 2 percent of the total estimated cost value.

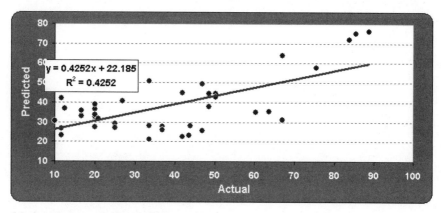

Figure 5.6: Actual versus predicted effort.

Summary

This chapter introduced the first of our seven patterns, which provides a firm foundation for planning the rest of your virtualization transformations. It provided a tested "divide and conquer" approach for server virtualization transformations that we have successfully leveraged for several large and complex virtualization projects. This approach will enable your organization to successfully plan and execute complex server virtualization transformations, while maximizing ROI within a favorable payback period.

The models and decision trees presented in this chapter, based on quantitative scorecards and representative testing, provide an effective means to plan and optimize large-scale, diverse virtualization transformations. A factory-based approach to project management offers an efficient implementation method for realizing large-scale virtualization transformations.

In short, the Segmenting Complexity pattern enables you to do the following:

- Build and use decision models and planning tools to achieve optimal server virtualization transformations
- Help your management and staff plan large-scale IT infrastructure virtualization transformations
- Build and use predictive cost and pricing models for infrastructure virtualization transformation proposals and their implementation
- Customize your models and continuously refine their prediction accuracy by feeding back the actual performance data

6

Redistributing Activities

Virtualization transformations often reach across complex organizational boundaries. Each organization or business unit within the organization might be facing different measurements from their management and trying to achieve different goals. When such organizational complexities are placed against the well-prepared technical plans of a virtualization transformation, care must be taken to avoid inter- and intra-organizational conflict, misalignment of goals, lack of adherence to architecture standards, team rivalries, miscommunication, and other harsh realities that can delay or detour even the best laid plans.

To drive a successful virtualization effort, transformation projects benefit from realigning key skills and redistributing activities under a common project management organization. Creating well-structured steering committees and architectural boards for organizational and architectural governance can keep the project on target and reduce additional costs.

The Client Scenario

This chapter builds upon the example of a financial services firm from Chapter 5. Assume the firm consists of these four revenue-generating business units:

- Global wealth management
- Commercial banking
- Financial advisory services
- Retail banking

The firm formed through the merger of three organizations, one providing wealth management and advisory services, another conducting retail banking, and the third conducting commercial banking. Each of the three divisions within the organization has, itself, undergone significant acquisition and merger activity. This results in a broad mix of infrastructure support models, including generalists dedicated to specific applications in an end-to-end model, as well as specialists devoted to the management of individual technology layers.

The firm's executive management has given the CIO full control of all the infrastructure, including facilities, servers, storage, and network, as well as all core IT operations. Application development, on the other hand, continues to be maintained as a separate function within each business unit, with the development teams not reporting to the CIO. Procurement and finance functions are provided by a corporate headquarters unit, distinct from either the central IT organization or any of the four business units. The CIO reports into the corporate headquarters organization, but is also accountable to the heads of each business unit for servicing their IT infrastructure needs.

The CIO's new infrastructure team is charged with supporting an environment that consists of 1,500 applications running on 5,000 heterogeneous servers, with seven data centers, and three network providers. The team has a range of skills that are aligned into technology-specific functional units. These include the following:

- There is a team of 20 architects, responsible for the design and structure of the overall infrastructure.
- There are 150 systems administrators, responsible for running distributed and mainframe platforms with a broad range of operating systems in use. Systems administrators are also sometimes called upon to serve as architects.
- There is a team of 30 facilities specialists, responsible for the planning and operations of the seven data centers.
- There is a team of 50 storage administrators, responsible for the management and operations of an advanced tier-one storage system. Most of the storage systems come from a single large vendor, but a variety of smaller storage technologies are also in play.
- There are 50 application administrators responsible for application operations. This team was culled from the business unit's application-development teams, and some of them resent being placed in an operational, rather than developmental, organization.

- A service desk is staffed by a team of 50, with significant turnover. This team is tasked with supporting three different main support structures, involving different telephone numbers and ticketing systems. The service desk's infrastructure varies across business units and operational teams, with much of the coordination needed to resolve problems being handled by email, instant messaging, and telephone.
- Network operations are outsourced to a service provider, but three different network vendors are used across the firm's seven data centers. The network architecture is mixed between the business unit's application development teams and the infrastructure architects.
- Overall, there are 100 application developers, split relatively evenly among the four business units.
- Procurement and finance are responsible for approving all capital spends as well as the annual budgeting process. They also provide contractual management of the outsourced network services.

The Redistribute Activities pattern addresses the five strategic objectives outlined in the previous chapter:

1. Reduce annual server operating expenses.
2. Align IT to service level expectations.
3. Simplify the IT environment.
4. Increase the agility of IT.
5. Optimize the use of IT resources.

The Redistribute Activities Pattern

The Redistribute Activities pattern's description is provided below

Name

The name of this pattern is Redistribute Activities.

Value Statement

This pattern overcomes the challenges of conflicting organizational missions and measurements by redistributing workforce skills to a common organizational structure and management system. The latter enables the virtualization transformation to address skills gaps, governance, architectural control, intra-organizational conflicts, and communications mishaps.

This pattern drives the establishment of a common management structure for the duration of the virtualization transformation, linking the disparate teams together into a unified force. This pattern can be leveraged beyond the life of the virtualization transformation project, to introduce consistent cross-organizational steady-state management of the virtualized IT environment.

Context

This pattern provides an effective solution in scenarios where the virtualization transformation project is mid-size to large, where disparate technical teams with disparate management chains (organizations) are involved, and where management goals are not necessarily aligned. This pattern influences a more fluid distribution and alignment of key virtualization-related skills within the same project management system, thus minimizing costs from rework, waiting, and workflow inefficiency.

Problem

The environments subject to virtualization transformations are rarely simple affairs. Applications and infrastructure are often heterogeneous and may range across a number of different guiding architectural principles. Also, all aspects of the infrastructure (such as storage, server, network, data center facilities, and applications) have complex dependencies among them.

Several technical teams, with different deep skill sets, are required to operate in a matrix environment during transformation. Challenges during the "team forming, storming, and norming" phase delay and negatively impact the performing phase. This leads to cost overruns and schedule misses. Individual technical teams are pursuing the goals established by their managements, which can be in conflict. Resolving differences involves delay and political maneuvering.

To add to the challenges facing a virtualization transformation, it is quite common for different IT infrastructure and business components to be managed by different teams within the larger organization, or even by different organizations altogether. In some examples, an individual application might be managed vertically by a single team, such as when one group is responsible for servers, storage, network, facilities, applications, and operations. Even so, such a group usually needs to interact with other applications, which might well be managed by other vertically aligned teams.

In other cases, organizations might run across functional technology components rather than application stacks or business alignment. In a structure such as this, one team might be responsible for server management, while another is responsible for storage management. A third team is responsible for middleware, and still others are responsible for the applications. Such separation of roles can lead to high degrees of efficiency, but can also create challenges for the virtualization transformation to transcend the silos of technology, as shown in Figure 6.1.

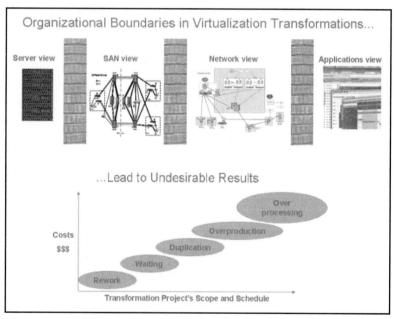

Figure 6.1: The negative impact of organizational silos on virtualization transformation projects.

These organizational complexities during a virtualization transformation, if not addressed properly, can be extremely detrimental to the success of the transformation project.

Forces

The difficulty of carrying out virtualization transformation projects for mid-size to large organizations with complicated organizational structures can be explained by the large number of variables and constraints involved. The main ones that deserve special mention in the context of the Redistribute Activities pattern are outlined here:

- Management goals might not be in alignment. An infrastructure support organization might well hold goals of standardizing the infrastructure and minimizing change. A development team, though, might be more focused on rapid application development and exploring new capabilities. In this kind of scenario, the infrastructure team could easily see the application team as "cowboys" or "out of control." From the alternate perspective, the application team might regard the infrastructure team as bureaucratic and behind the times. Unless their goals are aligned, these teams are likely to encounter significant conflict in a transformation effort that requires them to partner closely.
- Financial goals might be different for various support organizations, as well. A team responsible for reducing the cost of facilities operations, for instance, might strongly support an aggressive virtualization transformation. On the other hand, an applications support team tasked with minimizing the cost of supporting existing applications might well be unwilling to invest the time and resources needed to get their applications to work in the new environment.
- Some teams might simply not work well together and have histories of conflict and trouble. Centralized architecture organizations, for instance, can sometimes be perceived as arrogant and out of touch with the realities of the business. Sometimes organizations from different geographies regard each other as competitors for the same scarce resources and end up acting in conflict, withholding information from one another or subtly sabotaging each other's goals. A history of acquisitions, mergers, or divestitures could leave one part of the team feeling slighted or at risk of being eliminated, which could affect their behaviors and interactions.

These kinds of all-too-common scenarios affect businesses of all kinds and are a frequent subject of management attention. (Examples of discussion of managing organizational conflict abound in both the popular and IT-specific literature. One example is Rahim's "Toward a Theory of Managing Organizational Conflict," from *The International*

Journal of Conflict Management, 2002, Vol. 13, No. 3, pp. 206–235.) When they are encountered specifically within the context of executing a virtualization transformation project, we recommend the use of a service pattern to redistribute activities. This helps achieve effective cross-organizational management, adherence to architectural standards, identification of sources of conflict, and minimization of the disruptive effects of misalignment and miscommunications.

Selection Guidance

Establishing a simple project team, or simply gathering a few key leads from each area, might work well when the transformation initiative is small and where the teams are already tightly integrated. In a more complex organizational structure, however, the Redistribute Activities pattern might be more appropriate. This pattern should be considered when the following is true:

- Critical operational organizations do not have common management below the senior executive level.
- Multiple business units with competing measurements are required to closely collaborate to ensure success.
- Transformations require disparate geographical teams to march in lockstep through an extended period of analysis, architecture, design, and deployment.

Solution

In the example of our financial services firm, the skills needed to execute a virtualization transformation are spread across an architecture team, four operations teams (systems, storage, applications, and facilities), four distinct sets of application developers, and multiple business units. These are supported by a service desk, a third-party network operations team, and corporate-level procurement and finance organizations. To enable a complex set of interrelated organizations such as this one to effectively partner together during a virtualization transformation, the following actions are recommended:

- Establish an executive steering committee to oversee project governance, communications, and escalations.
- Consolidate key technical teams (such as Storage, Server Management, Application Services, and Network) under a single project management governance system.

- Establish architectural governance and controls around all architecture decisions.
- Establish a common measurement/management system to influence disparate technical teams.

The Executive Steering Committee

An executive steering committee should be established, comprised of senior executives from all stakeholder organizations, to provide management direction for the entire transformation initiative. While care should be taken to provide representation from each of the involved organizations, the steering committee itself must have clear authority to make and implement decisions. Communications to other corporate functions must come from the steering committee.

While the goal of such a steering committee should always be consensus, the outcome need not be all parties agreeing on all aspects of the solution. They just need to agree to implement the guidance that the executive steering committee provides. The work of the executive steering committee is summarized in Figure 6.2.

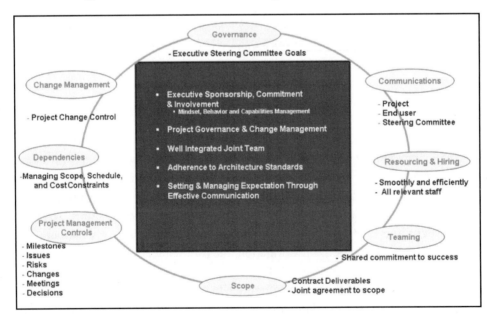

Figure 6.2: The executive steering committee integrates and manages a complex set of activities and organizational structure.

Without such a steering committee, the transformation project faces several risks. For instance, multiple operational organizations can bring forward to the finance team competing business cases based on alternate architectures. The storage team might suggest consolidation on a single, broad storage solution within a single site, based on the economic efficiencies of managing the storage. Another team, though, might recommend several geographically distributed storage solutions supporting individual computing centers, based on the revenue to be gained by providing local, low-latency solutions. If such disparate architectural and structural concerns are not addressed consistently across the entire transformation effort, the corporate finance function might well send the collective team into "analysis paralysis," as they model dozens of different scenarios for cost and revenue implications. While such analysis is critical to effective business management, in order to succeed, the transformation effort must efficiently select the optimal approach and present a coordinated view to which all teams will adhere.

In the case of our financial services firm, the steering committee is headed by the CIO. She is supported by the executives responsible for architecture, operations, and development. The operations executive, in turn, is supported by the managers responsible for each of its key areas (systems, storage, facilities, and applications). Development is represented by executives from each of the four business units. The steering committee also has participation from the project office responsible for network outsourcing, from the executives responsible for the service desk, and from the procurement and finance teams at the corporate level.

The final decision and authority for the steering committee rests with the CIO, but all organizations have agreed to adhere to the committee's decisions. This is particularly critical in the case of functions that do not report to the CIO, which include the four business units, finance, and procurement. The committee members from each of these organizations are responsible for securing their organization's commitment and buy-in to all decisions and for alerting the rest of the steering committee when issues arise.

In the case where an IT service provider is retained by an organization to assist with the virtualization transformation initiative, additional inter-organizational governance must be established to ensure that the vendor's and the contracting organization's goals are aligned at the strategic, tactical and operational level. Figure 6.3 is an example of the joint governance structure that needs to be established in this situation.

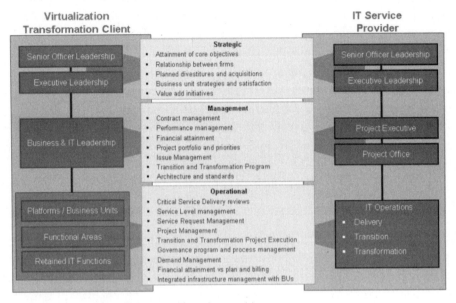

Figure 6.3: Joint governance model with an IT service provider.

Team Consolidation

In order to implement the virtualization transformation, activities of several technical and nontechnical resources need to be coordinated. (There are approximately 450 resources involved in our financial services example.) While the steering committee can address executive-level issues, resolve decision log-jams and escalations, and provide directions on business and technical directions, the architecture, design, and implementation must be accomplished deeper in the organization. To achieve this, the second aspect of the pattern should be implemented: the selective consolidation of key technical teams.

Reorganizing the entire team into a single organizational structure might not align well with the overall organizational goals, and it might introduce new problems, as well. To succeed in the virtualization transformation, an integrated view of all IT infrastructure components and teams should be developed, as shown in Figure 6.4. Key technical leads should be selected from each technical organization, with clear responsibilities for designing and implementing the transformation, communicating it to their teams, and ensuring that the concerns of their teams are recognized and addressed by the transformation efforts. For these reasons, representatives who communicate effectively within their organizations are critical.

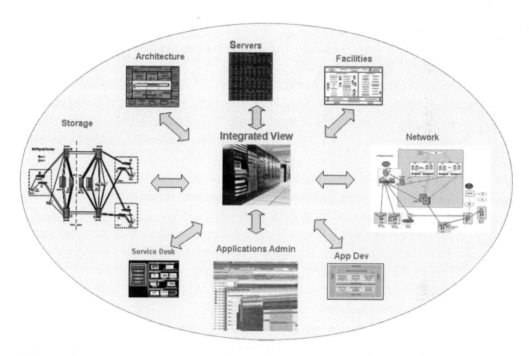

Figure 6.4: Establish an integrated IT Infrastructure and team view for the organizational and technical alignment during the virtualization transformation project.

For our financial services client, the overall technical implementation team is established under the leadership of a well-respected technologist drawn from the architecture team, who is charged as the chief engineer for the entire virtualization initiative. The chief engineer is the single, high-level technical resource who works to translate business strategy into technical vision and strategy. This person also builds "trusted advisor" relationships with internal and external stakeholders, to help them understand where best to optimize activities in the value chain through the appropriate application of technology. The chief engineer is responsible for technical governance across the organization, which is needed to drive sound technical decisions in support of the virtualization transformation project charter, business strategy, and technical management plan.

To establish the chief engineer's implementation team, an official representative is assigned from each of the following groups:

- *Architecture*—While the chief engineer comes from this group, since this role is now to oversee the overall transformation, it is preferable that another resource assist in unifying the disparate architectures that are currently overseen by the 20-person architecture team.
- *Systems administration*—In this case, two co-leads are established, representing distributed and mainframe operations systems.
- *Facilities*—An experienced specialist who has deep ties in both the facilities teams targeted for consolidation and those being consolidated is a critical part of the team.
- *Storage administration*—A lead from storage is brought into the team, assisting with architecture and ensuring that the transformation takes into account the needs of the storage team.
- *Application administration*—A lead from this area partners particularly closely with the developers from the business units, to ensure that all applications can be effectively run on the new infrastructure designs.
- *Application development*—Since this area represents four distinct business units, four leads are needed. In practice, they coordinate their activities through the application administration team, but the technical lead needs to ensure that they do not come to regard the transformation as something that affects only operations and that they do not become disconnected.
- *Service desk*—A manager from the service desk organization is assigned to the transformation effort. As with application development, the technical lead needs to reach out to this team at specific junctures. Otherwise, the service desk might become disconnected from the transformation and miss key impacts.
- *Network outsourcing*—A representative of the project office responsible for network outsourcing is key. While some contractual aspects of the outsourcing terms (such as limitations on intellectual property rights or freedom of action clauses) might limit how deeply the third-party vendor can be brought into detailed design, the technical implementation team will surely need deep participation from the network area. Such network discussions might need to be focused on specific topics. Further, they might need to be scheduled independently of, for instance, application-to-server mapping exercises. Nevertheless, the network must be a part of the technical team in order to realize success.

As part of the overall project management office, an experienced project manager should also be assigned, to work in collaboration with the chief engineer. The project manager develops plans, tracks issues, manages risks and project financials, ensures effective communications, and generally makes sure that the consolidated technical implementation team operates effectively.

Architectural Governance

The third aspect of the Redistribute Activities pattern is architecture governance and control, which is established to maintain the integrity of the overall enterprise architecture during the transformation process. Architecture governance helps identify and manage the cross-component technical linkages and dependencies created by the transformation design. Let's consider an example to illustrate the importance of architectural governance.

Consolidating storage might well offer significant cost savings opportunities for the storage operations team in our client example. This might, however, drive additional complexity and cost into the network team, based on the need to provide sufficient bandwidth and latency between the user base and the consolidated storage locations. Addressing some of the concerns introduced through consolidation by the use of technologies such as network performance optimization requires the close collaboration of the network provider and the systems administration teams, who might be required to run application acceleration devices. In this case, a storage consolidation design drives dependencies into the network team, which in turn creates requirements on the systems administration team, as well as the application development and application administration teams.

As the technical team defines the solution, determines key approaches, and provides recommendations to the steering committee, one further aspect of the pattern that becomes critical is the need to maintain effective architecture. Decisions on the placement of servers, storage, networks, and applications need to be evaluated and considered, not just in light of that specific decision but in light of the impact on the application architecture and the total enterprise architecture, as well.

To achieve this, the technical team should create reference architecture and an associated technology plan. Each application has its own architecture, but in order to be effectively consolidated, all of them must work together in an overall architecture design, detailing elements such as the relationship of servers to storage and storage to network, as well as the role of specific facilities, directions of technology in service desks, network equipment, storage providers, and so forth. Such reference architecture can be extremely valuable in arbitrating decisions between competing solutions, but in order to be effective, it must be maintained and governed.

Architectural governance structures go by many names, such as "Architecture Management Office," "Architecture Control Board," or "Architecture Committee." In all cases, though, some aspects are common. Architectures must be published and be capable of review by all stakeholders. New designs must be reviewed to determine if they adhere to the current architectural standards and the organization's business goals. If they do not, one of three things happens:

- The proposed architecture is modified to bring it into alignment with the standards of the enterprise.
- The overall reference architecture is modified to accommodate the new solution.
- A conscious risk is accepted that a specific solution deviates from the architectural standard, with its impact well known and a plan to address the deviation identified.

To drive successfully virtualization transformation initiatives, we recommend that technical solutions be developed and governed across the transformation team by leveraging an Architecture Management Framework. This framework defines the processes, roles, and responsibilities required to manage and implement an enterprise-wide architecture (covering business processes, applications, data, and technology) within a given client environment. The Architecture Management Framework defines how the enterprise architecture and all its component parts will be implemented, managed, and updated in response to changes in business needs and available technologies. The processes defined within this framework are fundamental to enabling the business to make conscious decisions about IT.

One of the key uses of this framework is the identification and definition of new processes, roles, and responsibilities that might not currently exist in the client environment, but are fundamental to the effective implementation of the strategic aims of the business. These new processes are used to enable the business to make conscious decisions about IT, the acquisition of IT assets, and the design and implementation of new systems and solutions to meet business needs.

The Architecture Management Framework consists of four sub-processes:

- The Architecture Review and Approval Process
- The Architecture Vitality Process

- The Architecture Exception and Appeals Process
- The Architecture Communications Process

To ensure the successful implementation of these processes, the Architecture Management Group (AMG), which is led by the chief engineer and the Business Steering Committee, must establish regular and ongoing informational and working meetings.

An Architecture Management Framework can take several forms, but it should contain the following:

- A textual description of the desired management processes, with appropriate process flow diagrams.
- A defined set of roles and responsibilities. These are normally textual, but diagrammatic or foil-based versions are valuable for aiding communication and gaining agreement.
- An organization chart showing the reporting structure for the newly defined roles.

The effective implementation and management of the enterprise architecture involves active participation by several key groups. Each group has specific responsibilities and must interact with the other groups, as summarized in Figure 6.5.

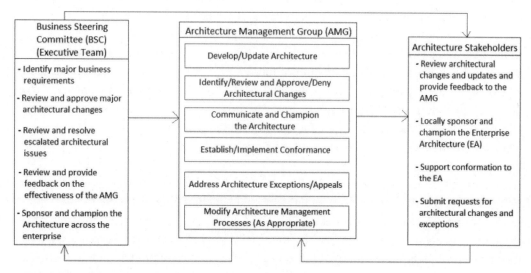

Figure 6.5: Architecture management roles and responsibilities.

In our example of a financial services firm, the solution is defined as an Architecture Management Group, which performs the following tasks:

- Quality assurance of changes in architecture
- Decisions on architecture proposals within areas of responsibility
- Identification of architecture questions for the AMG
- Preparation of architecture for authorization within the AMG
- Identification, prioritization of architecture projects, and introduction within the AMG
- Rating the consequences of new business requirements on architecture
- Suggestions for the development of architecture
- Development of proposals for review and acceptance by the steering committee and other stakeholders

A Common Measurement System

One further aspect of the pattern is critical to drive success in a proposed transformation initiative: the establishment of common measurement criteria. While a steering committee can create consensus, and a consolidated technical team can ensure a common view of the issues, if different teams continue to be managed according to different measurements, conflict is likely to occur. To minimize this effect, development of common measurements is a key part of the Redistribute Activities service pattern.

In the financial services firm, key performance indicators were laid out at the start of the initiative (refer to Chapter 5 for a listing of these KPIs). It is vital that these be managed across the entire organization. The technical team and total solution must be measured on how well they meet the objectives in balance, without, for instance, assigning Strategic Objective #4 (increase flexibility) to the business units, while the operations teams are tasked with Strategic Objective #1 (reduce IT costs).

A solution that reduces the time to deploy an OS to four days satisfies the flexibility objective, but if it does so by funding an increased bench of administrators to provision servers, it violates the cost reduction requirement. Finding solutions such as standardizing on an explicit number of images with limited configuration options, and then automating the provisioning of those images through technologies such as end-user-driven dynamic provisioning and cloud management platforms, can provide solutions to both measurement challenges. Such a solution might well introduce changes to the interdependencies among teams and to the core reference architecture. Those can be managed by fully implementing the service pattern.

An empowered executive steering committee ensures that the enterprise has the discipline and structure to implement the transformation. A consolidated technical team ensures that it has the skill. A plan that articulates the key dependencies gives a clear roadmap when conflicts occur and offers the opportunity to mitigate them. A reference architecture and a method for governing it ensure that the solutions match the needs of the enterprise and that changes can be adopted without introducing chaos. Finally, common measurement and management structures ensure that the organization acts as one, avoiding the infighting that can occur without this pattern.

Summary

We often find virtualization transformations occurring in enterprises that have complex organizational structures and boundaries. Executing an overall virtualization plan drives together teams that might normally tend to operate separately. They might even be held to different measurements and objectives, further complicating their opportunities to work together.

Implementing a well-defined service pattern for activity redistribution can dramatically increase the chances of virtualization success. Establishing clear executive leadership, a unified technical team, well-articulated interdependencies, a common and managed architecture, and integrated measurement plans, as described in this service pattern, can significantly improve the success rate of a virtualization transformation.

CHAPTER 7

Pooled Resources

Pooled resources provides for economies of scale, reducing the amount of facilities (power, space, and cooling) and IT (CPU, memory, disk, and network) necessary to meet customer requirements. Capacity management at the component, service, and business level minimizes the potential for sub-optimization of the overall IT environment.

The Value of Pooled Resources

Prior to virtualization, many IT organizations deployed multi-tier applications on separate physical servers. It was not uncommon to have one server for the database, one server for business logic, and one for Web content. In a high-availability environment, these servers were clustered, doubling the amount of production servers. In order to maintain and enhance the application, a separate set of servers was needed for testing reactive changes to the environment (such as bug fixes and security patches). Still another set of servers was needed for developing proactive changes, for new functions. This would bring the number of servers to 12 per application. Many IT organizations dedicated servers for each application to avoid cross-application conflict, resulting in thousands of servers for organizations with hundreds of applications. Each of these many servers took data center resources, in addition to IT resources. By pooling resources using virtualization, a significant amount of IT equipment can be eliminated. By putting more workload on fewer physical devices in a pool, resources can be shared among applications.

The goal of capacity management is to provide cost-effective facilities and IT resources to meet current and future business requirements. This can be viewed as a supply-chain paradigm, mapping supply (physical resources) with demand (business requirements) over time. By pooling the physical resources, we can share them for economies of scale.

The Pooled Resources services pattern focuses on leveraging virtualization technology to obtain economies of scale. This provides the agility needed to support business objectives. Capacity management processes are used to ensure proper resources are available in the pool.

The Client Scenario

The Pooled Resources pattern affects all of the strategic objectives originally outlined in Chapter 5:

1. *Reduce operational expense and capital expense.* By pooling resources, fewer physical devices are needed. This reduces the capital expense associated with obtaining the devices and the operational expenses (such as power) of running the devices.
2. *Align IT to service level expectations.* Typical application service levels include availability and performance requirements. Capacity management includes the performance management discipline to ensure that performance service levels such as response time are being met and to appropriately respond to performance incidents when service levels are not being met.
3. *Simplify and standardize the IT environment.* By pooling resources, fewer physical devices are needed. This simplifies the environment by, for example, reducing the number of network ports and associated cabling. Virtualization abstracts the hardware from the application, allowing an IT organization to standardize on fewer types of hardware, as the application no longer requires a specific type of hardware.
4. *Increase the agility of IT to respond to business needs.* An organization can better respond to business needs using the available resources in a pool. (See Chapter 9 for more on this issue.) Replacement hardware can be ordered to replenish resources to the pool asynchronously, resulting in an immediate response to a business need.
5. *Optimize the use of IT resources.* By pooling resources, an organization is able to optimize the use of IT resources. Resources can be shared, and the workload can be moved around in the pool when its characteristics change. This might prevent having to obtain additional resources for a particular application.

In addition, the Pooled Resource pattern affects the majority of the critical success factors and key performance indicators associated with the objectives.

The Pooled Resources Pattern

One of the design considerations for building new data centers is to have a modular approach, where you can non-disruptively add new resources to a data center with both facilities and IT equipment. Each of the major resource components can be combined to create a collective group, called a *resource pool*. The pattern for pooling resources is described below.

Name

The name of this pattern is Pooled Resources.

Value Statement

This pattern helps organizations leverage virtualization technology to meet business objectives such as improved service, at reduced cost and reduced risk.

IT service is often measured at the business, application, and component levels. A business service measurement might be how much pooling capacity is kept available for future growth. An application service measurement might be response time. A component-level service measurement might be server utilization. Pooling resources allows an IT organization to improve all three of these.

Cost is always a consideration for IT organizations. These organizations want to reduce costs to return value to the shareholders (e.g., profit) or to deal with anticipated growth without increasing costs. Pooling resources expedites the ability to increase or decrease resources within the pool, whether the virtual pool is the processing and storage of network IT resources or the power, space, and cooling of data center resources.

The relationship between IT resources and data center resources is often overlooked. It is not uncommon for an IT architect to develop a solution without regard to the availability of data center resources. Fortunately, with the exception of initial equipment, most virtualization pooling projects are justified based on their ability to decrease IT and data center resources, not increase them.

Along with service and cost, risk must be considered. *Capacity management* is the balance between the risk of having insufficient resources to respond to increases in demand and of having too many resources, resulting in unnecessary costs.

An example of this is the amount of fuel needed to be kept onsite for generators in high-availability data centers. Each generator has its own fuel supply. By pooling resources, a site can maintain an additional central storage fuel tank, resupplying fuel when needed to the different generators, which run at different loads and consume fuel at different rates. The risk is minimized by using the central storage tank as a pooled resource. The tradeoff then becomes a matter of service ("How long do I want to be able to run on generator power in the event of a utility power failure?") and cost ("How much fuel should I keep onsite?"). Pooling resources simplifies the situation, by not requiring separate decisions on how big to make each particular generator storage tank. Rather, the decision is made at the pool level, instead of the component level.

Context

This pattern provides an effective solution in scenarios where there is a large amount of IT workload deployed on numerous physical devices, energy costs have reached a point where it is cost-effective to change a physical server paradigm, or the data center is constrained from providing any room for IT growth.

With the advent of distributed computing, many organizations deployed servers and storage, connected via a network in numerous locations. As the size and quantity of applications at more and more locations grew, the support costs to maintain these applications increased, as well. Mergers and acquisitions also contributed to the geographically dispersed IT workload. Many organizations completed business cases indicating significant business value could be achieved with data center consolidation. Virtualized pooled resources were a key component of that analysis. This concept allowed applications to continue to appear to be run independently on a portion of a physical device. The device could be a server, disk storage, or connectivity to the network.

According to various sources, the cost of energy has increased in double-digit percentages over the last several years. There are also estimates indicating that U.S. data centers consume more than two percent of the energy produced in America, and this figure is expected to double in the next five years. Increases in per-unit costs and power requirements have resulted in an overall data-center energy bill that has caught the attention of corporate executives. As many IT budgets are flat or declining, IT organizations are looking to virtualized pooled resources as a major way to reduce the amount of energy being used.

The demand for IT resources is growing even faster than the cost of energy. The U.S. Environmental Protection Agency reported to Congress that the amount of processing in the United States would grow by a factor of six, and storage would grow by a factor of 69, between 2007 and 2017. The equipment represented by this growth has either already constrained data center resources or will constrain them in the near future. Virtualized pooled resources are being used to increase the IT capacity without the traditional corresponding increase in data center resources.

Problem

Figure 7.1 graphs workload consumption over time. In this example, each workload runs on a separate physical server. Each of the servers must be sized to handle the peak of that workload, which is often a multiple of the average workload (i.e., the peak-to-average ratio for the application is greater than two). Many applications have a ratio greater than two. Even at just a two rating, the size of the server must be twice the size of the average workload, meaning that the server, on average, has twice the capacity it requires. This is why many servers run low levels of utilization.

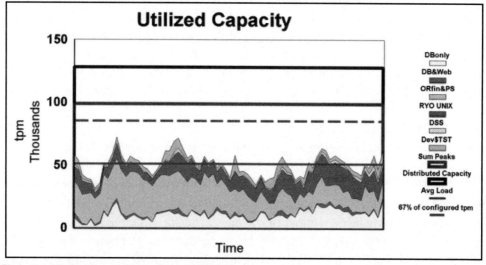

Figure 7.1: Workload usage for various applications.

Historically, it has been difficult to move an application, often requiring the application to be taken down. Therefore, capacity managers would further oversize the server, especially since they considered the cost of the excess resources to be small. Unfortunately, they did not consider the cumulative effect of these excess resources on thousands of servers or the amount of wasted data center resources needed to provide space, supply power, and cool these servers.

The blue line in the figure indicates that the sum of the peaks of each workload is 100,000 transactions per minute and the installed capacity is 130,000 transactions per minute. By using resource pools, an organization can create a pool of resources at the 100,000-transaction level and have sufficient capacity for all the workloads to peak at the same time. In reality, the workloads do not all peak at the same time, as indicated in the figure. This means that the pool can be further decreased without additional risk for needing resources for any specific workload. The dashed line, set to 67 percent of the configured (installed) capacity, represents this. The reduction of resources due to variability of individual workload peaks is the second benefit of pooled resources, in addition to the reduction provided by capacity planning for the total load versus individual loads.

IT environments typically refresh servers after about five years, since servers have mechanical parts and are subject to mechanical failure. In that time, processors historically increase in processing power by a factor of eight. (Moore's Law of doubling the amount of capacity per unit of space has taken place three times.) In the case where a new single-processor server replaces a single-processor server, the utilization decreases. For example, suppose a server with a utilization of 16 percent is replaced with a new server after five years. That new server is running at just 2 percent utilization. By pooling resources, you can use the excess capacity on these faster single-processor servers.

Pooling is not limited to server resources. Consider the example where 20 servers have 10-gigabyte drives, each of which has reserved 5 gigabytes for growth. Capacity planning must be done at the individual drive level. By moving the data to a network attached storage (NAS) device or a storage area network (SAN), the cumulative reserved space of 100 gigabytes can be reduced without risk to any particular virtual drive, since no single workload would have the need for growth that large. Capacity planning is done at the pooled level, reducing the number of metrics to manage from 20 to one. This results in a significant labor savings, in addition to the hardware savings.

Similar, if not larger, savings also occur with network resources. Network capacity increases by orders of magnitude (e.g. 10-megabyte ports, 100-megabyte ports, 1-gigabyte ports) in a period of years, compared to servers, which cut price/performance in half during similar time periods. A network port reduction has the ripple effects of not having to perform as much cabling and having fewer network devices.

We've spent the first few paragraphs of this section considering the problem we are looking to mitigate with this pattern and the last few paragraphs discussing the benefits of the pattern. To further highlight how the pattern applies to real-world situations, let's consider a few recent client examples:

- A client wanted to extend the life of its existing data center, which was constrained by power, space, and cooling to prevent installing new IT resources. By creating pooled resources, the organization was able to increase the amount of server capacity by a factor of eight, without the corresponding increase in facilities resources. In three years, it also reduced the amount of servers running under 5 percent from 60 percent of the servers to less than 15 percent. The utilization of the pooled resources was at periods ten times the amount of utilization when run as a physical server environment. The organization was also able to baseline the effect of peak utilization of multiple images on larger physical servers. As a result of this baseline, it was able to right-size the resources for each image and server, allowing it to reallocate $2.4 million in hardware to other projects and sell some of the excess equipment to other organizations.
- A client looked to rationalize its multiple-data-center environment. It had two data centers, which were geographically separated. The client wanted to leverage that fact, by designing disaster recovery into its multiple-data-center design, eliminating the need for a separate disaster recovery site. Pooled resources were used to create a production pool at one site and a development/test pool at the second site. Production virtual images were then created in the second site, and the production data was copied to that site to keep it up to date. As the production images in this site were not in use, they consumed minimal resources in the pool. The production images at the second site were set to have a higher dispatching priority. If a disaster occurred, production at the second site would take over the majority of the resources, but would still have resources for test and development at times when the production workload was smaller than the size of the second site's pool.
- A client looked to build a new data center for its cloud computing workload. The cloud was designed with pooled resources for servers, storage, and network. An

additional reduction in resources was obtained by understanding the relationship between processing, data, and network requirements for a particular virtual image and setting the pool size to leverage the synergy of requirements. The virtual pool was extended from the individual component (CPU, disk, and network) to a pool of combined resources, providing further simplification. The simplification allowed the capacity planner to order new units of cloud computing at the offering level, instead of the individual component pools.

Forces

Resource pooling optimizes existing equipment (traditionally considered performance management). It also allows for growth via pooled excess capacity and the ability to easily add resources to the pool (traditionally considered capacity management). In this respect, pooling has both reactive and proactive components.

Performance management is not the absence of tactical supply and demand mismatches, but the triumph over them. The effects of business changes to the IT environment are not always predictable. Even when they are, the anticipated effect on IT resources can often vary. For example, consider the release of a new song or video over the Internet. While the release of the media content is the known business event, the exact amount of sales upon release can only be calculated with a determined amount of accuracy.

The ability to redirect resources from a pool minimizes the effect of a performance problem. The more resources in the pool, the larger the amount of net additional resources available. These can be applied to a specific performance problem at any time. Incident resolution is performed without having to wait to approve hardware capital, order it, install it, and then mitigate the application performance situation.

On a more positive, proactive note, new technologies drive new IT business models. One of these models is associated with public cloud computing, which is defined as a highly virtualized pooled environment, with dynamically provisioned resources based on a standard service catalog accessed via a Web front-end. All of the current public cloud IaaS (infrastructure as a service) offerings are based on a virtual pooled resource environment. By pooling IT resources via virtualization, an organization positions itself for the use of cloud computing or other advances in technology that leverage the abstraction of the hardware from the application.

Selection Guidance

Use this pattern when your organization meets many of the following characteristics:

- You have a large number of low-utilization resources that, when combined, can leverage economies of scale.
- You are constrained by facilities resources (power, space, or cooling) and need to pool current hardware requirements to have room to grow.
- You are constrained by IT resources (CPU, memory, disk, network) and need to pool current hardware requirements to have room to grow.
- You are constrained by capacity-management labor and want to increase capacity management by converting from component capacity management to pooled capacity management.
- You are capital constrained and want to maximize your return on future capital expended.
- You need to reduce your facilities and IT operating expenses.
- You need to increase your equipment utilization.
- You want to position yourself for future IT business models, such as cloud computing.

Solution

This pattern leverages pooled resources via changes to the capacity management process.

Physical Resource and Virtual Resource Capacity Management

Before performing capacity management at the pooled resource level, you must first understand some of the basics of capacity management in a virtual environment. IT workload is still running on a physical device, so physical metrics such as overall capacity and utilization are still important to understanding how much resource is added to the pool with a particular device and how well the device performs compared to other devices in the pool. Adding a server to the pool with four physical processors and 64 gigabytes of memory increases the pool by that amount of resources.

Overall physical utilization of the pool is a normalized average of the resources in that pool. Consider a simple case of servers all with the same size processor. The overall utilization of a three-server pool with two single-processor servers at 40 percent and one dual-processor server at 80 percent is as follows:

$$\frac{((2*40)+(2*80))}{4} = 60 \text{ percent}$$

This is higher than the non-normalized straight average:

$$\frac{(40+40+80)}{3} = 53 \text{ percent}$$

In addition to physical resource metrics, virtual resource metrics provide information on the particular virtual image on a physical server. Virtualization provides for the sub-allocation of physical resources to a particular virtual image. Virtual resource capacity management contains the metrics required to manage the image. The first set of metrics represents the amount of allocation permitted to the workload. This is indicated by the minimum, maximum, and expected value of the resource. For example, an image might have a minimum of one-tenth of a processor, a maximum of two processors, and an expected value of half a processor, indicating a peak to average ratio of four. Different virtualization implementations use these values differently in assigning physical resources to the virtual images. IBM's AIX operating system, for example, will not allow another virtual image to come online if the minimum value of virtual processors cannot be dedicated to that virtual image.

Virtual metrics are also used for purposes other than capacity management. For example, software licensing in a virtual environment can be sized based on the maximum number of virtual processors, as virtual load balancers can restrict an image from using more physical processors than virtual processors assigned. In this way, a software license can be obtained for a portion of a physical server, instead of having to license the software based on the entire size of the physical server.

Eliminating the Debate Over Capacity Management Peak vs. Average Sizing

There have been many debates among capacity planners as to whether to size an environment for average utilization or for peak utilization. With pooled resources, you can do both. At a virtual image level, the peak utilization should be set to the maximum value of the resources (e.g. processors and memory), while the average utilization should be set to the expected value of the resource. In this way, the virtualization code understands how to mitigate changes in resource requirements. When a virtual image requests additional resources less than the maximum assigned to it, and physical resources are available on the device, the resources are allocated to that virtual image. When the physical resources are not available, a weighting system is used to determine the image to which the resources are made available. The lack of resources might or might not be a problem to the workload, depending on how much queue time is incurred waiting for resources to become available.

Wait time in a virtual environment is similar to wait time in a physical environment. It is inversely proportional to the utilization of the resource requested:

$$Wait\ Time = \frac{1}{(1 - Resource\ Utilization)}$$

To minimize the risk associated with converting images to a virtual environment, many capacity planners assign virtual images to a specific physical server with lower expected utilization (typically less than 50 percent utilization of peak expected workload). This low level of utilization is still several times higher than what was previously experienced in the physical environment, allowing multiple equipment devices to be removed. For example, four 10 percent utilized servers being replaced by one 40 percent utilized server eliminates 75 percent of the IT hardware required. At levels of less than 50 percent utilization, the extra queuing time incurred does not typically affect the response-time service level.

Right-Sizing the Pooled Resources after Initial Sizing

In creating a pool of resources, the capacity manager should understand the expected average and peak utilization of each physical device in the pool, in addition to the overall pool average and peak utilization. This is often performed by normalizing the average utilization of all workloads and the peak utilization of all workloads. These calculations are a conservative (worst case) approximation of utilization, since workloads do not have the same average or peak utilization at the same time.

To compute the benefit derived from the variation of peak workload, the capacity planner often compares the average and peak utilization of the device or pool after the workload has been given sufficient time to run in the new environment. This baseline is then compared against the expected utilization to understand the extent of the benefit from the economies of scale provided by multiple workloads on a physical device or pool. The amount of this benefit can then be removed from the pool, or left in the pool to provide for future growth. As mentioned in the "Problem" section, a single account was able to reallocate $2.4 million in hardware because of the value of right-sizing the environment.

Mitigating the Supply/Demand Mismatch: Performance Management

The frequency of constrained resources should be much smaller than the amount of mismatches in the physical environment, as the amount of additional resources that can be allocated to a particular image is often larger than the entire virtual image itself. Despite the large amount of available resources, mismatches occur, particularly when automation is not in place to allocate additional resources to a particular image.

It is a best practice to work to proactively identify and prevent mismatches. One way is to implement an early warning system that monitors utilization metrics at the virtual image, physical resource, and pooled resource levels. Alerts should be set low enough to provide time to mitigate the situation, without being set so low that they are tripped when there is not an imminent problem.

Once an alert has been triggered, the capacity manager has several options to mitigate the resource constraint. One option is to allocate more resources from the physical device to the virtual image. When there are insufficient resources on the physical device, another option is to move workload off the physical device to other devices in the pool, enabling additional resources to be assigned. This might mean moving the virtual image that is growing, or moving alternate images on the physical device and using the resources freed from the alternate moved images to allocate to the growing image. Moving a workload between physical devices used to make the workload unavailable during the move. By implementing the Flexible Resource Balancing pattern in the next chapter, however, you can move the workload non-disruptively, providing alternative capacity management solutions that were previously not possible.

Forecasting Pooled Resources: Traditional Capacity Management

Many IT models that describe capacity management include performance management as part of the capacity management discipline. Independent of this, the element of capacity management involved with forecasting resources is performed at the overall pool level.

On a predefined, periodic basis (at least annually, as part of the organization's overall capacity plan), the capacity planner should understand the historical growth pattern of each of the resource pools. The capacity planner should then forecast the future need for resources, adding to the historical projection any known changes to workloads (such as increased processing or storage needed for regulatory compliance, deployment of new applications, or adding new functionality to existing applications). The forecast is compared against the amount of resources that exist in the pool. If the forecast exceeds the amount of resources, the capacity planner should create a growth mitigation plan, which includes not only the resources that should be added to the pool, but when those resources should be added (with sufficient lead time to minimize the risk of running out of resources).

In addition to the annual forecasting of each pool, additional requests for IT resources (demand) are identified during the year. The mitigation of this demand is further described by the Reducing Incoming Hardware Infrastructure and Work pattern, in Chapter 9.

Implementing Policy-Based Pooled Resources

While capacity management is performed at the pooled resource level, there are often constraints that must be maintained within the pool. For example, in a high-availability environment, processing and storage are usually clustered. It is important to maintain the elimination of a single point of failure. This is the major purpose of policy-based pools. In the example from earlier in this chapter, a policy would be defined for the high-availability configurations, which would prevent the images from being deployed on the same physical server or the data from being stored on the same physical disk drive. These predefined policies increase in significance when organizations move away from statically assigned images per physical device to pooled resources, where dynamic image movement is performed to optimize the use of physical resources and prevent supply/demand mismatches.

Such is the case with VMware's Distributed Resource Scheduler (DRS), described in the next chapter. DRS dynamically moves the workload between physical devices in a pooled environment. By predefining the business constraints as policies, we prevent a situation that would result in a single point of failure should the clustered virtual workloads be allowed to reside on the same physical device.

Integrating the Effect of IT Changes on the Data Center

As mentioned previously, traditional IT solutions did not usually consider the effect of changes on the data center in which the solutions would reside. This did not cause a problem because the paradigm for building data centers was to build a very large center that would support years of IT growth and then slowly fill it up with IT resources over time. As the initial cost of data centers has increased and the capital to build them has become increasingly constrained, this has changed to a more modular approach. An IT organization non-disruptively adds power or cooling to an existing data center or adds power, space, and cooling to an adjacent part of an existing data center in a non-disruptive fashion.

The modular growth of data center resources should match or precede corresponding IT modular growth to the particular pooled resource. As part of the forecasting of IT resources, the capacity planner should forecast the need for facilities data center resources. As the lead time for data center modules is often longer than the lead time for an IT unit of supply, the capacity planner should improve service in decreasing risk, by having more data center resources available. For example, if it takes 12 months to add a data center module, the build of the next data center module should be started 12 months prior to the IT need for its resources.

The capacity planner should also understand and incorporate the effects of the data center on the financial value of pooled resources. Traditional multi-year business cases for IT requirements made assumptions about the price of refreshed IT equipment to be less per unit of IT resource. For example, it was assumed that the cost per megabyte of storage would decrease over time. Often, the costs of data center resources were not included in IT business cases at all. These assumptions and oversights are no longer valid, as the cost of energy is driving up the data center costs. Studies show that the power and cooling equipment is half the cost of a new data center build, while the space is less than 10 percent of the build.

To recover rising energy costs, many data center providers have moved from a single-space-based rate (such as $100 per square foot per year for 40 watt per square foot space) to a dual rate, one for space and one for energy (for example, $50 per square foot per year and $0.12 per kilowatt hour used).

Lastly, the capacity planner should incorporate the difference in efficiency of data centers. Five years ago, it was not uncommon for a data center to spend more energy on cooling than on powering the IT equipment it cooled. As energy costs increased and data centers became cooling constrained, significant improvements in cooling technology were developed. The Green Grid established a metric called Power Usage Effectiveness (PUE), which is defined as the amount of power coming into a data center divided by the amount of power used by IT equipment. A PUE of 2.0 indicates that, for every watt of energy consumed by IT equipment, an additional watt of energy is consumed by the data center for power and cooling distribution.

The PUE of a data center should be considered when pooling resources. For example, by installing a resource pool in a data center with a PUE rating of 3.0, an organization uses twice the energy of a data center with a PUE rating of 1.5. All other things being equal, resource pools should be added to data centers with lower PUE ratings, to optimize the overall IT environment.

Summary

The Pooled Resources pattern enables you to obtain economies of scale. The scale comes from taking the relatively small amounts of resources available on each physical resource and combining them into a pool of resources, which can be used to mitigate any resource concern in the pool.

This pattern applies to all of the strategic objectives in the client scenario and affects most of the associated critical success factors and key performance indicators.

The business value of implementing the Pooled Resources pattern in a virtual environment is that it increases IT service while decreasing risk and cost. The main benefit of this pattern is that it allows you to decrease the amount of reserve capacity required and to share the remaining reserve capacity over a larger number of servers.

Capacity management, which includes the performance management discipline, is used to manage existing resources and to forecast future resources needed within a pool. New metrics that represent virtual resources have been added to clarify the relationship between the virtual workloads and the physical workloads.

The Pooled Resource pattern is fundamental to the optimal virtual environment. It enables the implementation of other patterns that are based on it, such as the Flexible Resource Balancing pattern and the Reducing Incoming Hardware Infrastructure and Work pattern.

CHAPTER 8

Flexible Resource Balancing

R educing inflexibility is an important goal of virtualization transformations. To be lean, we must create an IT environment that can adapt to customer requirements with the minimum allocation of cost and resources.

Flexible IT systems are required by businesses to meet their objectives of leveraging resources with maximum elasticity. When client requirements increase, assets and resources have to be organized and optimized to complete each operation in less time. If the client demand decreases, the assets and resources must be reconfigured to reflect the new reality, while minimizing wastes such as waiting and inventory. The Flexible Resource Balancing pattern focuses on leveraging virtualization technology to ensure that the right resources are available when needed to support business and IT objectives.

Client Scenario

The Flexible Resource Balancing pattern primarily addresses the following strategic objectives, which were outlined in Chapter 5:

- SO 4, increase the agility of IT to respond to business needs
- SO 5, optimize the use of IT resources

The Flexible Resource Balancing Pattern

The pattern for Flexible Resource Balancing is described below.

Name

The name of this pattern is Flexible Resource Balancing.

Value Statement

This pattern helps organizations leverage virtualization technology to meet business objectives such as the following:

- Prioritize resources for critical applications in an automated manner.
- Increase the operational and energy efficiency of data centers.
- Optimize hardware utilization while responding in real time to changes in demand for resources.
- Implement minimal or zero downtime for server maintenance.
- Reduce the high costs associated with server hardware, network, and storage I/O.
- Implement flexible storage management and disaster recovery solutions.

This pattern can be used beyond the life of the virtualization transformation project to ensure that flexible resource balancing capabilities are consistently applied and leveraged by an organization during steady-state operations management of its virtualized IT environment.

Context

This pattern provides an effective solution in scenarios where the virtualization implementation and administration teams are tasked with ensuring that optimized IT resources are available to meet higher utilization and dynamic resource provisioning requirements. This pattern is also useful in the following scenarios:

- Data center energy conservation is critical.
- The costs of storage and I/O resources need to be constrained, along with server and storage hardware costs.
- Maintenance windows need to be reduced to minimize outages and the impact on production environments.
- System security and isolation of virtual resources are key considerations, from both a systems management and business requirements perspective.
- Labor productivity and tighter alignment of IT resources with business imperatives are key objectives.

Problem

Most organizations have fallen prey to increasing amounts of distributed server sprawl, disconnected islands of technology, and heterogeneity of hardware and operating systems. These problems impede flexible operations. They can be caused by natural growth, mergers, acquisitions, ongoing reliance on antiquated IT systems, or lack of architectural controls. In these organizations, IT is no longer an agile enabler that can fuel business growth rapidly, while staying in lock step with the shifts in client demands, business requirements, and technical imperatives.

Let's consider a few real-life client examples that highlight the problem:

- A server running one or more applications requires additional processing power to meet an increase in peak demand for computing resources. In most legacy IT environments, the IT staff has no choice but to spend considerable time, money, and effort to provision a new, more powerful machine that can address the additional computing requirements. Meanwhile, the business has to suffer days or weeks of slower computing until a more powerful platform is available. This delay can be detrimental to an organization's growth or revenue objectives, depending on the nature of the applications and the services they provide.
- A blade server is running multiple virtual machines. It is physically constrained in terms of the number of I/O connections per blade, thus limiting the deployment of additional storage resources. The applications vendor for the most critical application on this machine has released a new version and now recommends additional dedicated I/O resources for running it in virtual environments. However, there are no more free HBA (Host Bus Adapter) resources available on this machine. This situation creates a problem for the IT staff, who must add more physical resources to another machine and move either the critical application or another application to it. Delays in provisioning and potential change-management-related errors can be introduced in these moves, which can negatively affect the business.
- A client is facing capacity constraints within its existing data center, due to power limitations. Almost half of this client's servers are running idle during off-peak hours. Their average server utilization is 30 percent. As in any typical IT environment, the idle servers still consume 60 percent of their peak power draw, leading to a huge amount of wasted energy. This energy, if properly used on an as-needed basis, could alleviate the client's power-constraint issues in the existing data center. The client, though, is faced with the hard choice of either moving some

resources to another data center or investing in a new data center. Both of these are very costly propositions.

- A client needs to quickly add functionality to its retail Web application, in response to a change introduced by one of its competitors. It has a short window to develop the new functionality, test it in a pre-production environment, and then release it to the production environment. The functionality changes cannot be tested on existing test and development infrastructure, due to other high-priority work being handled by these systems. The IT procurement office is currently facing a backlog in its hardware acquisition and order management system, so there is a wait of three weeks before new test and development hardware can be acquired. Meanwhile, the business owners are seeing a decline in their revenue and an increase in their competitor's retail sales. They are faced with the hard decision of either reprioritizing the work done on their existing test and development systems, which means sustaining losses elsewhere, or waiting for new hardware to arrive, while watching their business revenues decline.

- During the financial quarter-closing timeframe, a server running a critical financial application is displaying signs in its event log that one of its hardware components will probably fail unless it is replaced immediately. The maintenance operation for hardware component replacement involves powering down the system, replacing the component (assuming a new component is available), powering the system back on, and then conducting several system tests. These tests ensure that the system upgrade is error-free and that the system can support its workload, while meeting expected SLAs. This entire maintenance operation is estimated to take five to eight hours. However, the business owners of the application cannot afford this untimely system outage, due to a high demand for it to continue processing the transactions required to close the books before the end of the quarter. Unless the system was designed for high availability (using techniques such as redundant hardware, clustering, and failover services), the business owners have a tough decision to make. They must decide whether to let the system run, with a strong chance that it will fail before it ends its quarter-closing processes, or shut down the system for maintenance and lose valuable time that might affect the quarter-closing deadline.

Forces

Once you have implemented virtualized storage, servers, and networking in your IT environment, you have taken the initial steps towards establishing a foundation for your organization to benefit from flexible resource utilization. However, you still have more work to do before you can fully exploit the benefits of virtualization technologies. There are many more challenges to overcome before you are in a position to dynamically allocate or deallocate resources in response to your business needs.

The solution offered in this pattern is based on applying technology and capability. In most cases, these come out of the box with virtualization systems and products. However, our experience has shown that these technologies are not always easy to implement and that they might not yield the expected benefits, unless you first align your organization and support structure to the change and flexibility offered by the new technology.

Therefore, before the technical capabilities described below are applied, organizations need to address the challenges covered in other patterns in this book, especially those covered in Chapters 5, 6, 7, and 11.

In general, the difficulty of implementing flexible IT systems can be explained by the large number of variables and constraints involved. The main ones we've found include the following:

- Poor architectural control and project governance (including change management policies)
- Dependencies on legacy IT systems management technology to meet the required IT infrastructure-related flexibility requirements
- Heterogeneity of IT infrastructure components (including diversity of hardware and operating system platforms, applications, software, and storage environment components)
- Aging data centers and facilities infrastructure, with constraints on power, cooling, and floor space
- Dependencies on business reliance, high availability, and disaster recovery objectives and requirements

Selection Guidance

Use the Flexible Resource Balancing pattern when your organization meets many of the following characteristics:

- The scope of your virtualization transformation includes a mix of heterogeneous server hardware, operating systems, middleware, applications, and storage environments.
- You are working on providing flexible storage management services.
- You are working on providing flexible server provisioning services.
- You are required to perform systems maintenance with minimal or zero downtime for supported servers and applications.
- You are working on optimizing power usage by IT infrastructure resources in a data center.
- You are designing disaster recovery and high-availability solutions.
- Your transformation includes capacity and performance optimization of servers, applications, or storage environments.

Solution

This pattern leverages technology features available within virtualization-enabling systems and software products to address flexible resource-balancing challenges such as those mentioned in the "Problems" section above. The virtualization-related technology features we most commonly leverage to provide greater systems management flexibility for our clients fall into three main capabilities:

- Dynamic workload mobility
- Dynamic resource provisioning
- Dynamic energy management

The following pages provide descriptions of these three capabilities, along with examples of vendor products that offer these capabilities and the benefits of leveraging them in conjunction with the other patterns described in this book.

Dynamic Workload Mobility

Consider the scenario in which a running application is moved from one server machine to another seamlessly, and with no downtime. Dynamic workload mobility provides you the systems management flexibility to do just that. This is a very powerful technology capability, as it provides the freedom to move application workloads from one server machine to another as needed, without any disruption to the business.

Several industry vendors have implemented the dynamic workload mobility technology in their systems/products. They refer to it by different names, including VMotion by VMware, Live Partition Mobility by IBM, and Hyper-V Live Migration by Microsoft. All of these technologies provide support for a flexible use of IT resources within an IT environment. When these technologies are applied within the constraints of rigorous architectural management and change management governance (as described in Chapter 6), they have proven to be extremely advantageous to our clients.

To demonstrate the dynamic workload capability in action, let's look at examples based on IBM's and VMware's products.

Live Partition Mobility Using IBM System Products

You can use IBM's Integrated Virtualization Manager (IVM) to move AIX and Linux partitions from one server to another. The mobility process transfers the system environment, including the processor state, memory, attached virtual devices, and connected users. (For more information about this process, see *IBM PowerVM Live Partition Mobility* by John E. Bailey, Thomas Prokop, Guido Somers, and Scott Vetter, IBM Redbooks, 2009.) Figure 8.1 shows a basic hardware infrastructure, with two distinct systems, enabled for dynamic workload mobility. (For illustration purposes, the device numbers are all shown as zero, but in practice they could be different.)

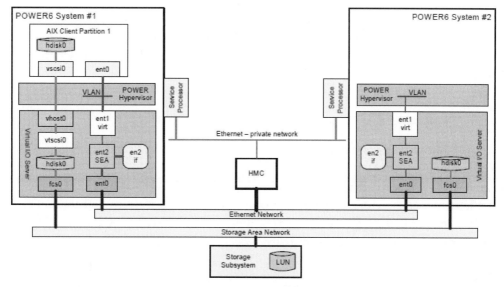

Figure 8.1: An example of hardware enabled for dynamic workload mobility.

The migration process creates a new partition on the destination system. This new partition uses the destination's virtual I/O server to access the same mobile partition's network and disks. During active migration, the state of the mobile partition is copied, as shown in Figure 8.2.

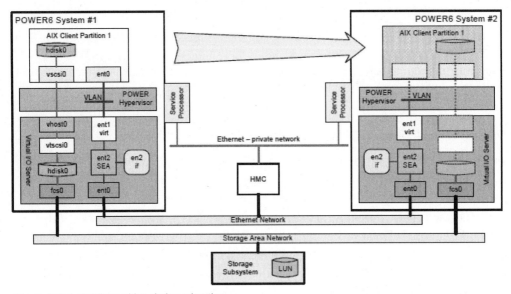

Figure 8.2: A mobile partition during migration.

When the migration is complete, the source virtual I/O server is no longer configured to provide access to the external disk data. The destination virtual I/O server is set up to allow the mobile partition to use the storage. The final configuration is shown in Figure 8.3.

VMware VMotion

VMware VMotion is a very effective technology provided by VMware. It exploits server, storage, and networking virtualization to dynamically migrate active virtual machines instantly from one server machine to another, as shown in Figure 8.4. During the dynamic migration process, the virtual machine's disk storage, network identity, and connections are migrated over to the target machine. (For more information about VMware's VMotion product, see *www.vmware.com/products/vmotion*.)

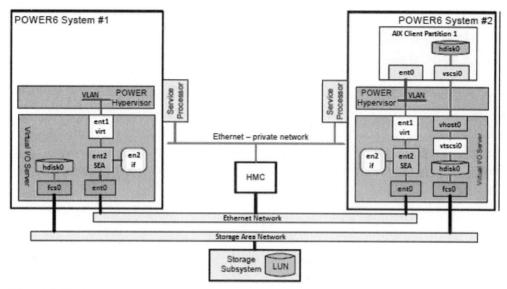

Figure 8.3: The hardware infrastructure after migration.

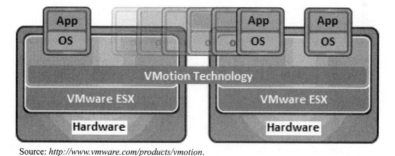

Source: *http://www.vmware.com/products/vmotion.*

Figure 8.4: VMware's VMotion dynamically migrates virtual machines across servers.

Dynamic Resource Provisioning

Based on our review of IT resource (server and storage) provisioning processes in many organizations, we have observed provisioning timelines that range anywhere from a few days to several months. The IT resource provisioning components include such things as the following:

- Financial and architecture reviews and approvals
- Change and configuration management reviews and approvals

- Hardware procurement
- Hardware installation and configuration
- OS and application installation and configuration
- Testing and deployment

Virtualization technology, by itself, cannot significantly streamline all component provisioning processes or drastically reduce the end-to-end provisioning timeline. However, when best practices for IT resource provisioning (including those for operating system and software/application provisioning) are in effect to optimize financial, architectural, change/configuration management, and procurement processes, virtualization can provide the additional "secret sauce" that brings the provisioning cycle time down to hours or even minutes.

The following are examples of tools and capabilities from IBM and VMware that we have leveraged extensively in our client engagements to facilitate dynamic resource provisioning.

IBM Tivoli Provisioning Manager

Leveraging IBM Tivoli Provisioning Manager (TPM) has helped our clients optimize efficiency, accuracy, and service delivery by automating best practices for data center provisioning activities. TPM has allowed us to automate best practices for activities such as the following:

- Change and release management processes
- Discovering and tracking data center resources to enable highly accurate server provisioning and software deployments
- Facilitating efforts to consistently follow client policies and preferred configurations, in support of corporate and regulatory compliance efforts
- Automatically provisioning software and configurations to Microsoft Windows servers and clients, as well as Linux and Unix servers
- Helping optimize availability by maintaining configurations and managing changes to resources
- Capturing and rerunning scenarios for even the most highly complex tasks
- Integrating with a variety of technologies and operating systems (such as AIX, Linux, Sun Solaris, and Windows)

TPM also incorporates advanced automation capabilities that allow administrators to develop workflows that respond to input changes from resource or service-level monitoring products. Based on these inputs, prioritized lists of resources, and provisioning workflows, TPM can dynamically allocate or reallocate resources and change resource configurations based on changes in IT infrastructure and business requirements. For example, as the processing requirements for a critical application change during the course of a business day, processing resources such as virtual machines may be created and deleted as needed, thus optimizing resource utilization and power consumption. (For additional details about TPM features and functions, visit its Website at http://ibm.com/tivoli/products/prov-mgr/platforms.html.)

VMware Dynamic Resource Scheduler

The VMware Dynamic Resource Scheduler (DRS) has proven extremely beneficial to our clients. It is a feature of the VMware product suite that combines computing capacity across a collection of servers into logical resource pools, as shown in Figure 8.5. DRS intelligently allocates available resources among the virtual machines, based on predefined rules that reflect business needs and changing priorities.

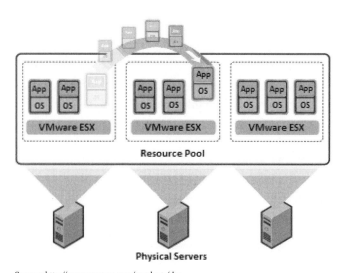

Source: *http://www.vmware.com/products/drs*.

Figure 8.5: VMware's DRS dynamically allocates resources among virtual machines.

VMware DRS continuously monitors utilization across resource pools. When a virtual machine experiences an increased load, DRS automatically allocates additional resources by redistributing virtual machines among the physical servers in the resource pool. By virtue of this capability, this product enables you to do the following:

- Allocate resources to the highest priority applications.
- Automatically adjust and optimize server utilization in response to changing conditions.
- Ensure that highly utilized and dedicated resources are available for applications based on business and technical requirements.
- Conduct zero-downtime server maintenance.

Xsigo Systems

In virtualized server environments, server connectivity is significantly more complex than in non-virtual environments. A virtualized server requires many more network and storage connections and more I/O bandwidth. Consider the example provided in the "Problems" section, where project delay and waiting is due to provisioning additional I/O connections required by the new release of an application. These types of challenges can be addressed by leveraging virtual I/O technologies provided by several vendors as part of their virtualization products and solutions.

Xsigo Systems is one of these vendors. Xsigo achieves dynamic resource provisioning in data center I/O virtualization by providing solutions that very efficiently connect any server to any network or storage device. It also manages connectivity on the fly, to meet changing application requirements. (More information about Xsigo is available at *www. xsigo.com.*)

By consolidating server I/O as shown in Figure 8.6, Xsigo increases the infrastructure's efficiency. It also provides software-controlled connectivity with virtual Network Interface Cards (NICs) and Hardware Bus Adapters (HBAs) that are deployed and migrated on demand. By leveraging a virtual I/O technology, such as the one provided by Xsigo, our clients can become more flexible in dynamically provisioning I/O resources in their IT environments.

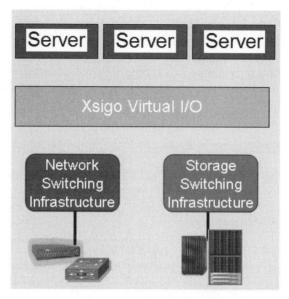

Figure 8.6: Xsigo Systems virtual I/O provides a switching layer between servers and the switching infrastructure.

Dynamic Energy Management

Chapter 2 explains the importance of optimizing energy management in data centers and IT infrastructure. This section briefly describes two vendor technologies that our clients have leveraged in virtualized IT infrastructures to optimize the use and allocation of energy to data center and IT resources. This provides higher returns out of every dollar they spend on energy.

IBM Active Energy Manager

Active Energy Manager™, shown in Figure 8.7, provides the ability to monitor energy in real time, as well as to record and analyze actual energy usage and thermal loading. This data is used to allocate energy on a server-by-server basis. It gives our clients the flexibility to set thresholds for individual server energy usage based on application priorities, time of day, and other factors. (The concepts discussed in this section are covered in depth in the International Technology Group's management brief *Aligning Platform and Service Management with IBM Systems Director and Tivoli Solutions*, Los Altos, California, January 2009.)

Active Energy Manager enables organizations to develop more effective data center energy-conservation strategies. Energy control functions such as power capping require knowledge of actual energy consumption. *Power capping* enables administrators to reduce the margin of power available to a server or group of servers. This approach is particularly valuable to organizations whose utility contracts penalize them if consumption crosses a particular threshold.

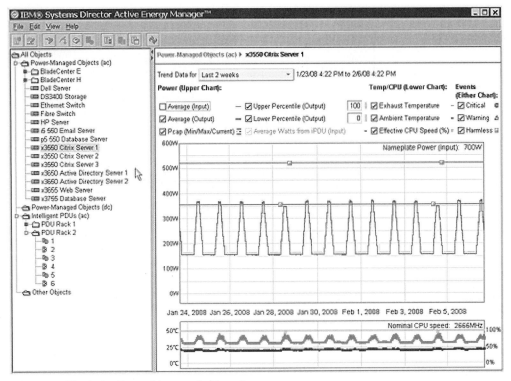

Figure 8.7: The Active Energy Manager dashboard.

VMware Distributed Power Management

VMware Distributed Power Management (DPM) is a technology that is part of the VMware DRS (described above). DPM, shown in Figure 8.8, automates power management and minimizes power consumption across a collection of servers. It continuously monitors resource requirements in a DRS cluster. When resource requirements of the cluster decrease during periods of low usage, DPM consolidates workloads to reduce power consumption by the cluster. When resource requirements increase during periods of higher usage, VMware DPM brings powered-down hosts back online to ensure service levels are met. Thus, DPM has allowed our clients to reduce energy (power and cooling) costs in data centers and to automate the management of energy consumption in servers. (For more information on VMware's DPM, see its Website at *www.vmware.com/products/drs*.)

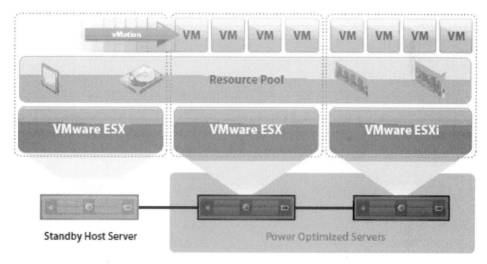

Figure 8.8: VMware's Distributed Power Management reduces power consumption in data centers.

Summary

The main benefits of applying the Flexible Resource Balancing service pattern are as follows:

- Organizations are able to avoid planned outages for hardware or firmware maintenance by moving workloads to another server and then performing the maintenance. This gives them the flexibility to work around scheduled maintenance activities.
- Organizations can avoid downtime for a server upgrade by moving workloads to another server and then performing the upgrade. This gives them the flexibility to continue their work without disruption.
- If a server indicates a potential failure, its workload can be moved to another server before the failure occurs. This gives organizations the flexibility to avoid unplanned downtime and any subsequent disaster recovery.

- Organizations are able to consolidate workloads running on several small, underutilized servers onto a single large server.
- Organizations can move workloads from server to server to optimize IT and energy resource use and workload performance.
- Organizations are able to schedule migrations at predefined times, and without an administrator's presence.

These benefits address the challenges described in the "Problem" section of this pattern.

CHAPTER 9

Reducing Incoming Hardware Infrastructure and Work

Although virtualization transformation programs significantly lower the costs associated with an IT infrastructure, additional programs should be implemented to ensure these costs remain low. The Reducing Incoming Hardware Infrastructure and Work pattern outlines a Hardware Resource Management (HRM) program that optimizes hardware-related costs and subsequently keeps the data center power and cooling costs low over the lifetime of an IT infrastructure.

Maintaining the savings from a virtualization transformation over the long term requires changing the cultural mindset among the IT stakeholders. Business users must start counting and requesting *IT services capability* (such as a service that processes payroll bimonthly and meets a specific set of SLAs) instead of *physical IT components* (such as servers, disk space, and memory). If you don't institute this cultural shift, you risk eroding any operational efficiency and cost savings gained during your virtualization transformation.

After virtualizing its IT infrastructure, an organization must not fall back into the trap of ordering additional hardware without first leveraging available capacity on its existing hardware. Keeping hardware costs down and increasing virtualized server utilization are key objectives of the Hardware Resource Management program discussed in this chapter.

The Client Scenario

The pattern in this chapter addresses the following strategic objectives, critical success factors, and key performance indicators outlined in the client scenario in Chapter 5:

- SO 5: Optimize the use of IT resources.
    - » CSF 5.1: Increase the average utilization of servers.
        - KPI 5.1.1: Keep the average CPU utilization across the entire production server landscape greater than 60 percent.
        - KPI 5.1.2: Complete provisioning and application readiness of standard offerings in less than five days.

The Reducing Incoming Hardware Infrastructure and Work Pattern

The Reducing Incoming Hardware Infrastructure and Work pattern is described in the following sections.

Name

The name of this pattern is Reducing Incoming Hardware Infrastructure and Work.

Value Statement

A key business objective of virtualization is to optimize IT hardware and maintenance costs. The HRM program ensures that an additional demand for IT services translates into the more efficient use of existing hardware, where possible, instead of an automatic request for additional hardware.

Of course, new hardware sometimes has to be purchased, incurring new costs both for the equipment and for the infrastructure and personnel surrounding it. Under an HRM program, however, the incremental costs diverge more and more from the incremental costs of a naïve hardware-purchasing program over time. This allows your savings to grow along with your business users' utilization, as shown in Figure 9.1.

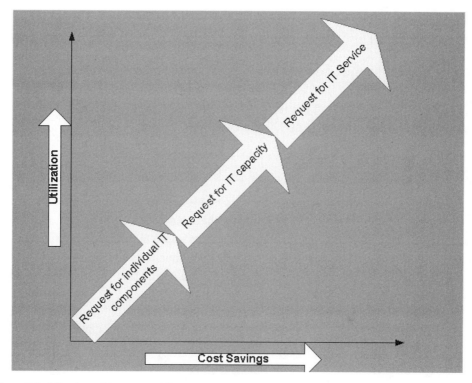

Figure 9.1: A Hardware Management Resource program saves more and more over time.

An HRM program uses detailed technical and business viability assessments to leverage existing hardware capacity to meet new IT service requests. Even when new hardware turns out to be needed, the HRM program helps you purchase additional capacity intelligently, preparing the way for its use with multiple business units, to allow higher utilization of the new hardware.

Context

This pattern is most useful where the common business and IT practice is to "buy and deploy" in response to every need. In many organizations, individual business units drive technology purchases. Each unit may have its own IT capital approval process and architectural controls, making it convenient to frame its needs in terms of end results (hardware and software), instead of in terms of business activities that can be met through commonly shared resources. When each department has its own hardware and software standards, collaboration and consolidation are even harder to achieve. A common symptom of the problem is a large, heterogeneous environment of underused servers.

Lack of synergy with respect to architectural controls, technology governance, and sharing of resources among business units can prove to be very costly for the larger organization. Virtualization will not rein in this practice by itself; the HRM program must be instituted in the new virtualized environment.

Problem

Figure 9.2 depicts the traditional hardware request process in most organizations. To move to a procedure that allows the IT group to share resources among business units efficiently, the whole organization must reexamine its approval processes. This must be done at the enterprise level as well as the individual business-unit level, to ensure that everyone supports the objectives of increasing and optimizing the use of existing hardware resources.

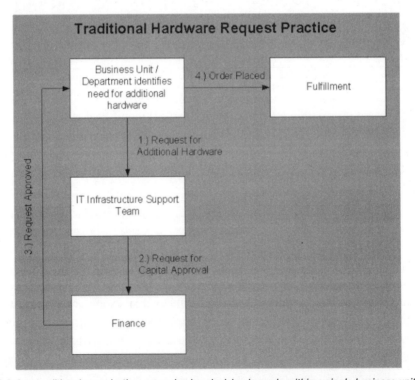

Figure 9.2: In a traditional organization, a purchasing decision is made within a single business unit.

Selection Guidance

Use this pattern when your organization meets many of the following characteristics:

- Your organization has several capital approval processes, which vary by individual organizational units.
- The hardware approval and acquisition process does not include an evaluation of the capacity of existing and requested hardware resources.
- You are relocating IT infrastructure components to a different data center.
- You are running a large-scale refresh project on the IT infrastructure or data center.
- Your organization needs to reduce hardware costs.
- You need to increase the utilization of existing server hardware.
- Your objectives include capacity and performance optimization of servers, applications, or storage environments.
- You are developing green IT solutions.

Forces

The idea behind the HRM program is quite simple: leverage the hardware you already have on the shelf before going out and buying more. However, the HRM program is challenging to implement and administer because of several competing forces. We review the main ones in the following sections.

Cultural and Organizational Challenges

In many organizations, the ownership and procurement control of IT assets resides with individual business units and/or IT service support teams. To implement the HRM program, a good portion of this ownership must shift to an IT organization servicing the entire firm. This shift initially poses several challenges, such as these:

- *Fear among business managers of losing control*—Groups still need a say in the architecture and design of their services in a virtualized environment. The key challenge here is to assure the business units and IT infrastructure support teams that their service level objectives, as well as their functional and nonfunctional architectural requirements, will be respected after the shift in the hardware acquisition and management policy.
- *Lack of understanding of how IT capacity relates to physical IT components*—The key challenge to address here is educating the IT service requesters, so they can frame their requests for IT in terms of required services and capacity. For instance,

in non-virtualized environments of non-cooperating business units, an organization might request a high-end Unix machine (such as a P570) with 16 CPUs and 256 GB of memory. In contrast, a request that can be handled effectively under an HRM program looks like this:

"We require the service to process 50,000 payroll checks monthly. Our IT staff estimates that we need at least 2 CPUs' worth of processing power at all times; an average of 3 CPUs' worth during the weekdays to process our transaction load; and a maximum of 4 CPUs' worth at least twice a month, for check processing."

- *Integrating the HRM process into overall business controls*—The HRM program must have strong buy-in from senior management and must be supported by a management system that measures its effectiveness and impact on the overall business.
- *General criticism and inherent fear of the unknown*—While the changes instituted by the HRM program will yield positive results for the business, getting everyone on board might not be easy. The sooner the business is able to embrace change and begin to transform itself, the quicker and more thoroughly the business results are achieved.
- *Communication, training, and support*—Proper communication and training, along with a staffed support structure, are required to reduce any growing pains experienced by an organization adopting the HRM program.
- *Lack of data about asset management, capacity planning, and performance*—Most organizations do not have well-managed technology and processes to discover and collect data about IT procedures. This data is required for implementing an HRM program, since it underlies decisions about the future deployment of IT services on existing hardware.

In order for the business to increase utilization of existing hardware, it is important to have a clear and consolidated view of all of its hardware assets. In particular, the organization needs ready access to information on the following:

- *Physical hardware resources*—These include such specifics as physical location (hosting data center, building/floor/aisle, machine specifications); network placement; storage and server connectivity information; and age.
- *Logical hardware resources*—These indicate how many virtual or logical servers are being hosted on each physical machine.
- *Hardware utilization and performance management*—These provide periodic resource utilization reports (such as daily, weekly, and monthly), along with views of total capacity, used capacity, and available capacity. The views should also include information related to specific hardware's performance when tasked with multiple types of transaction loads.

Managing the Scope of an HRM Program

The scope of the HRM program must be well defined relative to other IT disciplines, such as capacity and management and order fulfillment. An HRM program is not a replacement for capacity management or performance management. On the contrary, it leverages the output from these disciplines to drive decisions related to optimizing the use of hardware resources. Similarly, an HRM program does not replace the IT capital approval process. After the organization has assessed available IT capacity, the HRM step determines the approval of the hardware capital request or the substitution of existing resources.

Lack of Hardware Standardization

Lack of architectural standards and overall IT governance can result in the introduction of a large mix of hardware from multiple vendors into the IT environment. This diversity of hardware, in turn, restricts the ability to share workloads among machines. This frustrates the HRM process.

HRM Staffing Considerations

Most organizations have a misconception that an HRM program requires a large, separately staffed team that includes highly skilled subject matter experts (SMEs) for every IT system and application installed in the IT infrastructure. In fact, however, your HRM analysts should have general skills in capacity and performance management. These analysts can partner with existing IT specialists and SMEs as needed.

Your HRM analyst team should report directly to the organization's overall IT governance and architectural standards team, or at the very least be in close alignment with it. Close collaboration will ensure that hardware architectural standards are well understood and followed by the IT staff requesting additional hardware resources.

Solution

Our solution for the Reducing Incoming Hardware Infrastructure and Work pattern is to create and execute a Hardware Resource Management program. This relies on the coordination of activities among the following core components (teams, systems, and processes):

- HRM analyst team
- IT infrastructure support teams
- Server and storage capacity request tool
- Capacity management process
- HRM reports
- Idle hardware asset depot
- IT governance and architectural standards team
- Corporate finance
- Order fulfillment
- Hardware forecasting with key hardware vendors
- HRM measurement reporting

Figure 9.3 shows how each component feeds into the knowledge and decisions of the other components. Background about the role of each component follows.

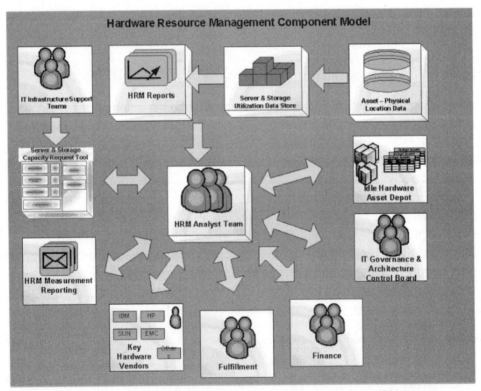

Figure 9.3: This model shows the relationships among teams and processes in an HRM program.

The HRM Analyst Team

The HRM analyst team is the core of the HRM program and is responsible for analyzing and responding to all hardware capacity requests. The team reviews current requests for hardware capacity, available capacity, and hardware standards and architectural constraints to find opportunities for extending and adding load to existing systems. The team also ensures that when the need arises, approved hardware models are ordered. The approval process follows the flow in Figure 9.4.

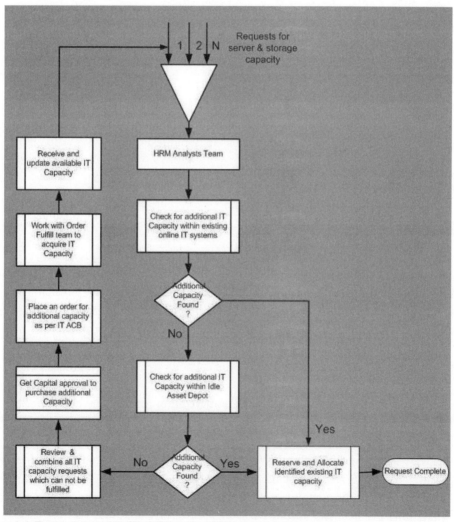

Figure 9.4: The hardware-capacity decision tree guides the HRM analyst team.

The IT Infrastructure Support Team

When IT management is not completely centralized within an organization, several instances of the IT infrastructure support team operate in various business units. Otherwise, this is one centralized team.

The team receives requests for IT services from the business and user community. It is responsible for the design, architecture, and deployment of the technologies to satisfy these requests. As part of its solution design phase, this team identifies the need for additional hardware. It submits the additional hardware capacity requirements to the HRM analyst team, via the server and storage capacity request tool.

The Server and Storage Capacity Request Tool

This tool is any system or COTS product that supports a workflow to allow collaboration between the HRM analyst team and the IT infrastructure support team. It receives, tracks, processes, audits, and reports on hardware capacity requests.

The Capacity Management Process

The capacity management process involves developing and maintaining tactical and strategic plans to ensure that the physical IT resources of supported operating environments accommodate the organization's growing or changing business requirements. This process provides the HRM analyst team with detailed information about the IT systems: their physical location (data center, floor, aisle); physical characteristics (such as model, type, individual components, and number of CPUs); total available capacity; used and unused capacity; and number of virtual machines.

The following basic activities performed in the capacity management process:

- Define metrics, data collection, and summarization for capacity and storage requirements.
- Define capacity-alert thresholds to support agreed-upon service levels.
- Track capacity measures against defined thresholds, and notify the customer when system resources reach critical or alert levels.
- Manage queues for incidents, problems, changes, and other service requests pertaining to capacity.
- Provide ad hoc capacity reporting for the analysis of incidents to restore service.

- Analyze capacity measures and forecasting of physical resource requirements.
- Track and document the use of physical IT resources, and provide the information to the customer to help determine future capacity requirements.
- Recommend corrective actions to resolve capacity problems and prevent possible future incidents.
- Recommend any system configurations or modifications necessary to maintain acceptable resource utilization.
- Define and maintain business process documents.

HRM Reports

The HRM process requires several capacity management reports, which can be generated via a COTS capacity management software product. These reports should include user-friendly graphical representations of the IT infrastructure's server and storage hardware placement. These reports assist the HRM analysts in identifying total, used, and available capacity at each data center location, at a system level (such as Enterprise Resource Planning or ERP) and the individual IT component level (such as for a single server or storage device).

The key reports required by the HRM analyst team are as follows:

- *Total capacity at the resource pool level*—A resource pool, as explained in Chapter 1, is a collection of components, such as servers and storage devices, which can be divided among users in a flexible manner.
- *Total used capacity at a system level*—This could be the total capacity used by an ERP system.
- *Total available capacity at a system level*—This could be the total capacity available to an ERP system.
- *Summary of individual component usage*—Suppose a system had four CPUs. This report could show the utilization of each of the CPUs over a specified period.
- *Total capacity per storage system*—This could be the total capacity available for each tier of storage allocated to an ERP application.
- *A visual map of each system*—This includes the number of virtual machines, network connections, storage system connections, and applications.
- *Data about physical location and system configuration*—This information comes from the organization's asset and configuration management reporting service. It should be combined with server and storage utilization data from capacity

planning, to generate a complete picture of each system and storage unit's physical location, as well as its total, used, and available capacity.

The Idle Hardware Asset Depot

Typically, every organization has idle assets. These assets are no longer in active use for a variety of reasons. For example, the services that an asset supported might no longer be required. Redeployment of these hardware assets can avoid additional spending on new hardware.

The depot is a warehouse of idle hardware assets. It includes both those that have been preordered for specific uses but not yet deployed and older assets that have been decommissioned but are still useful.

It is important to ensure that active and valid inventory controls are in place and that the HRM analyst team has access to the current and accurate state of the decommissioned hardware assets. Otherwise, the HRM process runs the risk of deploying a hardware asset that lacks the expected capacity. For example, suppose some RAM of an asset has been taken out and installed in another machine to serve another capacity request, but the inventory control systems were not accurately updated. HRM might incorrectly reassign the asset, resulting in schedule delays, client complaints, and the waste of valuable resources required to remedy problems down the road.

The IT Governance and Architectural Standards Team

The IT governance and architecture standards team is a corporate-level governance body that defines IT architecture standards based on corporate business strategy. The information technology standards include recommended hardware platforms, vendor type, hardware models, and standard configurations approved for use by the entire business. These hardware standards become guidelines for the HRM analyst team when the need to order hardware arises.

This team also defines the set of architectural constraints that the HRM team must review when they evaluate the IT infrastructure staff's request for additional capacity. This includes constraints such as a security policy and the applications and workloads that may not be shared on the same machine. For example, even if the HRM analyst team determines that existing hardware capacity exists to furnish a new request for hosting a new workload, there might be architectural standards related to security zoning, data privacy, or regulatory compliance to consider. These might necessitate the purchase of additional hardware to host the workload/application being evaluated.

Corporate Finance

The corporate finance team is responsible for approving the capital required to purchase hardware. Having performed an assessment of available IT capacity, HRM helps this team find the best course of action with respect to approval (or denial) of the hardware capital request.

Order Fulfillment

The order fulfillment team provides the basic services of placing hardware orders, tracking and receiving the hardware, and delivering it to the IT team responsible for its deployment. The HRM analyst team works with this team to ensure timely procurement that meets the service level expectations of the requesting support teams and business units.

Hardware Forecasting and Vendor Relations

The HRM program also establishes external relationships with key hardware vendors to speed up the hardware acquisition process. In contrast to the IT staff for each business unit, the HRM analyst team can review hardware capacity requirements for the entire business. The HRM team also has a view into the currently available in-house hardware capacity.

Thus, this team is uniquely positioned to understand current and future (near-term) hardware needs. It can forecast the business demand for hardware. By communicating its forecasts to vendors, the team puts them in a better position to respond to future hardware requests. Ultimately, the HRM program can reduce the costs of new hardware and can receive better discounts from OEM vendors.

HRM Measurement Reporting

The HRM program should provide measurements to report its effectiveness. The following types of measurement reports produced by the HRM team:

- The total number of open, in-progress, and completed requests within a specified period
- The average time required to satisfy hardware capacity requests

- The total dollar amount saved by reusing existing hardware for all requests, or any specified subset of requests

These measurements serve two purposes in the organization. First, they pinpoint areas of the HRM process that are working well, as well as those requiring improvements, therefore driving a feedback loop that leads to better HRM. Second, they quantify to the business the actual dollar amount saved by reusing existing capacity.

HRM for Processing a Hardware Request

Figure 9.2 shows the traditional hardware request process used by most organizations. Figure 9.5 highlights the new process, which leverages HRM components.

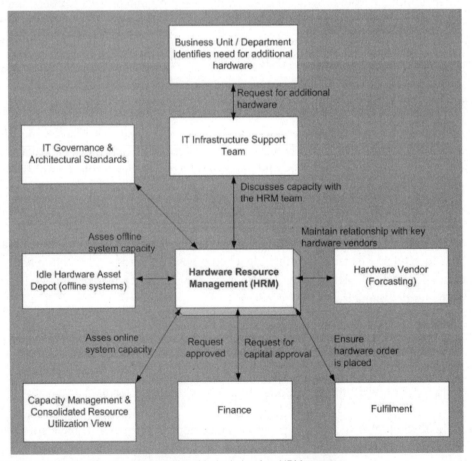

Figure 9.5: A purchasing decision is made, with the help of an HRM program.

The HRM-supported hardware acquisition process works as follows:

1. The business unit or individual department identifies the need for additional IT services.
2. The business unit engages its IT infrastructure support team, which reviews the IT service request, defines the architecture and design of the required IT service, and identifies the need for additional hardware capacity.
3. The request is then submitted to the HRM analyst team, which takes the following actions:

   a) Review the existing needs for additional hardware capacity.
   b) Assess the request by reviewing the capacity planning and maintenance reports to retrieve the total, used, and available capacity.
   c) Review the idle hardware asset depot.
   d) Identify any existing capacity.
   e) Validate identified capacity resources with the IT infrastructure support team, to ensure that the identified capacity is able to meet both capacity requirements and architectural constraints.
   f) If appropriate capacity is found, work with the IT infrastructure support team to provide it to the business unit.
   g) If existing capacity is not available or cannot be used for the requested purpose due to justifiable business and/or technical constraints, document the reasons and create a request for capital.

4. The HRM analyst team works with the capital finance team on a request for capital approval.
5. Upon receiving an approval for the request, the HRM analyst team places an order via order fulfillment, using standard procurement processes.
6. The HRM analyst team works with the order fulfillment team to complete the order.
7. The HRM analyst team informs the business unit's IT infrastructure support team of the status of the order.
8. The HRM analyst team updates the HRM measurement report.

By leveraging the new HRM-supported hardware acquisition process, we have generated substantial cost savings for several clients.

Summary

This chapter introduced the fifth of our seven patterns, which assists you in optimizing the use of hardware resources. In summary, the HRM program enables you to do the following:

- Increase utilization of existing hardware.
- Cut down on unnecessary hardware purchases and capital expense.
- Enforce hardware architectural standards across your business.
- Redeploy idle hardware assets and save money.
- Minimize data center power and cooling costs over the long term.
- Improve your hardware demand forecasting, to get improved delivery times and better discounts from hardware vendors.

CHAPTER 10

Reducing
Non-Value-Added Work

The lean methodology, discussed earlier in this book, breaks work into three types:

- Value-adding work
- Incidental work
- Waste

Value-adding work meets the customer's needs. The customer is willing and happy to pay for this work because it contributes to the customer's success. Incidental activities, by themselves, are not part of the customer requirements or specifications, but delivery of customer requirements is not possible without performing these tasks. Because the customer does not receive direct value from incidental work, it is always worthwhile to minimize it.

Waste provides no value to the customer and frequently is frustrating for the provider to perform. A key goal of the lean methodology is the total elimination of this type of work.

A key benefit of virtualization projects is the reduction of both capital and operational expenses. (We define the latter as the labor required to operate and deliver IT services.) The virtualization-related benefit of reducing capital expenses is easy to recognize. It results primarily from consolidating and reducing hardware resources and slimming down data center build-out and expansion plans. However, organizations struggle with the realization of operational expense reduction as it relates to virtualization in their IT environment.

All patterns in this book contribute toward reducing waste and incidental activities and enhancing the value an organization can gain from IT virtualization. This chapter, however, highlights those areas that contribute directly to reducing the operational expenses related to creating and managing virtualized IT environments.

You might find some repetition of the book's content in this chapter, since many of the concepts discussed here are also discussed in other chapters. However, we consider the topic of operational expense reduction important enough to dedicate a complete chapter to it. We concentrate here on the critical focus areas that must be considered to reduce operations expenses via virtualization. In this chapter, we provide summary-level explanations of each focus area and our prescribed approach to reduce non-value-added activities in that area. Refer to the appropriate pattern (chapter) for a more detailed discussion of the prescribed approach.

Client Scenario

The pattern in this chapter primarily addresses all of the strategic objectives outlined in our client scenario in Chapter 5:

1. Reduce annual server operating expenses.
2. Align IT to service level expectations.
3 Simplify and standardize the IT environment.
4. Increase the agility of IT to respond to business needs.
5. Optimize the use of IT resources.

The Reduce Non-Value-Added Work Pattern

The Reduce Non-Value-Added Work pattern is described in the following sections.

Name

The name of this pattern is Reduce Non-Value-Added Work.

Value Statement

This pattern provides you with insight into what areas of technology, process, and organization should be considered for removal of non-value-added work. This will drive a tangible reduction of operational expenses, while managing virtualized IT environments. Some of the areas of focus in this pattern have been mentioned in other patterns of this book, from different perspectives.

Context

This pattern is most useful where organizations need to identify means to lower their cost of operations, while managing a virtualized IT environment.

Problem

Many critics of virtualization say that virtualization does not lead to operational expense reduction. These critics contend that it takes more labor to manage a virtual image than it does to manage a physical image, because of the added complexity of managing the hypervisor.

Our client experiences have revealed that these critics' assertions, while based on their real experiences, are not valid if virtualization is implemented and managed using a best-practices approach, such as the one in this book. Later on in this chapter, you will see the results of a study conducted by our partners at VMware, Inc., to demonstrate that many organizations are realizing operational expense reduction and operational efficiencies with virtualization technology.

The problem common among many IT environments is that, while they are running their server images as virtualized systems, they have done very little to transform their IT processes and organizational structures. Many organizations today are managing virtualized IT resources the same way they used to manage non-virtualized IT resources. These organizations have also not completely embraced and exploited virtualization technology advancements. These come out-of-the-box with commercial virtualization system products, to reduce non-value-added tasks via automation. The result is that they are unable to generate a tangible reduction of operational expenses in their virtualized IT environments.

Forces

The difficulty of reducing operational expenses during and after a virtualization transformation can be explained by the large number of variables and constraints involved. Here are the main ones we've found:

- The heterogeneity of hardware and server images in the IT environment makes it more complex to manage the environment.
- The IT environment lacks architectural standards and controls.
- The new layer of complexity added by virtualization is not properly managed.
- There is a failure to exploit dynamic systems management capabilities and automation enabled by virtualization systems, to reduce complexity.
- "Simpler to virtualize" workloads are not prioritized during the virtualization transformation, and the project is not properly segmented.
- The organization relies on the same organizational structures and measurement systems that were in place to support the legacy (non-virtualized) IT environment.
- The organization relies on the same IT management frameworks and systems management tools that were in place to support the legacy (non-virtualized) IT environment.

Selection Guidance

Use this pattern when your organization meets many of the following characteristics:

- Your organization is planning on virtualizing its IT infrastructure.
- You are required to reduce operations costs for your organization's IT.
- You are required to demonstrate productivity gains from virtualization.
- You need to demonstrate the value that a virtualized IT environment can bring to your organization's stakeholders.
- You are enabling your virtualized IT environment to operate through the use of automated, repeatable ITIL-aligned processes.

Solution

To realize the benefits of virtualization related to operations expense reduction during and after virtualization transformations, we guide our clients to focus on removing non-value-added activities in the following areas:

- Implement standardized IT management processes and architectural control across the IT environment.
- Implement a "divide and conquer" strategy for virtualization transformations.
- Leverage automation and reusable templates during application migration when moving from physical to virtual systems.
- Focus on workload (application and middleware) consolidation/virtualization as part of the transformation effort.
- Reengineer or adopt new IT management processes, tools, and capabilities specifically designed to manage virtualized IT infrastructures.
- Leverage virtualization to optimize all infrastructure components: storage, servers, and networks.
- Establish an organizational staffing model that minimizes non-value-added work and wasteful activities.
- Leverage virtualization technology to enable new value-added services.

The following sections provide additional details around each of these focus areas.

Implement Standardized IT Processes and Control

Organizations that have diverse hardware, software, management processes, data center locations, and teams supporting an IT environment often lack IT standards that are uniformly deployed and adhered to. For example, we find that client organizations' lines of business might have problems such as the following:

- Different OS and application provisioning processes in place
- Different asset and configuration management processes
- Multiple security policies and compliance standards
- Varying procurement and approval processes for purchasing and installing hardware and software
- Diverse IT monitoring, metering, and charge-back processes

If architectural controls are not well-defined and strictly regimented, the issue of lack of standardized IT management processes arises, irrespective of the organization's size or complexity. In such an organization, virtualization rarely succeeds in driving organization-wide operational efficiency and productivity gains.

Chapter 6 discussed the approach of implementing architectural governance and an Architecture Management Framework for virtualization transformations and for the ongoing management of virtualized IT environments. It also highlighted the importance of executive sponsorship and oversight on architectural governance and described organizational constructs (such as the executive steering committee) to drive and enforce architecture standards and controls within the entire organization. With these governance and organizational constructs in place, organizations have the opportunity to reduce their operational expenses in virtualized environments. For example, an organization might standardize on a common OS and application provisioning process to provision virtual images and use fewer standardized OS images (which may be bundled with standard software/middleware stacks). This reduces the operations costs associated with doing work, compared to a virtualized environment that lacks these standard IT management processes.

Implement a "Divide and Conquer" Strategy

Organizations that fail to control transition costs upfront during the virtual transformation phase end up taking a long time to see a positive ROI in their virtualized IT environment. The complexity arising from different hardware, operating systems, applications, middleware, and so on contributes largely to the increase in operations costs during transformation. Attempting to virtualize "hard to virtualize" workloads in the initial stages of the project further exacerbates the situation.

The operations costs during virtualization transformations can be controlled significantly by focusing on virtualizing the "low-hanging fruit." Migrate these less-complex workloads first, learn from these transformations, and then apply the lessons learned to more complex workloads. Experienced IT service providers, who have already led several virtualization transformations, have learning and reusable assets from virtualizing workloads of varying complexity. This should be applied for any new project. In this way, you can tackle the less-complex ("sweet spot") workloads at the same time as those that are more complex but higher priority.

Chapter 5 recommended a "divide and conquer" approach to tackle and overcome the challenges of virtualizing very complex environments. The Segmenting Complexity pattern's solution, discussed in that chapter, consists of three stages:

- What to do
- How to do it
- Whether to do each part

In the "what to do" stage, project teams decide on a server-by-server basis whether a server can be migrated to a virtual state. For instance, the team might consider a "lift-and-load" move to a binary-compatible platform or a "platform refresh" that involves recompilation (and sometimes recoding).

In the "how to do it" stage, project teams identify servers and applications with similar characteristics that can be handled as a group to generate economies. The benefit of grouping efforts for different servers and applications not only saves money and time but also provides input to the next stage.

Finally, in the "whether to do each part" stage, the project teams can use a predictive model to estimate costs for each transformation defined in the previous step. Time and cost estimates help project teams define independent phases and schedule them in a way their staff and budget can support. Most organizations perform the simpler phases with lower costs and faster schedules before the more complex and costly phases, to maximize their ROI from virtualization.

Leverage Automation and Reusable Templates During Migration

Workload migrations from physical servers to virtualized machines can be operationally intensive and the source of a large portion of the operational expenses incurred during the virtualization transformation process. Workload migrations are especially expensive when a repeatable process is not followed and when teams performing migrations of different workloads are not coordinated. Coordinated teams learn from each others' experiences about avoiding common pitfalls and using best practices or reusable assets (such as code, documentation, migration processes) while migrating different classes of workloads to virtual environments.

To minimize waste and incidental activities in the workload migration effort, Chapter 5 recommended the binary, the like-for-like, and custom transformation options. (Their pros and cons were detailed in Table 5.1.) The chapter described decision support tools (such as application scorecards, application surveys, and decision trees) that help determine the best migration option for each type of workload. With the help of these tools and techniques, the virtualization project teams can determine the optimal path for each workload.

Chapter 5 also described the approach to find common elements that allow the IT staff to process and migrate several servers or applications at once. Large-scale transformation projects present many opportunities for organizing, automating, and timing transformations that can exploit the following efficiencies:

- Economies of scale based on the sheer repetition of tasks
- Reuse of the IT staff's expertise and their knowledge of resources
- Reuse of tools and code developed along the way
- Organizational structures mapped to dependencies within the applications being transformed

A workload/application migration approach during virtualization transformations that is based on reusable templates and automation leads to economies of reuse, economies of organization, and economies of integration (described in detail in Chapter 5). For example, there is the approach of identifying clusters of dependent applications that need to be transformed and placing codependent applications in the same transformation bundle. Such clustering allows integration testing on all the members of the cluster together in a target environment, instead of repeating the same integration points multiple times. Hence, waste and incidental activities are reduced.

Focus on Workload Consolidation/Virtualization

Most organizations undergoing virtualization transformations focus primarily on infrastructure (server, storage, and network) virtualization aspects and leave the workload consolidation and virtualization options untouched. The latter is understandable where organizations do not want to take on additional risk and complexity during the first few phases of the virtualization transformation process. However, by not consolidating and virtualizing workloads and middleware, these organizations miss the opportunity to lower their operations costs in the long term.

When not consolidated or virtualized, each instance of middleware adds operations overhead to an organization's cost structure. Separate backups, security patching, software upgrades, health checks, and other systems management tasks are required for every instance of middleware in the IT environment. Chapter 11 provides a virtualization maturity model (in Figure 11.1) that allows organizations to focus on workload virtualization and address workload consolidation opportunities in their IT environment.

Reengineer or Adopt New Processes, Tools, and Capabilities

Many organizations fail to reduce operations-related expenses in virtualized IT environments because of their failure to manage the lifecycle of these virtualized environments. This poses its own set of risks and challenges.

There are two common reasons for organizations' failure to properly manage the virtualized IT environment lifecycle:

- Not understanding up-front how virtualization might affect their IT and business processes
- Continuing to rely on IT systems management tools and capabilities that were originally put in place to manage the non-virtualized IT environment, which might not have the maturity and flexibility to help reduce costs for virtual IT environments

Chapter 11 describes how an organization can start adopting and applying technology, process, and organizational changes to its virtualized IT environment based on a virtualization maturity model. With this approach, organizations can overcome the challenges associated with complexity of managing virtualized IT environments, while benefiting from lower operations costs and higher responsiveness to business demands. The virtualization maturity model identifies several opportunities for generating increasing levels of benefits over time.

Chapter 11 also describes an approach to help organize plans derived from virtualization maturity model using a services management framework, which we have relied upon extensively in our client engagements. By having our clients consider the end-to-end services management paradigm, we have helped them understand how the service management capabilities can be applied and tuned along with their IT infrastructure and virtualization technologies.

Finally, Chapter 11 describes advanced virtualization management tools and capabilities (including products from IBM and VMware). We have leveraged these tools in multiple client engagements to address the virtualization management requirements and challenges.

Leverage Virtualization to Optimize All Infrastructure Components

A number of organizations virtualize their physical server environments, but do not leverage the full extent of virtualization capabilities in their storage and network infrastructure. For example, virtualization provides basic virtual I/O capabilities, which organizations use while running their servers as virtual machines. However, they do not extensively apply and use storage virtualization capability across their storage environments.

We have found that, by applying storage virtualization technologies (such as IBM's SAN Volume Controller) and organizing their data into different tiers of storage (determined by data access and performance requirements), organizations can distribute their data over multiple storage devices of varying price/performance. This reduces storage hardware costs. Specifically, storage-management-related operations costs are reduced by 25 percent or more.

Chapter 8 discussed an example of this using the Flexible Resource Balancing pattern. Xsigo System's technology increased an infrastructure's efficiency by providing dynamic I/O resources, while providing software-controlled connectivity with virtual NICs and HBAs, deployed and migrated on demand. By leveraging advanced virtualization I/O technology, such as the one provided by Xsigo, our clients can further reduce their operations costs related to provisioning I/O resources.

Establish a Staffing Model That Minimizes Non-Value-Added Work

The programs managing virtualization transformations and ongoing steady-state operations often reach across complex organizational boundaries. Each organization or business unit within the organization might be facing different measurements from their management and be trying to achieve different goals. In these situations, be careful to avoid inter- and intra-organizational conflict, misalignment of goals, lack of adherence to architecture standards, miscommunications, and other activities that can result in wasteful and incidental activities. Such activities have a negative impact on operations costs.

Chapter 6 reviewed the Redistribute Activities pattern. To drive success in virtualization, implementing a well-defined service pattern for activity redistribution can dramatically increase the chances of success. This will also lead to lower operations costs.

The virtualization transformation projects benefit from realigning key skills and redistributing activities under a common project management organization. Creating well-structured steering committees and architectural boards for organizational and architectural governance helps keep the project on target and reduces additional costs. Establishing clear executive leadership, a unified technical team, well-articulated interdependencies, a common and managed architecture, and integrated measurement plans, as described in this pattern, significantly improves the success rate of a virtualization project.

Leverage Virtualization Technology to Enable New Services

Infrastructure and application virtualization techniques tend to focus primarily on core technologies, such as logical partitions, shared resources, and underlying hypervisors. While this drastically reduces the bottom-line cost associated with delivering IT, major cost savings can also be achieved by changing the way that IT is offered and managed. IT services and associated service management capabilities ensure that automated, repeatable processes and technologies are in place to manage the IT lifecycle.

Virtualization has the potential to enable scenarios that were not possible before. However, it brings along a set of concerns that make the management of an environment containing virtual elements challenging. For example, virtualization might change the usage behavior of traditional software, therefore requiring a more specific licensing approach. The VMs can be moved around for different reasons, such as for disaster recovery or for a performance requirement. The traditional agreements might not be able to cope with this.

IT services represent the third level of maturity in the model described in Chapter 11. The key to IT services is that they represent an abstracted view of the underlying technology to the consumer. This virtualization of IT through the use of services allows the provider to manage the infrastructure in a cost-effective and optimized manner.

IT services in virtualized environments need to be composed and built so that IT consumers can understand what to expect and subscribe to it. Such services hide all the technology layers and expose just IT's capabilities as consumable services. The abundance of primary IT resources (CPU, storage, and network) has led to the commoditization of IT elements. This has influenced IT businesses to innovate by making

IT accessible as a service, rather than selling in "nuts and bolts." This model forms the basis for the most touted utility computing paradigm and helps to realize the on-demand and cloud computing vision.

VMware Study Findings

To gain perspective into the operational impact of virtualization on IT organizations and staff, VMware conducted a formal study of 30 unique customers in their Technical Account Manager (TAM) program. (Soumen Chowdhury and Gerod Carfantan, *The Operational Impact of Virtualization in the Datacenter: A Research Study of VMware Customers*, VMware, Inc., 2010.)

Study Methodology

The following criteria were used to select the participants:

- *Experience*—Organizations with more than two years of enterprise virtual infrastructure deployment experience, with staff investment
- *Scale*—Organizations running more than 50 VMs, where the deployed VMs represent more than 20 percent of their IT x86 compute infrastructure

In a two-step research process, participants completed an online survey to collect quantitative data about their virtualization deployment, staffing, policies, system management tasks, and barriers to adoption. Respondents were then segmented according to role and industry and invited to participate in a series of roundtable discussions with their peers. These discussions were designed to gather more contextual and qualitative information about survey responses, as well as uncover best practices in deploying virtualization solutions.

The research focused on the effect of virtualization on specific tasks associated with server management. Administrative tasks were divided into two categories to determine the overall impact of virtualization on operational activities:

- *One-time tasks* are discrete tasks, such as provisioning and decommissioning. They happen very few times in a server's lifecycle, primarily to get a new service online.
- *Day-to-day tasks* occur on a regularly scheduled or ad hoc basis. Examples include scheduled activities, such as backups, patching, and disaster recovery

(DR) testing, as well as unscheduled activities, such as outages, bugs, and capacity issues. Given that scheduled activities occur in different cycles—twice a year, once a quarter, daily, and weekly—these activities are considered day-to-day tasks.

The Organizations and Their Structures

The firms surveyed included small, medium, and large enterprises, across a variety of industries. Of the respondents, 73 percent had more than 500 server VMs under management. The number of server VMs ranged from 55 to 5,500, with a median of 1,000 VMs.

Respondents' organizational models and interpretations of server/administrator ratios differed. Therefore, the survey results focused on the actual tasks performed as part of a normal system administrator role, and the impact that virtualization had on those tasks, as measured by task-based time savings. While organizations varied by services delivered, technology portfolio, and operating model, significant commonalities were observed on specific operational tasks.

Virtualization's Effect on Operational Efficiency

Server virtualization with VMware inserts an abstraction layer between server hardware and operating system software. The abstraction layer enables considerable flexibility around how availability, business continuity, provisioning, and other system management tasks are accomplished. However, there is a specific skill set associated with managing the virtual layer.

While organizations have absorbed this skill set in different ways, the results of this survey show that, despite adding an additional layer of software, virtualization improves productivity. In fact, 94 percent of respondents said their IT organization experienced improved productivity as a result of virtualization.

Accelerating One-Time Tasks

More than three-quarters of IT professionals surveyed experienced significant efficiency gains for one-time tasks in a virtual environment over a physical environment. One-time tasks resulted in the greatest savings of time—both elapsed time and actual person-hours spent on the task. As shown in Figure 10.1, 83 percent of respondents reported one-time server management tasks improved by at least 25 percent.

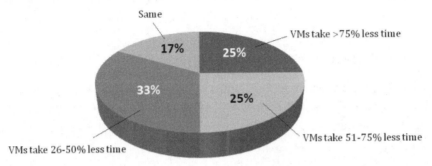

Figure 10.1: The overall time savings for one-time tasks in a virtual environment, compared to a physical environment.

For the specific one-time task of provisioning a server/VM, more than 60 percent of all respondents cited at least a 75 percent improvement. For that one-time service provisioning task, four out of five IT professionals surveyed said they spent up to 25 percent less time than "business as usual." This is shown in Figure 10.2.

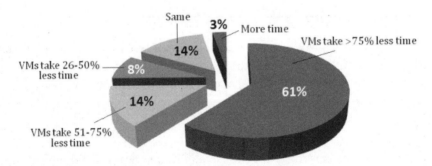

Figure 10.2: The time savings for provisioning servers.

The time savings for the one-time tasks of migrating servers between data centers and decommissioning servers are shown in Figure 10.3. As you can see, more than two-thirds of all respondents cited greater than a 75 percent improvement. For server migration tasks, 92 percent of respondents spent at least 25 percent less time with virtualization.

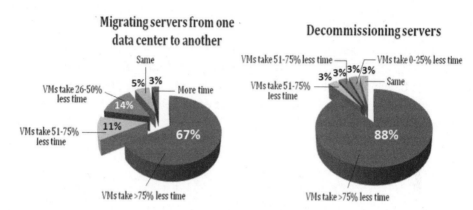

Figure 10.3: The time savings for migrating and decommissioning servers.

More than half of those surveyed estimated VMs take at least 75 percent less time for deploying a new OS instance compared to traditional physical servers. More than half found configuring a new OS instance took at least 50 percent less time. As shown in Figure 10.4, no respondents cited either of these tasks taking more time with virtualization.

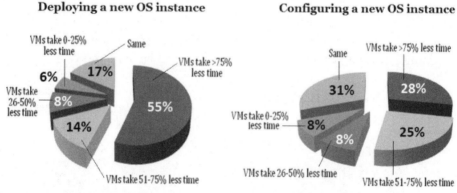

Figure 10.4: The time savings for deploying or configuring a new OS instance.

In addition to compressing elapsed provisioning time from months to days, roundtable participants stated that the ease of VM service decommissioning and re-provisioning enabled rapid asset reuse.

Reducing the Time Spent on Low-Value, Day-to-Day Activities

Survey respondents also reported productivity gains in day-to-day tasks accomplished in a virtual environment. The vast majority of IT professionals surveyed, 97 percent, found virtualization to be equal to or better than physical environments in terms of productivity gains, as shown in Figure 10.5. Only three percent of those surveyed noted any decrease in day-to-day productivity.

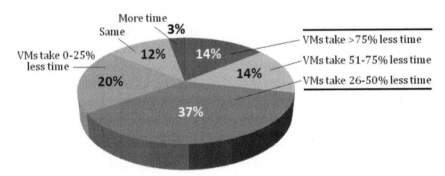

Figure 10.5: The time savings for day-to-day tasks.

The day-to-day tasks of performing hardware maintenance and reverting to a previous configuration (when a problem occurs during patch rollout) can be time-consuming and difficult. In a virtualized environment, both tasks resulted in a time savings of at least 75 percent, according to roughly half of all respondents, as shown in Figure 10.6.

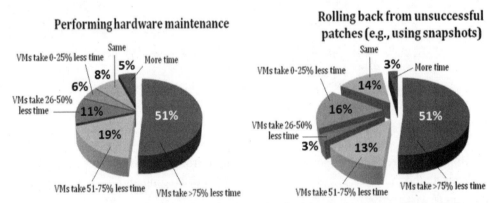

Figure 10.6: The time savings for the day-to-day tasks of maintaining hardware and rolling back after a problem.

Similarly, half of all respondents reported they spent at least 75 percent less time reversing configuration changes. Sixty-nine percent of respondents achieved at least a 25 percent improvement, as shown in Figure 10.7.

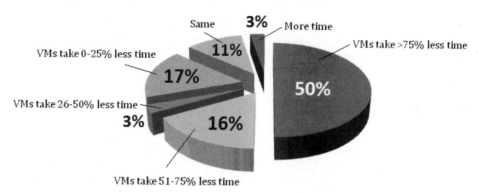

Figure 10.7: The time savings for reversing configuration changes.

Survey respondents also reported material improvements in the time it took to perform the day-to-day tasks of troubleshooting and fixing hardware problems, as well as managing and testing DR plans. Fifty and 41 percent of respondents, respectively, reporting these tasks were now taking at least 50 percent less time. For testing upgrades, patches, and configuration changes and maintaining documentation (runbooks and DR plans), roughly half of those surveyed said VMs saved them time.

The following specific, day-to-day activities also showed improvement:

- On system restores, 57 percent of respondents spent at least 25 percent less time.
- On patch deployment, 30 percent saw improvement, spending between 25 and 90 percent less time.
- On troubleshooting and fixing software problems, 21 percent spent at least 50 percent less time.
- On backups, 30 percent reported improvement, spending between 25 and 95 percent less time.
- On file-level restores, 29 percent of respondents spent at least 25 percent less time.

A full two-thirds of respondents stated their virtual infrastructure administration staff was at least 25 percent more efficient overall, operating VMs. This increase in operational efficiency equates to 1.25 days saved per week, per administrator, or a reduction in low-value IT activity time spent by 65 days per year, per administrator.

Summary

This chapter described the pattern for reducing non-value-added activities. By leveraging this pattern, you will get insight into the areas of technology, process, and organization that should be considered for removal of non-value-added work. This will drive a tangible reduction in operational expenses while better managing the virtualized IT environment.

Standard Operations

A plan that includes virtualization management from the outset can lead to productivity gains and operational efficiencies over the whole lifetime of a virtualized IT infrastructure.

Virtualization can lead to such productivity gains as managing more machines with less staff, improving server availability, and improving the utilization of physical resources. However, for these to be sustained, you need to put in place processes, tools, and capabilities that are significantly more evolved and efficient than those generally used in non-virtualized IT environments.

This chapter focuses on virtualization management as part of an organization's post-virtualization standard operations. You will learn to leverage the *virtualization maturity adoption model*, to incorporate virtualization benefits over the long term into your IT processes.

To unveil the wealth of possibilities in virtualization management, the virtualization maturity model categorizes the various types of tools, processes, and optimizations available to you. This chapter also describes a management structure that can drive adoption and proper use of the tools and processes, and it discusses the services offered in the industry to carry out your transformation.

Objectives Addressed by This Pattern

The Standard Operations pattern in this chapter addresses the following strategic objectives (SOs), critical success factors (CSFs), and key performance indicators (KPIs), outlined in Chapter 5's client scenario:

- SO 1: Reduce annual server operating expenses.

  » CSF 1.2: Reduce IT labor costs needed to support the target state for distributed servers.

    - KPI 1.2.1: Reduce server administration staff by more than 20 percent.
    - KPI 1.2.2: Reduce the average server burden on administrators by more than 30 percent, through simplification and automation.

- SO 3: Simplify and standardize the IT environment.

  » CSF 3.1: Leverage repeatable processes, procedures, and technology standards.

- SO 4: Increase the agility of IT to respond to business needs.

  » CSF 4.1: Automate and accelerate the operational readiness of new or modified servers.

    - KPI 4.1.1: Keep the average request-to-readiness time for new OS images to less than four days.

- SO 5: Optimize the use of IT resources.

  » CSF 5.1: Increase the average utilization of servers.

    - KPI 5.1.2: Complete provisioning and application readiness of standard offerings in less than five days.

The Standard Operations Pattern

The Standard Operations pattern is described in the following sections.

Name

The name of this pattern is Standard Operations.

Value Statement

A virtualization maturity adoption model, along with the tools and processes for virtualization management, can provide significant benefits to an organization. The model allows an organization to do the following:

- Improve total cost of ownership (TCO).
  - » Reduce management cost.
  - » Raise asset utilization.
  - » Reap savings from IT optimization.
    - Decrease the number of servers, the amount of storage, and the number of network devices.
    - Decrease the required floor space and environmental factors.
    - Reduce power and cooling requirements.
    - Reduce per-server network and environmental costs.

- Reduce response time.
  - » Reduce the time to provision servers from weeks to hours, and in some cases even minutes.
  - » Enable rapid provisioning of incremental capacity.
  - » Reduce outages due to system maintenance.
  - » Reduce recovery time by dynamically moving resources.
  - » Lower the costs of disaster recovery.
  - » Permit seamless data migration.

- Integrate the enterprise to accommodate business flexibility and future growth.
  - » Accelerate the IT and business integration required as a result of mergers and acquisitions.
  - » Increase growth via global expansion and the addition of new clients.
  - » Marshal resources based on business priorities.
  - » Manage virtual and physical storage pools with a single management console.

Context

This pattern is most useful where organizations need to optimize their steady-state IT standard operations, while managing their virtualized IT infrastructure to generate added value for their stakeholders.

Problem

In several post-virtualization IT environments, organizations have failed to see a positive ROI for their virtualization transformation project within an acceptable timeframe. This is because of their failure to manage the complex lifecycle of virtualized IT environments.

A common reason for this failure is not applying insights and consideration up-front for how virtualization might affect business processes, organizations, and the technologies used to manage the IT environment. Another contributing factor is that organizations fail to proactively adopt the virtualization management model, reference architecture, and appropriate virtualization management toolset. These can provide them the advanced capability to manage the virtualized environments more efficiently than their previous, non-virtualized IT environment.

Although virtualization simplifies the implementation of various complex IT management functions (such as moving workloads across physical machines, disaster recovery, and managing multiple machines through pooling), it also adds another layer of IT management. This layer, like any other needs constant attention from IT staff and management to prevent it from failing or having performance issues. Additionally, even after a virtualization transformation, the IT environment is rarely 100 percent virtualized.

There will always be stand-alone physical servers in the IT environment running non-virtualized workloads because of a number of IT or business constraints. For example, an application vendor might not support their application in a virtualized environment due to performance-degradation concerns. In another example, data privacy and security considerations might necessitate that certain types of workloads be kept on completely isolated physical machines.

You should expect your environment to be a hybrid, comprising both systems that run natively on physical machines and others running on virtual machines. IT management goals should involve creating applications and processes to seamlessly handle the hybrid IT environment.

Selection Guidance

Use this pattern when your organization meets many of the following characteristics:

- Your organization is planning on virtualizing its IT infrastructure.
- You are required to reduce the standard operations costs for your organization's IT.
- You are required to demonstrate productivity gains from virtualization.
- You are developing a virtualization maturity model for your IT environment.
- You are planning to develop a virtualization management architecture at the outset of your virtualization transformation project.
- You need to demonstrate the value that a virtualized IT environment can bring to your organization's stakeholders.
- You are enabling your virtualized IT environment to operate through the use of automated, repeatable, ITIL-aligned processes.

Forces

Virtual IT environments require a different level of care than non-virtualized IT environments. Many organizations move to virtual environments to save money on hardware, energy, and space. Although managers also recognize the potential savings that virtualization enables through easier management and greater availability, most IT organizations are quite set in their ways in terms of how they manage IT resources. IT management rarely focuses proactively on process, technology, and organizational changes that might enable them to exploit the benefits of virtualization in reducing operational expenses over the long term.

Many organizations also fail to take into account the new layer of management responsibilities added by virtualization. Virtual environments pose their own sets of risks and challenges that must be properly managed. Otherwise, any benefits expected from virtualization may easily fade away.

Here are some examples of the management-related challenges of virtualization:

- *Server consolidation*—The number of physical servers might be reduced and capacity utilization improved, resulting in lower physical resource-management costs. However, the complexities of IT systems management might increase significantly. Additional administration tools and skills are required. In addition to learning the basic tools and skills of managing virtualization, for example, the team might need more focused usage monitoring and capacity management for IT resources, if virtual server workloads are unstable or unpredictable.

- *Server provisioning*—New virtual servers may be created in a fraction of the time, and with significantly lower costs, than new physical servers. However, more intensive capacity planning and spare physical server capacity might be required to ensure that workloads do not overload available capacity.

- *System availability*—While planned downtime may be reduced or eliminated for such tasks as hardware maintenance, operating system updates, and patch management, vulnerability to hardware failures might increase. This is because multiple virtual servers can be disabled by the failure of a single physical server. Failover and recovery processes for both hardware and applications might, therefore, become more complex to implement and manage.

- *Backup and recovery*—The costs and time required for backup processes might be reduced because multiple virtual servers may be backed up simultaneously. Also, recovery can be coordinated for multiple system instances. However, administrative complexity might increase, along with the need for network capacity and more expensive backup systems.

- *System security*—While many virtual servers hosted on a single physical server represent a smaller attack profile, a single exploit might affect multiple virtual servers. System patches might be required for virtualization software, as well as operating systems. The overall complexity of security administration increases for a virtualized infrastructure.

- *Storage management*—While virtual servers may be migrated between disk arrays without configuration changes, storage capacity planning and management becomes less predictable. Additional tools, processes, and skills might be required.

Solution

To realize the benefits of virtualization outlined in the "Value Statement" section, and to avoid the types of challenges outlined in the "Forces" section, we employ the following three elements of a plan:

- Virtualization maturity model
- End-to-end services management
- Leveraging of virtualization management tools

Virtualization Maturity Model

As Chapter 1 showed, virtualization goes much further than simply moving systems off their physical hardware and onto a virtualized platform. This fairly mechanical process is the lowest level of thinking about virtualization. Managers and staff must also think on higher, more conceptual levels, such as planning for the migration of entire environments and for apportioning resources to meet business needs. As the staff, technologies, and processes move to higher and higher levels, we can talk about virtualization *maturing*.

We have developed a virtualization maturity model to help us make plans with our clients and get them to the highest available level of maturity. This, in turn, lets them take advantage of the technological advancements, process improvements, and organizational changes and benefits that virtualization offers.

As the maturity of virtualization increases, the services, processes, organization, and technologies evolve in parallel. For example, implementing a new tool often means developing or redesigning a set of processes that use the tool. A new process or service will drive a change in the organizational structure necessary to manage the virtualized infrastructure.

Figure 11.1 shows the four stages of the virtualization maturity model. The horizontal axis of the diagram lists the following four stages, with increasing level of maturity as you move from left to right:

1. *Infrastructure virtualization*—This stage describes physical-to-logical virtualization. This includes technologies such as hypervisors, SANs, virtualized storage, and virtual networking. It also includes hardware consolidation and application stacking. This infrastructure virtualization stage is usually what customers associate with virtualization.
2. *Application virtualization*—As their systems move to virtual platforms, applications should be consolidated and standardized to reuse functionality. Among several industry solutions available, IBM's Websphere Extended Deployment, Grid Computing, and Workload Management are typical tools enabling this move.
3. *IT service virtualization*—On top of the infrastructure and application layers, this level of the model builds a set of IT services that end users invoke in a self-service request model. The key is to offer IT services to customers without exposing the underlying IT specifications. Each IT service should be defined in IT terms, so that the underlying virtualized IT resources can be configured and optimized based on

managing to service levels. Using IT services to abstract underlying technologies gives the IT provider the flexibility to constantly optimize the IT infrastructure.

4. *Business service virtualization*—At this level, currently the highest in the model, services are defined in business terms, so they can be advertised and managed according to business-driven service levels. The customer is not concerned with the underlying IT. An optimized, cost-effective IT infrastructure can be managed through the use of technologies such as policy-based orchestration.

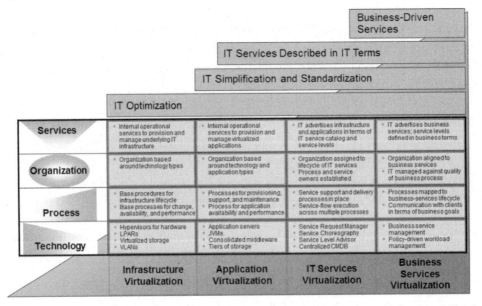

Figure 11.1: In the virtualization maturity model, increasing levels of virtualization enable improved IT delivery to the organization.

This figure also shows how the four levels of maturity view the major building blocks of technology, process, organization, and service. The cells of the diagram suggest different opportunities or areas for improvement that can significantly enhance the value derived from a virtualized IT environment.

Each cell of the virtualization maturity model depicted in the figure demonstrates opportunities for operational cost savings and productivity gains that can be attained by navigating through the model. The cell at the intersection of "Infrastructure Virtualization" and "Technology," for example, covers tasks such as the following:

- Consolidating several standalone server machines onto a single virtualized server machine to reduce hardware, maintenance, power, space, and cooling costs.
- Virtualizing storage subsystems using a technology such as IBM's SAN Volume Controller to combine storage capacity from multiple disk systems into a pool that can be managed more efficiently. This lowers the operational costs for storage management services. (See *www-03.ibm.com/systems/storage/software/virtualization/svc* for more information.)

The cell at the intersection of "Infrastructure Virtualization" and "Service" covers such tasks as automating the provisioning of virtual servers. Such activities can lower the costs of configuring and provisioning servers in response to end-user requests.

The cell at the intersection of "Application Virtualization" and "Technology" covers tasks such as these:

- Consolidating and virtualizing middleware and instances of application servers. This can reduce ongoing operations and management costs.
- Segmenting an organization's storage environment into multiple tiers of storage subsystems, ranging from highly responsive and expensive storage systems at the high end to off-site tape backups and archives at the low end. The use of low-end options allows an organization to lower its existing storage management operations costs, while freeing up capacity on high-end storage systems to accommodate new demands for data.

The cell at the intersection of "Application Virtualization" and "Process" includes new processes to manage high availability and performance stability in virtualized applications. This can reduce operations costs by reducing downtime for servers and applications, time spent on failover and recovery processes, and the costs of reacting to problems in application performance.

The cell at the intersection of "IT Services Virtualization" and "Process" includes changes such as the implementation of a Hardware Resource Management (HRM) service, described in Chapter 9. This can make better use of existing hardware resources and capacity to meet new demands for IT infrastructure, thus reducing the hardware footprint and its associated hardware operations management costs.

The cell at the intersection of "IT Services Virtualization" and "Organization" includes changes such as placing some staff into a Hardware Resource Management (HRM) analyst team, described in Chapter 9. This makes it easier to provide capacity as a service to end users.

The cell at the intersection of "IT Services Virtualization" and "Service" includes changes such as providing a Web application with a service level that defines a minimum level of throughput. Using infrastructure and application virtualization techniques, such Web applications can be hosted on a series of logical partitions. The IT staff can modify the size, type, and location of the underlying virtualized resources to meet the promised service level. As long as the service levels associated with each offered service are not breached, the decisions about which resources support which service are left to the provider.

The cell at the intersection of "Business Services Virtualization" and "Service" includes changes such as implementing business continuity services, organizing the IT services underneath into a policy-based offering. This supports the seamless, non-disruptive movement of operating systems, middleware, and applications to a new site after the failure of a hardware or virtual server, while maintaining the integrity of transactions, data, and end-user experiences.

The cell at the intersection of "Business Services Virtualization" and "Technology" includes such technologies as VMware's VMotion and Distributed Resource Scheduler to move workloads dynamically to another system in support of the business continuity service. This contributes to operations savings, as well as efficient recovery after a disaster or other failure.

We have found that many organizations initially restrict virtualization discussions to the infrastructure phase. During our consulting, we have leveraged the maturity model shown in Figure 11.1 along with virtualization management tools, processes, organizational models, and engagement models to help move our customers through all four of the virtualization phases, particularly in the areas of service management and process work.

You can get a sense of the tools we leverage to support the four phases of maturity at IBM's services management Web site (*www.ibm.com/ibm/servicemanagement*). Additional information detailing the capabilities we have leveraged in services management software is at *www.ibm.com/ibm/servicemanagement/solutions.html*.

End-to-End Services Management

The previous section shows that leveraging the virtualization maturity model can help you identify opportunities for generating increasing levels of benefits. The next step is to organize plans into a framework. One such structure we rely upon extensively is the IBM Service Management Solution™ (ISM) framework, discussed in this section. The ISM framework outlines the underlying capabilities necessary to deliver optimized services and benefits to clients.

Figure 11.2 represents the high-level management capabilities necessary to deliver quality IT services, end-to-end. By having clients consider the end-to-end services management paradigm, we have helped them understand how the service management capabilities can be applied along with their IT infrastructure and virtualization technologies. The latter focus has benefited our clients in terms of very effective management of their virtualized IT environments through the use of automated, repeatable, ITIL-aligned processes.

Figure 11.2: The ISM scoping model.

The goal of leveraging the ISM architecture is to provide the building blocks that enable an organization to make good IT decisions and drive optimum IT service levels. It also encourages more productive and cost-effective behavior through IT automation and self-service capabilities within virtualized IT environments. Figure 11.3 identifies the components within a services-driven infrastructure and how they relate to the capabilities noted in Figure 11.2.

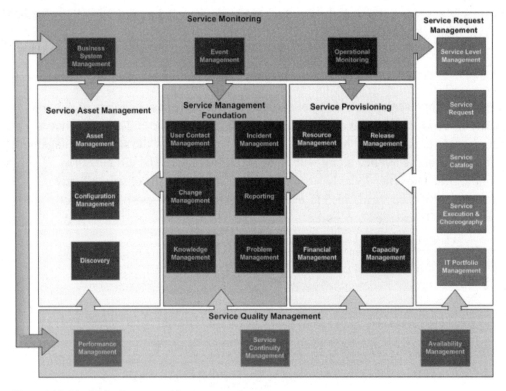

Figure 11.3: The ISM reference architecture overview.

Each of the capabilities depicted in this figure is described further below:

- *Service management foundation*—This capability identifies the fundamental building blocks for deploying the core process systems that will establish consistency and control over the operational IT service environment. Most customers start with this domain in building an integrated service management environment. The foundation building blocks include two of the ITIL service management processes. They are supplemented with the IBM Process Reference Model for IT™ (PRM-IT) to include knowledge management and user contact management. More information about PRM-IT can be found at *www-01.ibm.com/ software/tivoli/governance/servicemanagement/welcome/process_reference.html*.

- *Service request management*—This capability identifies the building blocks for managing the portfolio of IT services, as well as the integration of service authentication, entitlement, and subscription capabilities with an operational IT service catalog for user requests. This capability includes a framework for defining service offering types. These are mapped to a standardized stack of technologies and/or activities within the portfolio and published via the catalog. Managing the service catalog includes the customer view of what services the IT provider offers in support of business processes, business services, and vital business functions, as well as the operational user access to agreed-upon IT services.
- *Service provisioning*—This capability provides the integration of resource capacity allocation (conversion and distribution), metering, billing (including cost allocation), and managing operations that control the behavior of an IT service during use. This capability includes both the technical and business aspects for supporting IT service consumer activities.
- *Service monitoring*—This capability focuses on correlating the performance and availability of a customer's information systems with its business goals. The objective here is to monitor all pieces of infrastructure that support a given business process or activity.
- *Service asset management*—This capability defines an integrated approach to managing configuration and asset information. This capability includes the components required to provide accurate details about the IT environment, which includes the supporting resources (people, applications, infrastructure, and information), as well as the services provided with them. This capability not only includes traditional configuration information, but also the physical location and financial status of all service assets within the enterprise.
- *Service quality management*—This capability establishes the framework for the end-to-end collection of quality metrics, real-time monitoring, and historical reporting of service levels (achievements and breaches). This is required for service assurance, process ownership accountability, and proactive continuous improvement programs.

Now that you have an overview of end-to-end services management capabilities, let's look at the areas where you can leverage commercially available tools to address your virtualization management requirements.

Leveraging Virtualization Management Tools

While managing the challenges of a virtualized environment, our clients still need to execute many of the same management tasks associated with any data center, virtualized or not. Our clients still have to discover and monitor resources, manage the overall storage needs of the organization, provide resource billing and chargeback to their lines of businesses, and so forth. Therefore, management tools now have to be smart enough for a virtualized environment.

Managing virtual systems is a complex undertaking that raises a number of tough questions:

- How will you handle new application provisioning?
- How can you increase server and storage utilization?
- How will you allocate capacity on the fly, as application requirements change?
- How are you going to optimally manage increasing demand for virtual resources?
- What about software license management, metering, and performance management?

Addressing these kinds of questions successfully requires effective tools to visualize, control, and automate the virtual environment.

For many organizations, cost reduction might initially be the primary driver for deploying virtualization. The full value of virtualization, however, comes with being able to master the following management challenges:

- Discover and visualize the physical and virtual environments and their relationships.
- Rapidly provision the virtual environment.
- Optimize the execution and maintenance of workloads.
- Manage virtualized storage efficiently.
- Manage software licensing to ensure cost-effectiveness.
- Allocate IT costs appropriately.
- Keep it all running.

While remaining vendor-agnostic, Table 11.1 lists the tool categories you can leverage to address the above challenges.

Table 11.1: Tools to Leverage Virtualization Management	
If your organization needs to do this:	**Leverage virtualization management tools for this:**
Discover and visualize physical and virtual environments, understand configurations, and map applications and changes.	Discovery and dependency mapping
Rapidly provision the virtual environment.	Provisioning management
Ensure that workloads run on schedule without disruption.	Workload automation
Achieve better storage utilization and standardize management of disparate storage systems.	Storage virtualization
Manage software licensing to ensure compliance and identify opportunities to reduce costs.	License management
Allocate IT costs appropriately, optimizing cost structures and providing visibility into spending.	Usage and accounting management
Keep it all running, meeting availability requirements and optimizing resource utilization.	Monitoring and system automation

For additional information, the appendices at the end of this book list toolsets from two leading virtualization management software vendors, IBM and VMware. We have employed tools from both these vendors successfully to address the virtualization management challenges faced by our clients. Of course, you might choose to evaluate toolsets from other vendors, as well, based on your organization's procurement commitments and preferences.

Summary

This chapter introduced the last of our seven service patterns, Standard Operations. It will assist you in optimizing the costs of managing ongoing standard operations in a virtualized IT environment. In summary, virtualization management standard operations will enable you to do the following:

- Improve the total cost of ownership (TCO) of managing your IT environment (such as reducing the annual server operating expense).

- Develop a virtualization maturity model for your organization.
- Simplify and standardize the IT environment.
- Exploit the capabilities offered by virtualization to achieve desired productivity gains and operational efficiency.
- Increase the agility of IT to respond to business needs.
- Integrate the enterprise for business flexibility and future growth.
- Manage both the virtual and physical IT environment with a single management toolset.

CHAPTER 12

Virtualization Transformation Deployment

T he past seven chapters have described the virtualization patterns. This chapter presents a deployment process that leverages these patterns to achieve a successful virtualization transformation. This deployment process view is especially helpful to project managers responsible for driving an end-to-end virtualization transformation to a successful completion.

As described in Chapter 5, we recommend that an IT virtualization transformation be managed in a phased approach, with the goal of minimizing risk while maximizing ROI. This requires a detailed approach to planning and cost estimates, along with comprehensive program management to set up and achieve planned results. The deployment process follows four well-defined phases: planning, diagnostic, future state design, and implementation.

The following sections outline these four phases. Project managers should use these phases to plan their virtualization transformation deployments. During the design phase, they should apply the appropriate virtualization patterns, based on the context and selection criteria described in the earlier chapters of this book.

The Planning Phase

The planning phase entails the formation of a transformation organization and developing a coherent transformation plan to achieve the objectives of the virtualization. Revamping the IT infrastructure and data center facilities via virtualization transformation can be a very complicated and expensive endeavor. Without careful design, planning, and execution, it can result in unaffordable costs or even disaster.

The virtualization of a large site usually requires a specifically tailored plan that makes the most of efficiencies and cost savings available to that particular site, taking into account the training and expertise of the staff. It also requires firm governance at a high level. Organizations that bypass this planning stage risk failing to generate a positive ROI, due to cost and schedule overruns.

The first step is to define an organizational construct to deploy the transformation. A recommended organization has an executive steering committee, center of excellence (CoE), and a transformation team. The organization starts at the top, with full executive support represented by the executive steering committee. The transformation technical specialists, represented by subject-matter experts on the CoE team, enable, train, verify, and manage the transformation deployment process. The transformation team mostly represents the team responsible for updating and maintaining the environment.

The Executive Steering Committee

An executive steering committee, comprised of senior executives from all stakeholder organizations, should be formed to provide management direction for the entire transformation initiative. The steering committee should represent architecture, operations, development, project office, service desk, procurement, and finance teams at the corporate level. The committee members from each of these organizations are responsible for securing their organization's commitment and buy-in to all decisions and alerting the rest of the steering committee when issues arise.

The decisions of the steering committee should be supported by the company leadership, such the CIO and the CEO. It is key to establish architectural governance and controls around all architecture decisions and have a common measurement system to influence various technical teams.

The Center of Excellence (CoE)

The purpose of the CoE is to provide subject-matter expertise and competence on how the transformation is conducted. CoE members are technical leaders in various areas of the transformation process. They have the skills necessary to perform and manage various aspects of a successful transformation. They develop the training material and manage the overall transformation. The training includes guidelines on how to perform the various transformation phases. They also provide reference designs and templates for common and repeatable parts of the transformation process.

The CoE members train the transformation team, review their deliverables, and determine if a phase's exit criteria is met before entering the next phase. This team also conducts the checkpoint reviews and provides recommendations on how the transformation should proceed. CoE members provide guidance and recommendations to the steering committee on detailed technical matters of the transformation. They function as the technical link between the transformation team and the executive steering committee.

The CoE may also shoulder an additional responsibility of supporting the various OS transformations in the virtual environment. Some CoEs could be responsible for taking the application code from the source environment and making the code changes needed to run the application in the target environment, with the new OS and third-party components. The CoE also performs system testing on the migrated application, to verify its operations in the target environment.

By concentrating OS and third-party software expertise in the CoE structure, you ensure continuity and retention of knowledge and experience, as well as the reuse of tools and other assets.

The Transformation Team

The transformation team is a representative sample of the operational teams that run the environment. This team has the technical expertise and details of the environment's complexities and constraints, which helps determine if the virtualization is optimized. The transformation team is led by the *change agent* role, which is given to an influential individual by the organization. The change agent is responsible for making the transformation successful. After the transformation is complete, this team is responsible for maintaining and updating the transformed environment to minimize the deployment of any non-compliant systems.

Prior to each phase, the CoE trains the transformation team on how to perform their transformation duties and how to achieve the phase deliverables. The transformation team is primarily responsible for executing the transformation as instructed by the CoE. The transformation team follows the project plan approved by the steering committee and executes the transformation process developed by the CoE. If an IT service provider is retained by an organization to assist with the virtualization transformation initiative, the service provider must also be trained on the methodology, to complement the internal transformation teams.

Establishing a small project team, or simply gathering a few key leads from each area, might work well when the transformation initiative is small and where the teams are already tightly integrated. In a more complex situation, a more integrated team is required to achieve the task. Examples of complications include the operation teams not having a common management structure below the senior executive level, or having multiple business units, each involved with its own priorities.

The Wave Plan

A large transformation that includes multiple organizations, multiple data centers, or multiple locations cannot be done in one step. It must be segmented into multiple well-defined projects and performed in stages or waves.

The Segmenting Complexity pattern in Chapter 6 shows how to break down the transformation into projects of compatible complexities and develop a project plan to execute these projects. This allows managing and allocating the available resources to support the transformation objectives.

The scope of each project is determined by examining a number of business and technical variables and objectives. It is managed as an independent end-to-end project, governed by rigorous project management. Each project contributes to the efficiency and progress of the organization as the virtualization transformation continues.

The different projects are grouped together to be executed over a period of time. Each group of projects that follow a similar time line is bundled together into a wave. The organization can define a reasonable timeframe for the waves. This structure ensures that each phase within a wave is completed before proceeding. It also applies enough pressure on the various teams to stay in synch.

Each wave follows the standard four-phase approach of planning, diagnostic, future state design, and implementation shown in Figure 12.1. At the end of each phase, the CoE formally reviews the deliverables of that phase to ensure that the transformation team is ready to proceed to the next phase.

After the wave plan is complete, the wave execution starts with a kick-off meeting, to train the transformation team on performing the diagnostic phase. The diagnostic phase ends with the checkpoint review and training on future state design. Similarly, the future-state design ends with a checkpoint review and training on implementation. The wave ends with the checkpoint review of the implementation phase. This concludes the wave implementation accomplishments.

After a wave is complete, best practices and things to avoid should be documented, to enhance the success of the next wave. Also, any part of the plan that is not completed within the wave should be documented in a follow-up plan, to be completed later.

To leverage the skills acquired within the wave and minimize the training requirements, some of the transformation team should be applied to the next wave. Also, future wave resources could be included in earlier waves, to expedite the application of the best practices.

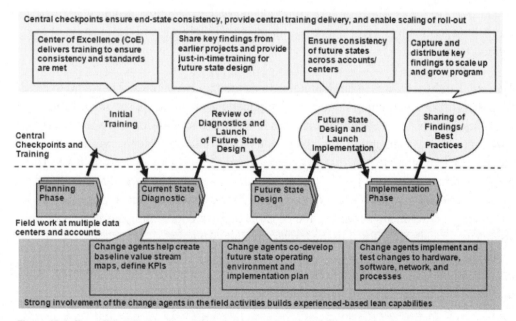

Figure 12.1: Formalizing the lean transformation approach to build virtualization capabilities.

The Diagnostic Phase

The diagnostic phase endeavors to identify the current state. The output of this phase consists of all key areas of the environment, such as accounts, user requirements, and the data center's assets of hardware, software, network, storage, applications, and personnel. It includes all dependencies between all the components of the environment. It is essential for all components to be included in the analysis; otherwise, there is a risk that something is not accounted for in the next phase.

At the start of the diagnostic phase, the CoE staff trains the transformation team on how to perform the diagnostics. The transformation team members must attend this training. The training covers the concepts of how to determine the current state, which is how the environment works today. The training should include specific exercises to get a good understanding of how to achieve the deliverables of the diagnostic phase.

It is common for the current state to consist of a heterogeneous environment. For example, some of the hardware resources might be located in data centers while others are scattered, some might use legacy technologies while others use the latest high-performance technology, and all might be on different platforms. It is critical to identify all attributes of the IT infrastructure components, such as location, installed applications, capabilities, criticality, performance requirements, availability, and the location of the support team.

Typical IT infrastructures in large organizations are highly complex. They tend to have thousands of servers running hundreds of applications on a diverse set of hardware, operating systems, COTS components, and homegrown applications, in a multi-vendor, multi-version environment. In this phase, you have to examine each server to determine its viability to migrate to a virtual environment and the best way to accomplish it. To complete this task for each server, technical staff must assess its hardware, operating systems, applications, linkages to other servers, storage systems, and applications in its existing environment, as well as the possible hardware, operating systems, and applications available offered in the transformed environment.

As the current state is being identified, all the wastes also need to be documented, as discussed in Chapter 3. Later, in the future state, lean levers determined by the seven service patterns are applied to eliminate these wastes. The future state design should have these wastes minimized.

The deliverables of the diagnostic phase are reviewed and approved by the CoE at the diagnostic review checkpoint. Any gaps identified must be addressed with corrective actions prior to proceeding to the next phase. The checkpoint review process functions as a best practice sharing opportunity among the transformation teams.

The Future State Design Phase

The future state design (FSD) phase determines the desired future state and the transformation path from the current state to the desired state. You have to factor in all of the current environment variables, such as requirements, future growth, constraints, and customer needs. The design will specify important new environment parameters, such as hardware and software application configurations, technologies, performance, cost, and location. In addition, migration plans must take into account such business considerations as how critical each application is to the functioning of the organization.

The transformation team carefully examines all transformation options that apply to each component in the current state, for consideration in the future state design. The seven service patterns (discussed starting in Chapter 5) are applied to remove the waste and optimize the transformation. They represent the preferred method for the transformation process. The transformation team follows specific guidelines and reference designs developed by the CoE, guided by these service patterns.

The deliverables of the FSD phase are reviewed and approved by the CoE at the review checkpoint. The FSD exit criteria must be met before proceeding to the implementation phase.

The Implementation Phase

A detailed implementation project plan must be developed, with clear tasks, schedules, and entry and exit criteria.

Although there are many possible approaches to implement the FSD, we'll review two primary options here: the Big Bang and the Prove-and-Grow, both shown in Figure 12.2. In the Big Bang approach, all of the transformation is implemented at once. Prove-and-Grow is a phased approach, aimed at minimizing the risk in large transformations.

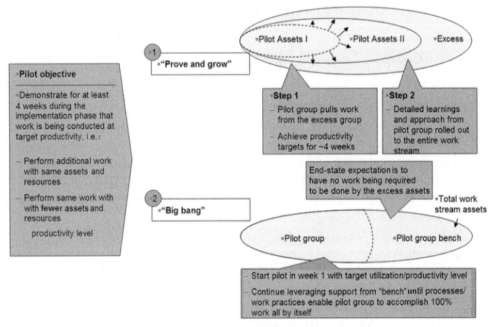

Figure 12.2: Two fundamentally different approaches to implementation.

The implementation must be tested for several weeks to verify its capability to support the steady-state environment. Different performance levels and seasonal variations should be tested, to demonstrate that capability.

The deliverables of the implementation phase are reviewed and approved by the CoE at the review checkpoint. The implementation phase exit criteria must be met before the wave is considered complete.

The Big Bang (Lift-and-Load) Approach

In Big Bang, the transition from the current state to the future state is done in a single step. The new environment goes live, and the old environment is disabled. The transition is abrupt.

Big Bang works well for small projects that have lower risk. For this approach to be successful, the team must have high confidence in the FSD, as well as a backup plan if an unexpected outcome is encountered. This approach is simple and provides immediate benefits of the transformation.

This approach is considered when major parts of the environment are being migrated to the transformed environment with minimum replacement and the reuse of the operating systems. For instance, the virtual environment might use the same hardware and operating system as the original. If the platform remains the same, the migration can be a Big Bang approach, where the original binary runs on the new server. As mentioned in previous chapters, testing must be done to verify the migration of code binary.

This approach can also be considered when a major part of the environment is being replaced with new systems, and the old systems will be deactivated.

The Prove-and-Grow Approach

In the implementation phase, the environment can be segmented into different groupings with compatible complexities and challenges. This allows you to transform one group at a time and grow the transformed content gradually. Move to the next group once the first group transformation is operating satisfactorily and any unexpected issues are resolved. The transition must be transparent to the customer, with minimum service disruption; therefore, the new design must be tested prior to going live. The transformation must be planned and staged perfectly.

In the Prove-and-Grow approach (also called "Refresh-and-Build"), the transformation is divided into multiple stages. The next stage starts once the current stage is demonstrated and the objectives are realized. Each stage has a well-defined entry and exit criteria. The functionality of the current stage must be proved before growing in the next stage.

This method allows a smooth transition of parts of the environment to the future state design. It gives the benefits of virtualization while preparations continue for the next stage. Fine-tuning the current stage proceeds until the target function and performance levels are achieved. The learning from the current stage is incorporated into the next stage, to avoid repeating a mistake.

The Prove-and-Grow approach leads to a robust implementation plan with a reasonable schedule. The plan mitigates risks to scope, schedule, and costs, while providing the foundation for managing the implementation in phases.

Summary

This chapter described how to deploy the virtualization transformation in four phases: planning, diagnostic, future state design, and implementation. The planning stage includes the organization of a steering committee, center of excellence, and transformation teams and the creation of a wave plan. In the diagnostic phase, you uncover the way the current state works and design the desired virtualized state. In the future state design, you apply one or more of the seven virtualization patterns, based on the context and selection criteria described for each pattern in the earlier chapters of this book. The future design is put into action in the implementation phase, using either the Big Bang method or the Prove-and-Grow method.

Developing the Business Case for Virtualization

Despite the broadly published and generally acknowledged benefits of IT infrastructure virtualization, virtualization projects that do not have compelling business cases are not likely to be funded. Virtualization projects with business cases developed solely on technical considerations, likewise, frequently lose their funding when "hidden" or underestimated costs begin to appear during project execution.

Most technical staff members are not experts in business case development, and their high-level financial justifications frequently miss or mishandle critical areas of both costs and savings related to IT infrastructure virtualization. We recommend that IT staff members always consult with their finance organization to develop a business case for virtualization. This helps ensure that the financial analysis for a virtualization project accurately depicts the financial benefits of moving to the target virtualized platform. Such a business case must properly take into consideration migration costs, operations costs, cost savings, avoidance factors, and cash flows—all properly distributed over time.

This chapter provides you with the essentials for building a virtualization business case. Use this information to help demonstrate the financial returns that your virtualization project can bring to your organizational stakeholders. We again remind you to consult with your finance team, however, to validate your business plan before reviewing it with your project sponsors.

Business Case Fundamentals

Business investments are not made on impulse, the way you might buy a music CD. They are also not made to give personal satisfaction, the way you might buy a vacation. Business investments are made to provide stakeholders with a return on their investment—and not just any return, but a return greater than what they could make elsewhere. A business case is a systematic way to determine whether to proceed with an investment, or which of several alternative projects to select. Business cases can be made to judge whether it would be beneficial to move into a new line of business, for example. Within an existing activity, a business case might help decide if it makes sense to, for example, replace an old machine with a new one.

To demonstrate the concepts of building a business case, we present several in this chapter. You'll read about simple cases first, to learn the typical components of a business case. Then, we will move on to business cases for virtualization.

Example 1: Investment in a New Line of Business

Suppose someone is thinking about starting a business to make hats. This person believes he can sell 6,000 hats per year, at $100 per hat. From his research, he determines the following:

- The cost of machinery is a $500,000 one-time cost. The tax authority allows depreciation over five years.
- Maintenance of the machinery is zero in the first year because of the included manufacturer's warranty. Thereafter, it is $40,000 per year.
- Materials cost $150,000 per year.
- Labor costs $220,000 in the first year to set up the business. Thereafter, it is $200,000 per year.
- Rent is $30,000 per year.
- Electricity is $10,000 per year.
- Advertising and general expenses are $30,000 in the first year. Thereafter, these expenses are $20,000 per year.

If, instead of starting a hat business, he invests his money in the bank, he can generate a return of 6 percent. The tax rate on company earnings is 30 percent.

Should he go ahead with the investment? The business case looks like Figure 13.1. The section from row 3 to row 13 determines the tax to be paid. Rows 15 to 25 provide the after-tax cash flows. Finally, the section from row 27 to row 31 shows the decision criteria. (Within the business case, from the perspective of the investor, negative numbers mean payments and positive numbers mean receipts.)

row	Case 1	Business Case - Base Case					
1		Year		1	2	3	4	5
2								
3	Tax to pay	Revenue: 6000 hats @ $100/hat		600,000	600,000	600,000	600,000	600,000
4		Depreciation		-100,000	-100,000	-100,000	-100,000	-100,000
5		Maintenance		0	-40,000	-40,000	-40,000	-40,000
6		Materials		-150,000	-150,000	-150,000	-150,000	-150,000
7		Labor		-220,000	-200,000	-200,000	-200,000	-200,000
8		Rent		-30,000	-30,000	-30,000	-30,000	-30,000
9		Electricity		-10,000	-10,000	-10,000	-10,000	-10,000
10		Advertising and general expenses		-30,000	-20,000	-20,000	-20,000	-20,000
11		Basis of taxation		60,000	50,000	50,000	50,000	50,000
12		Tax rate	30%					
13		Tax to pay		-18,000	-15,000	-15,000	-15,000	-15,000
14								
15	After tax cash flow	Revenue: 6000 hats @ $100/hat		600,000	600,000	600,000	600,000	600,000
16		Capital expenditure		-500,000	0	0	0	0
17		Tax		-18,000	-15,000	-15,000	-15,000	-15,000
18		Maintenance		0	-40,000	-40,000	-40,000	-40,000
19		Materials		-150,000	-150,000	-150,000	-150,000	-150,000
20		Labor		-220,000	-200,000	-200,000	-200,000	-200,000
21		Rent		-30,000	-30,000	-30,000	-30,000	-30,000
22		Electricity		-10,000	-10,000	-10,000	-10,000	-10,000
23		Advertising and general expenses		-30,000	-20,000	-20,000	-20,000	-20,000
24		After tax cash flow		-358,000	135,000	135,000	135,000	135,000
25		Cumulative cash flow		-358,000	-223,000	-88,000	47,000	182,000
26								
27	Decision criteria	Discount rate	6%					
28		Discounted cash flow		-358,000	127,358	120,150	113,349	106,933
29								
30		Net Present Value	109,789					
31		Breakeven in years	3.7					

Figure 13.1: The business case for a hat-making business.

Row 13 shows the tax to be paid in each year. This is positive in year 1, indicating that the business owner gets a rebate. Row 4 shows how the $500,000 cash cost of the machine is depreciated over five years, at $100,000 per year. The depreciation schedule is determined by the tax authority, according to the type of equipment. The cost of the machine is depreciated to even out the company's tax payments. Suppose, for the tax calculation, we used the full $500,000 cost in year 1 (and nothing in years 2 to 5). The tax rebate in year 1 would be much higher, but so would the tax payments in years 2 to 5. This would mean big swings in the receipts of the tax authority and big swings in the payments made by companies. To smooth things out, it is typical for major investments to be depreciated.

Row 27 shows the discount rate, which is what the business owner could earn if he invested his money elsewhere. In this case, the discount rate is 6 percent per year. Row 28 takes the after-tax cash flows from row 24 and discounts them at 6 percent per year, to give the discounted cash flows expressed at their present value.

What does *present value* mean? If the businessman in this scenario put money in the bank on day 1, then after a year, he would have 6 percent more. So, $100 is worth $106 after one year, and $112.36 after two years. Looked at the other way, if you know you will have $106 in one year, and the interest rate is 6 percent, then if you divide (discount) $106 by 1.06, you can calculate that the present value is $100. This is shown on row 28 of the business case, which calculates the discounted after-tax cash flows, i.e., the cash flows at their present value. We assume the payments and receipts are made at the start of each year.

For year 1, we do not discount. If the payments and receipts are made at the start of the year, then they are at their present value. The discounted cash flow for year 1 on row 28 equals the non-discounted cash flow for year 1 on row 24. For year 2, the payments and receipts are made at the start of year 2, which is one year from today. So, these must be discounted by 1.06. For year 3, the payments and receipts are made at the start of year 3, which is two years from today. So, these must be discounted by 1.06 to the power of two.

Rather than assuming all payments and receipts occur at the start of each year, we could make a calculation showing the monthly cash flows and record exactly when they take place. The concepts would be the same, but clearly, the table would be much bigger. Usually, this level of detail is not required, and annual cash flows suffice. Another refinement would be to change when payments and receipts occur during the year. For example, we could assume payments are made at the start of the year and receipts at the end, or that all payments and receipts occur in the middle of each year. To keep things simple, however, we assume all payments and receipts occur at the start of each year.

Row 30 adds up the discounted cash flows (i.e., the present values) from row 28. Row 30 is labeled "Net Present Value" to reflect that it is the sum of both the positive and the negative cash flows. Row 30 shows a positive net present value (NPV) of $109,789. This means that the business owner should go ahead with the investment, because he will earn this much more over five years, after tax (expressed in present value), than if he invested his money in the bank at 6 percent.

Row 31 shows the time to break even. This is when the cumulative non-discounted cash flows on row 25 turn from negative to positive, which in this case is after 3.7 years. So, the owner would have to wait 3.7 years to recover his investment.

How do you use the time to break even to help decide whether to go ahead with an investment? Use it to think about the risk of whether you will recover an investment.

Let's consider a different example. Suppose you were thinking about building a bridge over a large river. Your income will come from charging vehicles a toll for driving over the bridge. In this case, 3.7 years is not a very long time. Also, there is little chance that, in the next 3.7 years, someone else will build a competing bridge, taking customers away. In this case, a breakeven time of 25 years might be acceptable.

When thinking about making hats, however, 25 years is an unacceptable breakeven time. A small company would not be able to finance itself for that long before recovering its costs. Also, who knows what would happen in the hat market over such a long time? Fashions would change, and competitors would enter the market. For a small company, even 3.7 years might be a little long to break even.

To summarize, the NPV tells you if a project delivers a better return than investing elsewhere. The time to breakeven tells you about the risk associated with recovering an investment. The further into the future it is, the more uncertainty there is about what will happen in the market.

Now, let's consider case 2. Suppose that the businessperson from case 1 could earn a 20 percent return elsewhere, instead of 6 percent. Should he start making hats or take the alternative investment?

As shown in Figure 13.2, the information from row 1 to row 26 is the same as the previous case. The new discount rate is 20 percent, shown on row 27. The present value of the discounted cash flows is on row 28. The sum of the discounted cash flows gives the net present value on row 30.

row				1	2	3	4	5
	Case 2	Business Case with higher Discount Rate						
1		Year		1	2	3	4	5
2								
3	Tax to pay	Revenue: 6000 hats @ $100/hat		600,000	600,000	600,000	600,000	600,000
4		Depreciation		-100,000	-100,000	-100,000	-100,000	-100,000
5		Maintenance		0	-40,000	-40,000	-40,000	-40,000
6		Materials		-150,000	-150,000	-150,000	-150,000	-150,000
7		Labor		-220,000	-200,000	-200,000	-200,000	-200,000
8		Rent		-30,000	-30,000	-30,000	-30,000	-30,000
9		Electricity		-10,000	-10,000	-10,000	-10,000	-10,000
10		Advertising and general expenses		-30,000	-20,000	-20,000	-20,000	-20,000
11		Basis of taxation		60,000	50,000	50,000	50,000	50,000
12		Tax rate	30%					
13		Tax to pay		-18,000	-15,000	-15,000	-15,000	-15,000
14								
15	After tax cash flow	Revenue: 6000 hats @ $100/hat		600,000	600,000	600,000	600,000	600,000
16		Capital expenditure		-500,000	0	0	0	0
17		Tax		-18,000	-15,000	-15,000	-15,000	-15,000
18		Maintenance		0	-40,000	-40,000	-40,000	-40,000
19		Materials		-150,000	-150,000	-150,000	-150,000	-150,000
20		Labor		-220,000	-200,000	-200,000	-200,000	-200,000
21		Rent		-30,000	-30,000	-30,000	-30,000	-30,000
22		Electricity		-10,000	-10,000	-10,000	-10,000	-10,000
23		Advertising and general expenses		-30,000	-20,000	-20,000	-20,000	-20,000
24		After tax cash flow		-358,000	135,000	135,000	135,000	135,000
25		Cumulative cash flow		-358,000	-223,000	-88,000	47,000	182,000
26								
27	Decision criteria	Discount rate	20%					
28		Discounted cash flow		-358,000	112,500	93,750	78,125	65,104
29								
30		Net Present Value	-8,521					
31		Breakeven in years	3.7					

Figure 13.2: The same basic case as Figure 13.1, with a different discount rate.

This time, the net present value is negative. This means it would be better for the person not to undertake this investment, but to go for the alternative, paying 20 percent. The breakeven is the same, as this is calculated from the non-discounted cash flows, which have not changed. In this case, the knock-out criteria is the negative NPV. We do not need to consider this investment any further.

Example 2: Investment in a New Machine

Assume you have been in business making hats for some time, and you are considering replacing your machine with a new one. How do you make a business case to determine whether to buy a new machine or continue with the old one?

First, consider the business case for buying a new machine, shown in Figure 13.3. Row 1 shows the evaluation starting at year 5 because you have already been in business with the old machine for four years. Revenue, in row 3, remains the same, indicating that the new machine will make the same number of hats per year as the old one. The cost of the new machine is $300,000, shown on row 17. As before, this amount is depreciated over five years (row 4).

Case 3	Business Case for New Machine						
row							
1	Year		5	6	7	8	9
2							
3	Tax to pay	Revenue: 6000 hats @ $100/hat	600,000	600,000	600,000	600,000	600,000
4		Depreciation	-60,000	-60,000	-60,000	-60,000	-60,000
5		Write-off book value	-100,000	0	0	0	0
6		Maintenance	0	-20,000	-20,000	-20,000	-20,000
7		Materials	-130,000	-130,000	-130,000	-130,000	-130,000
8		Labor	-200,000	-200,000	-200,000	-200,000	-200,000
9		Rent	-30,000	-30,000	-30,000	-30,000	-30,000
10		Electricity	-7,000	-7,000	-7,000	-7,000	-7,000
11		Advertising and general expenses	-20,000	-20,000	-20,000	-20,000	-20,000
12		Basis of taxation	53,000	133,000	133,000	133,000	133,000
13		Tax rate	30%				
14		Tax to pay	-15,900	-39,900	-39,900	-39,900	-39,900
15							
16	After tax cash flow	Revenue: 6000 hats @ $100/hat	600,000	600,000	600,000	600,000	600,000
17		Capital expenditure	-300,000	0	0	0	0
18		Tax	-15,900	-39,900	-39,900	-39,900	-39,900
19		Maintenance	0	-20,000	-20,000	-20,000	-20,000
20		Materials	-130,000	-130,000	-130,000	-130,000	-130,000
21		Labor	-200,000	-200,000	-200,000	-200,000	-200,000
22		Rent	-30,000	-30,000	-30,000	-30,000	-30,000
23		Electricity	-7,000	-7,000	-7,000	-7,000	-7,000
24		Advertising and general expenses	-20,000	-20,000	-20,000	-20,000	-20,000
25		After tax cash flow	-102,900	153,100	153,100	153,100	153,100
26		Cumulative cash flow	-102,900	50,200	203,300	356,400	509,500
27							
28	Decision criteria	Discount rate	6%				
29		Discounted cash flow	-102,900	144,434	136,258	128,546	121,270
30							
31		Net Present Value	427,608				
32		Breakeven in years	1.7				

Figure 13.3: A business case for buying new equipment.

Because only four years have passed since you bought the old machine, and the value is depreciated over five years, only four-fifths of the purchase price of $500,000 has been depreciated away. This means that a "book value" of $100,000 remains. If you scrap the old machine, this book value must be written off, which is what happens in row 5. Writing off book value is not a use of cash, but it does affect the tax you pay, just like depreciation. For this reason, the write-off appears in the upper part of the table, in the "Tax to pay" section, but not in the lower part of the table ("After tax cash flow").

Maintenance of the new machine is included in the warranty for the first year. Thereafter, it costs $20,000 per year, as shown in row 6. The new machine uses materials more efficiently, allowing a reduction in the cost of materials to $130,000 per year (row 7). Costs of labor, rent, advertising, and general expenses are unchanged from the first case, but the lower electricity consumption of the new machine is shown on row 10.

With the discount rate of 6 percent, the NPV is $427,608, and the time to breakeven is 1.7 years. Next, you need to compare this result with the business case for continuing to use the old machine. This is shown in Figure 13.4.

row	Case 4	Business Case for Old Machine		5	6	7	8	9
1		Year		5	6	7	8	9
2								
3	Tax to pay	Revenue: 6000 hats @ $100/hat		600,000	600,000	600,000	600,000	600,000
4		Depreciation		-100,000	0	0	0	0
5		Write-off book value		0	0	0	0	0
6		Maintenance		-40,000	-100,000	-120,000	-140,000	-160,000
7		Materials		-150,000	-150,000	-150,000	-150,000	-15,000
8		Labor		-200,000	-200,000	-200,000	-200,000	-200,000
9		Rent		-30,000	-30,000	-30,000	-30,000	-30,000
10		Electricity		-10,000	-10,000	-10,000	-10,000	-10,000
11		Advertising and general expenses		-20,000	-20,000	-20,000	-20,000	-20,000
12		Basis of taxation		50,000	90,000	70,000	50,000	165,000
13		Tax rate	30%					
14		Tax to pay		-15,000	-27,000	-21,000	-15,000	-49,500
15								
16	After tax cash flow	Revenue: 6000 hats @ $100/hat		600,000	600,000	600,000	600,000	600,000
17		Capital expenditure		0	0	0	0	0
18		Tax		-15,000	-27,000	-21,000	-15,000	-49,500
19		Maintenance		-40,000	-100,000	-120,000	-140,000	-160,000
20		Materials		-150,000	-150,000	-150,000	-150,000	-15,000
21		Labor		-200,000	-200,000	-200,000	-200,000	-200,000
22		Rent		-30,000	-30,000	-30,000	-30,000	-30,000
23		Electricity		-10,000	-10,000	-10,000	-10,000	-10,000
24		Advertising and general expenses		-20,000	-20,000	-20,000	-20,000	-20,000
25		After tax cash flow		135,000	63,000	49,000	35,000	115,500
26		Cumulative cash flow		135,000	198,000	247,000	282,000	397,500
27								
28	Decision criteria	Discount rate	6%					
29		Discounted cash flow		135,000	59,434	43,610	29,387	91,487
30								
31		Net Present Value	358,917					
32		Breakeven in years	<1					

Figure 13.4: A business case for continuing to use old equipment.

In this case, you keep the old machine, which becomes fully depreciated in year 5, as shown in row 4. Maintenance of the old machine becomes progressively more expensive as the machine gets older (row 6). Other costs remain unchanged from the previous case.

The outcome is a net present value of $358,917. Actually, you could just call it the "present value" because all the discounted cash flows on row 29 are positive, so there is no netting of negative and positive numbers. For this reason, the breakeven is less than one year.

You can now compare the cases in Figures 13.3 and 13.4 to make a decision. The higher NPV of the case in Figure 13.3 indicates that you should buy the new machine, not carry on with the old one.

If you wanted to, you could also make a "delta business case," as shown in Figure 13.5. Here, each row considers the difference between the two cases. The delta NPV of $68,690 on row 31 is the difference between the NPVs of the cases in Figure 13.3 and 13.4, respectively: $427,608 minus $358,917, which equals $68,690.

row	Case 5	Delta Business Case for New Machine versus Old					
1		Year		5	6	7	8	9
2								
3	Tax to pay	delta Revenue		0	0	0	0	0
4		delta Depreciation		40,000	-60,000	-60,000	-60,000	-60,000
5		delta Write-off book value		-100,000	0	0	0	0
6		delta Maintenance		40,000	80,000	100,000	120,000	140,000
7		delta Materials		20,000	20,000	20,000	20,000	-115,000
8		delta Labor		0	0	0	0	0
9		delta Rent		0	0	0	0	0
10		delta Electricity		3,000	3,000	3,000	3,000	3,000
11		delta Advertising and general exp		0	0	0	0	0
12		delta Basis of taxation		3,000	43,000	63,000	83,000	-32,000
13		Tax rate	30%					
14		delta Tax to pay		-900	-12,900	-18,900	-24,900	9,600
15								
16	After tax cash flow	delta Revenue		0	0	0	0	0
17		delta Capital expenditure		-300,000	0	0	0	0
18		delta Tax		-900	-12,900	-18,900	-24,900	9,600
19		delta Maintenance		40,000	80,000	100,000	120,000	140,000
20		delta Materials		20,000	20,000	20,000	20,000	-115,000
21		delta Labor		0	0	0	0	0
22		delta Rent		0	0	0	0	0
23		delta Electricity		3,000	3,000	3,000	3,000	3,000
24		delta Advertising and general exp.		0	0	0	0	0
25		delta After tax cash flow		-237,900	90,100	104,100	118,100	37,600
26		delta Cumulative cash flow		-237,900	-147,800	-43,700	74,400	112,000
27								
28	Decision criteria	Discount rate	6%					
29		delta Discounted cash flow		-237,900	85,000	92,649	99,159	29,783
30								
31		delta Net Present Value	68,690					

Figure 13.5: A delta business case.

When making a delta business case, it is critical to remain consistent. Always think about "case 1 minus case 2" or "case 4 minus case 3," but never mix these up. For this reason, it might be safer to avoid delta business cases.

Example 3: Lease or Buy

Let's consider one last situation to complete the examples of simple business cases. What happens if you lease the machine, instead of buying it? Assume everything is as per the original case in Figure 13.1, and you are deciding whether to start making hats. Instead of buying the machine, however, you would lease it. The details of this case are shown in Figure 13.6.

row	Case 6	Business Case for Lease		1	2	3	4	5
1		Year		1	2	3	4	5
2								
3	Tax to pay	Revenue: 6000 hats @ $100/hat		600,000	600,000	600,000	600,000	600,000
4		Lease		-140,000	-140,000	-140,000	-140,000	0
5		Maintenance		0	-40,000	-40,000	-40,000	-40,000
6		Materials		-150,000	-150,000	-150,000	-150,000	-150,000
7		Labor		-220,000	-200,000	-200,000	-200,000	-200,000
8		Rent		-30,000	-30,000	-30,000	-30,000	-30,000
9		Electricity		-10,000	-10,000	-10,000	-10,000	-10,000
10		Advertising and general expenses		-30,000	-20,000	-20,000	-20,000	-20,000
11		Basis of taxation		20,000	10,000	10,000	10,000	150,000
12		Tax rate	30%					
13		Tax to pay		-6,000	-3,000	-3,000	-3,000	-45,000
14								
15	After tax cash flow	Revenue: 6000 hats @ $100/hat		600,000	600,000	600,000	600,000	600,000
16		Lease		-140,000	-140,000	-140,000	-140,000	0
17		Tax		-6,000	-3,000	-3,000	-3,000	-45,000
18		Maintenance		0	-40,000	-40,000	-40,000	-40,000
19		Materials		-150,000	-150,000	-150,000	-150,000	-150,000
20		Labor		-220,000	-200,000	-200,000	-200,000	-200,000
21		Rent		-30,000	-30,000	-30,000	-30,000	-30,000
22		Electricity		-10,000	-10,000	-10,000	-10,000	-10,000
23		Advertising and general expenses		-30,000	-20,000	-20,000	-20,000	-20,000
24		After tax cash flow		14,000	7,000	7,000	7,000	105,000
25		Cumulative cash flow		14,000	21,000	28,000	35,000	140,000
26								
27	Decision criteria	Discount rate	6%					
28		Discounted cash flow		14,000	6,604	6,230	5,877	83,170
29								
30		Net Present Value	115,881					
31		Breakeven in years	<1					

Figure 13.6: A business case for leasing equipment.

You will probably be able to negotiate the duration of the lease with the lease provider, which will typically be either a bank or the manufacturer of the machine. Assume you decide to lease the machine over four years, perhaps because you believe, after that time, a new machine will become available.

Instead of a purchase price of $500,000, lease payments of $140,000 per year for four years are shown on row 4. The total lease cost of $560,000 includes interest payments to the provider of the lease (the lessor). The interest is to compensate the lessor for effectively buying the machine on day 1 and giving it to you. In this case, the effective annual interest rate of the lease is 4.7 percent. (The mathematics of determining this is beyond our scope.)

The outcome of the business case is that compared with the case in Figure 13.1, the NPV is higher, and the time to breakeven is lower. Both indicate that in this situation, you should lease rather than buy the machine.

Why is this? If you buy the machine, you have to pay a large sum of money on day 1, namely $500,000. If you lease, you only pay $140,000 on day 1. You can keep the rest earning interest at 6 percent annually. A year later, you make another payment of $140,000, but you have earned 6 percent interest on the $360,000 invested for a year, which is $21,600. With the lease, you are effectively borrowing money at 4.7 percent and investing it at 6 percent. In this situation, it makes sense to take advantage of the lower cost of financing.

Now that we have looked at simple examples to understand the concepts of the business case methodology, let's move on to examples for virtualization.

Business Cases for Virtualization

Assume a subset of servers in one data center (referenced in the client scenario of Chapter 6). These are non-virtualized servers that have almost reached the ends of their lives. You can either replace them with 20 virtualized servers with an average of six images per server or replace them with 120 non-virtualized servers. The key cost elements are hardware, hardware maintenance, software, data center space, utilities, operating labor, transition, and installation.

Let's start by looking at the option in which you use virtualized servers. This is shown in Figure 13.7.

row	Case 7	Business Case for Virtualization					
1		Year	1	2	3	4	5
2							
3	Tax to pay	Revenue	5,000,000	5,000,000	5,000,000	5,000,000	5,000,000
4		Depreciation	-400,000	-400,000	-400,000	-400,000	-400,000
5		Write-off book value	-65,000	0	0	0	0
6		Sale of old machines	35,000	0	0	0	0
7		Maintenance	-170,000	-170,000	-170,000	-170,000	-170,000
8		Operating Labor	-360,000	-360,000	-360,000	-360,000	-360,000
9		Transition Cost	-900,000	0	0	0	0
10		Installation	-400,000	0	0	0	0
11		Software (op. systems & apps.)	-700,000	-700,000	-700,000	-700,000	-700,000
12		Power, cooling, DC space	-400,000	-400,000	-400,000	-400,000	-400,000
15		Penalties for SLA misses	0	0	0	0	0
16		Basis of taxation	1,640,000	2,970,000	2,970,000	2,970,000	2,970,000
17		Tax rate	28%				
18		Tax to pay	-459,200	-831,600	-831,600	-831,600	-831,600
19							
20	After tax cash flow	Revenue	5,000,000	5,000,000	5,000,000	5,000,000	5,000,000
21		Capital expenditure	-2,000,000	0	0	0	0
22		Tax	-459,200	-831,600	-831,600	-831,600	-831,600
23		Sale of old machines	35,000	0	0	0	0
24		Maintenance	-170,000	-170,000	-170,000	-170,000	-170,000
25		Operating Labor	-360,000	-360,000	-360,000	-360,000	-360,000
26		Transition Cost	-900,000	0	0	0	0
27		Installation	-400,000	0	0	0	0
28		Software (op. systems & apps.)	-700,000	-700,000	-700,000	-700,000	-700,000
29		Power, cooling, DC space	-400,000	-400,000	-400,000	-400,000	-400,000
31		Penalties for SLA misses	0	0	0	0	0
33		After tax cash flow	-354,200	2,538,400	2,538,400	2,538,400	2,538,400
34		Cumulative cash flow	-354,200	2,184,200	4,722,600	7,261,000	9,799,400
35							
36	Decision criteria	Discount rate	15%				
37		Discounted cash flow	-354,200	2,207,304	1,919,395	1,669,039	1,451,338
38							
39		Net Present Value	6,892,877				
40		Breakeven in years	1.1				

Figure 13.7: A business case for switching to virtualized servers.

The revenue derived from running the servers is $5 million per year, as shown on row 3. The new virtualized hardware costs $2 million, as shown on row 21. This is depreciated over five years, as shown on row 4. The old machines you are replacing have a remaining book value of $65,000, which will be written off (row 5), but these old machines can be sold for $35,000 (row 6). Annual maintenance and operating costs of the new servers are $170,000 (row 7) and $360,000 (row 8), respectively.

Because some of the old software applications require conversion to run in the new virtualized environment, there is a transition cost of $900,000 (row 9). This is a one-time cost in the first year. It is estimated using the techniques described in the Segmenting Complexity pattern in Chapter 6. Similarly, year 1 includes the installation cost of the new setup, assumed to be $400,000 (row 10).

The annual cost of software for the operating systems and applications is $700,000 (row 14). Power, cooling, and data center (DC) space come to $400,000 annually (row 15). With the virtualized hardware, you should be able to meet all of Service Level Agreements (SLAs) with your customers, so you will not have to pay any penalty payments (row 16).

With a discount rate of 15 percent, the net present value is almost $6.9 million, and the breakeven is 1.1 years. So, it appears to be attractive to use virtualized hardware. But would it be more attractive to use non-virtualized hardware?

The next case, shown in Figure 13.8, gives the details. Because the end users of the IT service probably do not care if the servers are virtualized or not, the revenue is assumed to be $5 million in both cases, as shown in row 3.

row	Case 8	Business Case for Don't Virtualize		1	2	3	4	5
1		Year		1	2	3	4	5
2								
3	Tax to pay	Revenue		5,000,000	5,000,000	5,000,000	5,000,000	5,000,000
4		Depreciation		-500,000	-500,000	-500,000	-500,000	-500,000
5		Write-off book value		-65,000	0	0	0	0
6		Sale of old machines		35,000	0	0	0	0
7		Maintenance		-250,000	-250,000	-250,000	-250,000	-250,000
8		Operating Labor		-400,000	-400,000	-400,000	-400,000	-400,000
9		Transition Cost		0	0	0	0	0
10		Installation		-300,000	0	0	0	0
11		Software (op. systems & apps.)		-700,000	-700,000	-700,000	-700,000	-700,000
12		Power, cooling, DC space		-800,000	-800,000	-800,000	-800,000	-800,000
15		Penalties for SLA misses		-50,000	-50,000	-50,000	-50,000	-50,000
16		Basis of taxation		1,970,000	2,300,000	2,300,000	2,300,000	2,300,000
17		Tax rate	28%					
18		Tax to pay		-551,600	-644,000	-644,000	-644,000	-644,000
19								
20	After tax cash flow	Revenue		5,000,000	5,000,000	5,000,000	5,000,000	5,000,000
21		Capital expenditure		-2,500,000	0	0	0	0
22		Tax		-551,600	-644,000	-644,000	-644,000	-644,000
23		Sale of old machines		35,000	0	0	0	0
24		Maintenance		-250,000	-250,000	-250,000	-250,000	-250,000
25		Operating Labor		-400,000	-400,000	-400,000	-400,000	-400,000
26		Transition Cost		0	0	0	0	0
27		Installation		-300,000	0	0	0	0
28		Software (op. systems & apps.)		-700,000	-700,000	-700,000	-700,000	-700,000
29		Power, cooling, DC space		-800,000	-800,000	-800,000	-800,000	-800,000
31		Penalties for SLA misses		-50,000	-50,000	-50,000	-50,000	-50,000
33		After tax cash flow		-516,600	2,156,000	2,156,000	2,156,000	2,156,000
34		Cumulative cash flow		-516,600	1,639,400	3,795,400	5,951,400	8,107,400
35								
36	Decision criteria	Discount rate	15%					
37		Discounted cash flow		-516,600	1,874,783	1,630,246	1,417,605	1,232,700
38								
39		Net Present Value	5,638,733					
40		Breakeven in years	1.2					

Figure 13.8: A business case for using non-virtualized servers.

This time, you are buying a large number of smaller servers, which will not be virtualized. The total cost of the hardware is $2.5 million (row 21). Don't forget that, although the virtualized example uses far fewer machines, they are likely to be larger and more complex than the non-virtualized servers. So, although you would expect hardware cost savings in the virtualized case, this needs to be confirmed for each project.

You would expect that maintenance and operating costs for the much greater number of machines in the non-virtualized example would be higher than in the virtualized case. These costs are shown as $250,000 (row 7) and $400,000 (row 8), respectively.

In the non-virtualized case, there is no need to convert applications to run on virtualized hardware (row 9). The installation cost may be lower ($300,000, on row 10) because there is no need to prepare the virtualized environments. You simply need to install the software on the non-virtualized machines.

Power, cooling, and data center space will likely be significantly higher in the non-virtualized example. Clearly, you will require much more space and power for 120 non-virtualized machines than for 20 virtualized ones. This is shown as $800,000 on row 12.

Finally, in the non-virtualized example, you do not have the flexibility to increase the size of partitions and to move workload between machines on-the-fly. These are abilities you would have with virtualized hardware. Realistically, this lack of flexibility might cause you to miss some customers' SLAs, leading to the payment of penalties. This is assumed to be $50,000 (row 15).

With the same discount rate of 15 percent as the previous case, the NPV is a little over $5.6 million, and the breakeven is after 1.2 years. The difference in the time to breakeven is not that significant, but the business case with virtualized hardware gives a much higher NPV, indicating you should go the virtualized route.

Figure 13.9 shows the delta business case for "virtualized minus non-virtualized." This gives the same delta between the NPVs, indicating that the virtualized option is the one to pick.

row		Case 9 Delta Business Case for Virtualize versus Don't Virtualize		1	2	3	4	5
1		Year		1	2	3	4	5
2								
3	Tax to pay	Revenue		0	0	0	0	0
4		Depreciation		100,000	100,000	100,000	100,000	100,000
5		Write-off book value		0	0	0	0	0
6		Sale of old machines		0	0	0	0	0
7		Maintenance		80,000	80,000	80,000	80,000	80,000
8		Operating Labor		40,000	40,000	40,000	40,000	40,000
9		Transition Cost		-900,000	0	0	0	0
10		Installation		-100,000	0	0	0	0
11		Software (op. systems & apps.)		0	0	0	0	0
12		Power, cooling, DC space		400,000	400,000	400,000	400,000	400,000
15		Penalties for SLA misses		50,000	50,000	50,000	50,000	50,000
16		Basis of taxation		-330,000	670,000	670,000	670,000	670,000
17		Tax rate	28%					
18		Tax to pay		92,400	-187,600	-187,600	-187,600	-187,600
19								
20	After tax cash flow	Revenue		0	0	0	0	0
21		Capital expenditure		500,000	0	0	0	0
22		Tax		92,400	-187,600	-187,600	-187,600	-187,600
23		Sale of old machines		0	0	0	0	0
24		Maintenance		80,000	80,000	80,000	80,000	80,000
25		Operating Labor		40,000	40,000	40,000	40,000	40,000
26		Transition Cost		-900,000	0	0	0	0
27		Installation		-100,000	0	0	0	0
28		Software (op. systems & apps.)		0	0	0	0	0
29		Power, cooling, DC space		400,000	400,000	400,000	400,000	400,000
31		Penalties for SLA misses		50,000	50,000	50,000	50,000	50,000
33		After tax cash flow		162,400	382,400	382,400	382,400	382,400
34		Cumulative cash flow		162,400	544,800	927,200	1,309,600	1,692,000
35								
36	Decision criteria	Discount rate	15%					
37		Discounted cash flow		162,400	332,522	289,149	251,434	218,638
38								
39		delta Net Present Value	1,254,144					

Figure 13.9: A delta case for virtualization.

Summary

This chapter highlighted the importance of a compelling business case. Without this, it is very hard to get management sponsorship and buy-in with any virtualization project. The IT staff should partner closely with the organization's finance team to develop a business case that takes both the technical and business aspects of the project into consideration.

In this chapter, you walked through the essential building blocks of a business case and learned the various concepts related to supporting project investment related decision-making. Then, you saw a series of business cases that demonstrated the net financial benefit of virtualizing infrastructure hardware.

Based on the content in this chapter, you should be able to quantify the financial benefits of your virtualization projects via a formal business case. Consequently, you will have better success with gaining management support and investment for your virtualization project.

IBM's Integrated Virtualization Management Toolset

This appendix provides an overview of IBM's integrated virtualization management toolset, which we have leveraged extensively to address the virtualization management requirements of our global clients. Using this toolset, we have demonstrated repeated success in lowering our clients' IT infrastructure management costs.

IBM Systems Director

Note: Information in this section is derived from the management briefs Aligning Platform and Service Management with IBM Systems Director and Tivoli Solutions *(Los Altos, California: International Technology Group, January 2009) and* Value Proposition for IBM Systems Director: Challenges of Operational Management for Enterprise Server Installations *(Los Altos, California: International Technology Group, October 2008).*

IBM Systems Director™ provides a unified management solution for IBM System x and BladeCenter, Power, and (for Linux guests) System z platforms, as well as for distributed disk systems and SAN resources. Recent versions of Windows Server 2003, Red Hat Enterprise Linux (RHEL), SUSE Linux Enterprise Server (SLES), and the IBM AIX and i operating systems are all supported, along with Windows Server 2008 and VMware ESX, Microsoft Virtual Server, PowerVM (for Power servers) and z/VM (for System z servers) hypervisors, and the Xen components of RHEL and SLES.

Overview

IBM Systems Director allows for the use of a standardized set of management tools and processes for all physical and virtual resources for all supported server platforms, operating systems, and hypervisors. Access is provided through a common management console, using a single Web-based administrator interface.

IBM Systems Director forms the core of a product family that consists of a set of base plug-in modules, along with a number of advanced function products. These are summarized in Table A.1.

Table A.1: The IBM Systems Director Product Family	
Systems Director 6.1 Base Plug-Ins	
Discovery Manager	Discovers physical and virtual resources; maintains hardware and software inventory; visualizes network relationships.
Status Manager	Monitors hardware, power, and update status, and provides event notifications; summary, dashboard, and scorecard functions display and analyze the status of managed resources.
Configuration Manager	Provides a central point and single framework for configuring physical and virtual resources and performing OS- or device-specific configuration functions; manages configuration settings, templates, and plans; automatically configures newly discovered systems.
Update Manager	Manages the download and installation of software updates; tracks update statuses and alerts system administrators of out-of-compliance resources.
Automation Manager	Automates customized responses to events; manages task activations.
Remote Access Manager	Provides an integrated toolset for remote access and control.
Virtualization Manager	Provides lifecycle management, including creation, editing, relocation, and deletion of virtual resources, including virtual servers and farms; tracks system statuses and alerts and creates automated event-response plans.
Security Features	Provide user authentication and role-based access control.
Advanced Function Products	
Active Energy Manager	Provides multiple functions that may be implemented at the rack or server level. These include monitoring, recording, and analysis of energy usage and thermal loading; capping; and setting of energy and temperature thresholds. Also monitors data center support devices, including PDS, UPS, CRAC equipment, and SynapSense nodes, and receives alerts from third-party facilities-management applications.
BladeCenter Open Fabric Manager (BOFM)	Manages I/O and network interconnects for up to 100 BladeCenter chassis with up to 1,400 servers. Provides a single administrator login to these. Also detects failures, automates failover to and restart of alternate blade servers, and transfers MAC and WWN network addresses to alternate I/O ports.

Table A.1: The IBM Systems Director Product Family (Continued)	
Systems Director 6.1 Base Plug-Ins	
Tivoli Provisioning Manager for OS Deployment (TPMfOSD)	Enables automated network deployment of server firmware and software, including BIOS and driver updates, and IBM AIX, Windows Server and Vista, Linux, Solaris, and Mac operating system images.
Service and Support Manager	Identifies and reports hardware-related problems; interfaces to Status Manager; and uses Electronic Service Agent to gather service information and report problems to IBM.

Main Components

There are four main components of a Systems Director deployment:

- Systems Director Server acts as the central management server. It may be deployed on AIX, Windows Server, Red Hat, or SUSE Linux. It may also be configured for High Availability (HA) operations. Apache Derby (for small environments), IBM DB2, Oracle®, or SQL Server may be employed for management databases.
- Management Console provides a common browser-based interface for administrators to access the full set of Systems Director tools and functions for all supported platforms.
- Common Agent and Platform Agent reside on managed servers running supported operating systems and hypervisors. Common Agent enables the use of the full suite of Systems Director services. Platform Agent implements a subset of these. It provides a small-footprint option for servers that perform limited functions or are equipped with less powerful processors.
- Agentless support is provided for x86 servers that run older versions of Windows or Linux, along with other devices that conform to the Distributed Component Object Model (DCOM), Secure Shell (SSH), or Simple Network Management Protocol (SNMP) specifications.

For Power servers, Systems Director support extends to logical partitions (LPARs), Virtual I/O Servers (VIOS), and other virtual resources enabled by PowerVM technology. The principal PowerVM tools for management of these technologies are the Hardware Management Console (HMC) and the Integrated Virtualization Manager (IVM). They may be accessed through the Systems Director administrator interface.

Systems Director interfaces directly with embedded Flexible Service Processors (FSPs), which provide local resource monitoring, data collection, and alerts for Power as well as

System x servers. Systems Director also interfaces with the System x Remote Supervisor Adapter II (RSA II), which provides remote management functions for System x servers.

Systems Director servers may also be employed to manage IBM server RAID controllers; DS3000, DS4000, and DS6000 disk systems; SAN Volume Controller software; and IBM-supported SAN switches from such vendors as Brocade, Cisco Systems, Nortel Networks, and Qlogic.

A single Systems Director 6.1 server can manage thousands of physical and/or logical servers equipped as Common or Platform Agents. There is no limit to the number of SNMP devices that may be managed. The overall Systems Director environment is summarized in Figure A.1.

Tivoli Solutions

Note: Information in this section is derived from the management briefs Aligning Platform and Service Management with IBM Systems Director and Tivoli Solutions *(Los Altos, California: International Technology Group, January 2009).*

We integrate the Tivoli solution offering with IBM System Director for managing virtualized and hybrid IT infrastructure environments. Tivoli solutions can be grouped into 13 main categories, described briefly here and listed in Table A.2 (on page 264):

1. *Business service management* consists of tools and processes for service level management, which includes definition and monitoring of SLAs as well as goal-setting, performance measurement, and service strategy planning. The core component of this category is Tivoli Business Service Manager, which enables continuous measurement of service availability and performance against business goals. It incorporates analytical and visualization tools, as well as scorecarding, key performance indicator (KPI) tracking, and other monitoring functions.

   Other key components include Omnibus, a former Micromuse offering for real-time data center and network operations monitoring; the Tivoli Service Request Manager service desk application; Service Level Advisor for designing and evaluating SLAs; and data integration tools that enable the cross-organizational collection and aggregation of service-related data.

2. *Change and configuration management* consists of two main components. Tivoli Application Dependency Discovery Manager (TADDM) provides for the discovery

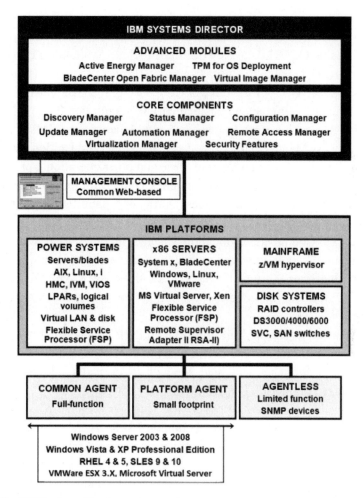

Figure A.1: The IBM Systems Director environment.

of a wide range of IBM and non-IBM IT resources, including virtualized resources. It establishes relationships among these resources and maps them to business applications.

The Change and Configuration Management Database (CCMDB) acts as the central enterprise repository of resources and relationships discovered by TADDM. Combined with the latter, it provides the bridge between conventional IT asset and operations-management functions and higher-level business service management processes.

3. *Process management* consists of a set of customizable workflow-based tools and best practice models that enable organizations to automate key operational processes using CCMB data. Key offerings include Availability Process Manager (for event management), Business Continuity Process Manager (for disaster recovery), Capacity Process Manager (for capacity management) Change Process Manager (for change management), Configuration Process Manager (for configuration management), Release Process Manager (for release management), Storage Process Manager (for storage management), and Unified Process Composer (for the documentation of these and other operational processes).

4. *Monitoring and event management* includes Tivoli Monitoring and Composite Application Manager, which provides additional capabilities for complex multiplatform environments.

    Specialized Composite Application Manager modules are offered for the management of service-oriented architecture (SOA), IBM WebSphere, Java 2 Platform Enterprise Edition (J2EE), Web services, and Microsoft applications; Internet service and transaction processing systems; and other software environments.

    An extension to Tivoli Monitoring, Tivoli Performance Analyzer adds capacity-utilization monitoring and predictive analysis functions. It allows for the early detection of performance bottlenecks, which are critical to address proactively in any virtualized or hybrid IT infrastructure environment.

5. *Provisioning* includes Tivoli Provisioning Manager, which provisions and configures a wide range of IBM and non-IBM servers, operating systems, middleware, applications software, and storage and network resources. It also includes Tivoli Intelligent Orchestrator, which enables the automation of provisioning-related processes based on organization-specific requirements.

6. *Workload automation* includes the core IBM Enterprise Workload Manager solution for complex workload management, along with Tivoli Workload Scheduler for job scheduling and Tivoli Dynamic Workload Broker for automated workload routing.

    Tivoli Workload Scheduler includes specialized modules for the management of ERP workloads (Workload Scheduler for Applications), grid environments (Workload Scheduler for Virtualized Data Centers), and parallel processing systems employed for high-performance computing applications (LoadLeveler).

7. *High availability* includes Tivoli System Automation for Multiplatforms, which automates failover and recovery processes for Veritas Cluster Server, and IBM

High Availability Clustered Multiprocessing (HACMP) for AIX and Linux servers. It also includes Tivoli System Automation for z/OS, which provides comparable services for Parallel Sysplex and Geographically Dispersed Parallel Sysplex (GDPS) clusters.

8. *Storage management* includes IBM TotalStorage Productivity Center, the company's strategic storage resource management suite; Tivoli Storage Manager for data backup and recovery; System Storage Archive Manager for policy-based archiving; and SAN Volume Controller.

9. *Network management* includes Tivoli Network Manager (formerly Netcool/Precision), which is the principal IBM solution for the management of IP networks, and the Tivoli NetView suite for managing conventional mainframe-based networks. Tivoli Network Manager includes IP Edition and Transmission Edition layers 2 and 3, and layer 1 networks, respectively.

10. *Financial management* includes Tivoli Usage and Accounting Manager (TUAM) for resource usage metering, accounting, and billing. Originally developed by CIMS Lab, which was acquired by IBM in 2006, TUAM is commonly used to implement chargebacks.

    Other financial management applications include Tivoli License Compliance Manager, which maintains inventories of and determines license costs and compliance requirements for IBM and third-party software; and IBM License Metric Tool, which assists in calculating license costs for IBM software based on processor value unit (PVU) pricing.

11. *Asset management* consists primarily of the Maximo®-based IBM Tivoli Asset Management for IT and Tivoli Integration Composer, a data integration tool that enables the collection and aggregation of IT asset-related data from diverse sources.

12. *Security, risk, and compliance* covers a broad portfolio of security-related solutions. These include the core Tivoli Access Manager and Tivoli Identity Manager solutions, along with Tivoli Federated Identity Manager for partner data sharing, Tivoli Risk Manager for security event management, and Tivoli Directory Server. Also forming part of this portfolio are Tivoli Compliance Insight Manager for security compliance monitoring, Tivoli Key Lifecycle Manager for the enterprise-level management of encryption keys, and the zSecure mainframe audit management suite.

13. *Data center transformation* includes products such as Tivoli Monitoring for Energy Management in data centers.

Also forming part of the Tivoli solution portfolio is Tivoli Data Warehouse, a DB2-based framework designed to interface to the principal Tivoli data collection solutions.

Table A.2: IBM Tivoli Solution Categories		
Business Service Management		
Business Service Manager	Service Request Manager	Service Level Advisor
OMNIbus		Data Integration Tools
Change and Configuration Management		
Change and Configuration Management Database		Application Dependency Discovery Manager
Process Automation		
Availability Process Manager	Business Continuity Process Manager	Capacity Process Manager
Change Process Manager	Release Process Manager	Storage Process Manager
Monitoring and Event Management		
IBM Tivoli Monitoring (ITM)	Composite Application Manager	Performance Analyzer
Workload Automation	**Provisioning**	**High Availability**
Enterprise Workload Manager	Provisioning Manager	System Automation for Multiplatforms
Dynamic Workload Broker	Provisioning Manager for OS	
Workload Scheduler	Provisioning Manager for Software	System Automation for z/OS
	Intelligent Orchestrator	
Storage Management	**Network Management**	
Archive Manager	**IP Networks**	**Mainframe Networks**
Storage Manager	Network Manager	NetView for z/OS
TotalStorage Productivity Center	IP Edition Manager	NetView Distribution
SAN Volume Controller	Transmission Edition Monitor	NetView Performance
Asset and Financial Management		
Usage and Accounting Manager	License Compliance Manager	Asset Management for IT
License Metric Tool	License Compliance Manager for z/OS	Maximo Suite
Security, Risk, and Compliance		
Access Manager	Federated Identity Manager	Key Lifecycle Manager
Identity Manager	Directory Server	Compliance Insight Manager
Identity Manager for z/OS	Directory Integrator	zSecure Suite
Data Center Transformation		
Energy Management		
ITM for Energy Management		

VMware's Virtualization Management Toolset

This appendix provides a list of VMware's virtualization management toolset. We have leveraged these tools extensively to address the virtualization management challenges of our global clients. We have succeeded in demonstrating repeated success in lowering our clients' IT infrastructure management costs using this toolset.

The following set of tools make up the VMware Data Center products:

- VMware vSphere
- VMware vCenter Product Family
- VMware vCenter Server
- VMware Server
- VMware ESXi

Virtualization Management Solutions from VMware

VMware's vCenter management platform, shown in Figure B.1, provides a proven approach to managing the virtualized data center. For the x86 server spaces, it offers one of the most comprehensive virtualization management solutions for optimizing critical IT processes and workflows in a data center.

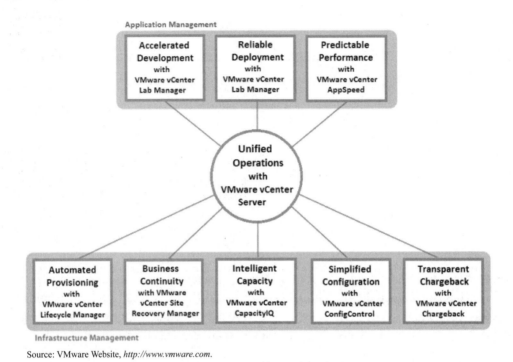

Source: VMware Website, *http://www.vmware.com*.

Figure B.1: VMware's vCenter management platform.

Currently, VMware's vCenter solution includes the following:

- VMware vCenter Server
- VMware vCenter AppSpeed
- VMware vCenter Chargeback
- VMware vCenter Lab Manager
- VMware vCenter Lifecycle Manager
- VMware vCenter Site Recovery Manager
- VMware vCenter CapacityIQ

All of these tools solutions integrate with VMware's vCenter Server, which is at the center of VMware's management platform.

For additional details and the latest updates regarding VMware's solutions and products, visit VMware on the Web, at *http://www.vmware.com/products*.

Index

NOTE: **Boldface** indicates illustrations and code; *t* indicates a table.